STUDY GUIDE 1-14
FESS & WARREN

Accounting Principles

SEVENTEENTH EDITION

Prepared by
JAMES A. HEINTZ
Professor of Accounting
University of Connecticut, Storrs

CARL S. WARREN
Professor of Accounting
University of Georgia, Athens

COLLEGE DIVISION South-Western Publishing Co.

Cincinnati Ohio

AB70RD3

Publisher: Mark Hubble
Senior Developmental Editor: Ken Martin
Developmental Editor: Mary Draper
Production Editor: Mark Sears
Production House: Berry Publication Services
Cover Designer: Craig LaGesse Ramsdell
Cover and Title Page Illustration: David Lesh
Marketing Manager: Martin Lewis

ISBN: 0-538-81853-0

2 3 4 5 6 7 DH 8 7 6 5 4 3

Printed in the United States of America

CONTENTS

Chapter 1
Accounting Principles and Practices

QUIZ AND TEST HINTS

The following hints may be helpful to you in preparing for a quiz or a test over the material covered in Chapter 1.

1. Terminology is important in this chapter. Review the chapter Glossary of Key Terms. Expect multiple-choice or true-false questions to include the terms introduced on pages 8-14 of the text. For example, you should recognize accounting as an information system (often called the language of business) and distinguish between CPA and CMA. Pay special attention to the three accounting concepts and principles—business entity concept, cost principle, and business transactions—discussed on pages 12-14.

2. Know the accounting equation: Assets = Liabilities + Owner's Equity. Be able to compute one amount when given the other two. For example, if assets equal $100,000 and liabilities equal $60,000, owner's equity must equal $40,000. Be able to determine the effect of change in the basic elements on one another. For example, if assets increase by $10,000 and liabilities decrease by $5,000, owner's equity must increase by $15,000.

3. Be able to record business transactions within the framework of the accounting equation. Use the illustration on pages 14-17 as a basis for review and study. Pay particular attention to items that are increased and decreased by transactions a through h. Note the introduction of new terms such as account payable, account receivable, revenue, and expense. These new terms are highlighted in color in the text.

4. Be able to describe each of the financial statements listed on page 18. You may be required to prepare a short income statement, statement of owner's equity, and balance sheet. You will probably not be required to prepare a statement of cash flows.

5. Review the summary data for Computer King on page 17. Trace the numbers into the statements shown in Exhibit 4 on page 19. Know the format of each statement such as the number of columns and placement of dollar signs. Some of the numbers in Exhibit 4 appear on more than one statement. Sometimes a quiz or a test question will provide partially completed statements, and you will be required to complete the statements. Recognizing amounts that appear on more than one statement will aid you in answering this type of question.

CHAPTER OUTLINE

I. Accounting as an Information System.
  A. Accounting is an information system that provides essential information about the economic activities of an entity to various individuals or groups for their use in making informed judgments and decisions.
  B. Accounting provides a framework for gathering economic data and the language for reporting these data to different individuals and institutions.
  C. Management, those individuals charged with the responsibility for directing the operations of enterprises, depends upon and makes the most use of accounting information.
  D. The process of using accounting to provide information to users involves (1)

1

identification of user groups and their information needs, (2) the gathering and processing of economic data by the accounting system, and (3) the generation of reports communicating the information to users.

E. Individuals engaged in all areas of business need not be expert accountants, but they are more effective if they have an understanding of accounting principles.

F. The importance of understanding accounting is not limited to the business world, but extends to nonbusiness areas such as engineering, law, etc.

II. Profession of Accountancy.

A. Accounting has experienced rapid development during this century.

B. Factors contributing to the increased growth of accounting include the increase in number, size, and complexity of business organizations; frequent changes in the tax laws; and other governmental restrictions on business operations.

C. As professionals, accountants typically are engaged in either (1) private accounting or (2) public accounting.

1. Accountants employed by a particular business firm or not-for-profit organization are said to be engaged in private accounting. The certificate in management accounting (CMA) and the certificate in internal auditing (CIA) recognize the professional competency of private accountants.

2. Accountants who render accounting services on a fee basis are said to be engaged in public accounting.

a. Public accountants who meet state laws may become certified public accountants (CPAs).

b. CPAs must adhere to codes of professional conduct.

D. The specialized fields of accounting include the following: financial accounting, auditing, cost accounting, managerial accounting, tax accounting, accounting systems, budgetary accounting, international accounting, not-for-profit accounting, social accounting, and accounting instruction.

III. Principles and Practice.

A. Based upon research, accepted accounting practices, and professional pronouncements, generally accepted accounting principles evolve to form an underlying basis for accounting practice.

B. Authoritative accounting pronouncements are issued by such bodies as the FASB.

C. The business entity concept is based on the applicability of accounting to individual economic units in society.

D. Businesses are customarily organized as sole proprietorships, partnerships, or corporations.

E. Under the cost principle, monetary accounting records are expressed in terms of cost.

F. The exchange price, or cost, agreed upon by buyer and seller, determines the monetary amount to be recorded.

IV. Business Transactions.

A. A business transaction is the occurrence of an event or of a condition that must be recorded.

B. A transaction may lead to an event or a condition that results in another transaction.

V. Assets, Liabilities, and Owner's Equity.

A. The properties owned by a business enterprise are referred to as assets and the rights or claims to the properties are referred to as equities.

B. Equities may be subdivided into two principal types: the rights of creditors (called liabilities) and the rights of owners (called owner's equity).

C. The accounting equation may be expressed in the following ways: assets = equities; assets = liabilities + owner's equity; assets - liabilities = owner's equity.

VI. Transactions and the Accounting Equation.

A. All business transactions can be expressed in terms of the resulting change in the three basic elements (assets, liabilities, and owner's equity) of the accounting equation.

B. A purchase on account is a type of transaction that creates a liability, account payable, in which the purchaser agrees to pay in the near future.

C. Consumable goods purchased are considered to be prepaid expenses or assets.

D. The amount charged to customers for goods or services sold to them is called revenue.

E. A sale on account allows the customer to pay later and the selling firm acquires an account receivable.

F. The amount of assets consumed or services used in the process of earning revenues is called expense.

G. In recording the effect of transactions on the accounting equation, the following observations should be noted:

  1. The effect of every transaction can be stated in terms of increases and/or decreases in one or more of the accounting equation elements.

  2. The equality of the two sides of the accounting equation is always maintained.

  3. The owner's equity is increased by amounts invested by the owner and is decreased by withdrawals by the owner.

  4. Owner's equity is increased by revenues and is decreased by expenses.

VII. Financial Statements for Sole Proprietorships.

A. The income statement is the summary of the revenue and expenses of a business entity for a specific period of time.

  1. The excess of revenue over expenses incurred in earning the revenue is called net income or net profit.

  2. If the expenses of the enterprise exceed the revenue, the excess is a net loss.

  3. In the determination of periodic net income, the expenses incurred in generating revenues must be properly matched against the revenues generated.

B. The statement of owner's equity summarizes the changes in owner's equity that have occurred during a specific period of time.

1. Three types of transactions may affect owner's equity during the period: (1) investments by the owner, (2) net income or net loss for the period, and (3) withdrawals by the owner.

2. The statement of owner's equity serves as a connecting link between the balance sheet and the income statement.

C. The balance sheet lists the assets, liabilities, and owner's equity of a business as of a specific date.

  1. The form of balance sheet with the liability and owner's equity section presented below the asset section is called the report form.

  2. Assets are listed in the order in which they will be converted into cash or used up in the near future.

  3. In the balance sheet, liabilities are reported first, followed by owner's equity.

D. The statement of cash flows is the summary of the cash receipts and cash payments of a business entity for a specific period of time.

  1. It is customary to report cash flows in three sections: (1) operating activities, (2) investing activities, and (3) financing activities.

  2. The operating activities section includes cash transactions that enter into the determination of net income.

  3. The investing activities section reports cash transactions for the acquisition and sale of relatively long-term assets.

  4. The financing activities section reports cash transactions related to cash investments by the owner, and borrowings and cash withdrawals by the owner.

MATCHING

Instructions: A list of terms and related statements appear below. From the list of terms, select the one that relates to each statement. Print its identifying letter in the space provided.

A. Account payable
B. Account receivable
C. Accounting equation
D. Assets
E. Balance sheet
F. Cost principle
G. Equities
H. Expense
I. Income statement
J. Liabilities
K. Net income
L. Prepaid expenses
M. Revenue
N. Statement of cash flows
O. Statement of owner's equity

_F_ 1. The most objective measurement used in recording the purchase of properties and services is in accordance with the (?).

_D_ 2. The properties owned by a business enterprise.

_G_ 3. The rights or claims to the properties owned by a business enterprise .

_J_ 4. The rights of creditors represent debts of the business and are called (?).

_N_ 5. A summary of the cash receipts and cash payments of a business entity for a specific period of time.

_C_ 6. Assets = Liabilities + Owner's Equity

_A_ 7. The liability created by a purchase on account.

_L_ 8. Consumable goods purchased, such as supplies, are considered to be assets, or (?).

_B_ 9. The amount charged to customers for goods or services sold to them.

_M_ 10. When sales are made on account, allowing the customer to pay later, the business acquires a(n) (?).

_H_ 11. The amount of assets consumed or services used in the process of earning revenue.

_E_ 12. A list of the assets, liabilities, and owner's equity of a business entity as of a specific date, usually at the close of the last day of a month or a year.

_I_ 13. A summary of the revenue and the expenses of a business entity for a specific period of time, such as a month or a year.

_O_ 14. A summary of the changes in the owner's equity of a business entity that have occurred during a specific period of time, such as a month or a year.

_K_ 15. The excess of the revenue over the expenses incurred in earning the revenue is called (?).

4

TRUE / FALSE

Instructions: Indicate whether each of the following statements is true or false by placing a check mark in the appropriate column.

		True	False
1.	Accounting is often characterized as the "language of business"...................	✓	
2.	Accountants who render accounting services on a fee basis, and staff accountants employed by them, are said to be engaged in private accounting		✓
3.	Standards of conduct which have been established to guide CPAs in the conduct of their practices are called codes of professional responsibility		✓
4.	Accounting systems is the special field concerned with the design and implementation of procedures for the accumulation and reporting of financial data .	✓	
5.	The financing activities section of the statement of cash flows includes cash transactions that enter into the determination of net income.......................		✓
6.	A separate legal entity, organized in accordance with state or federal statutes and in which ownership is divided into shares of stock, is referred to as a corporation	✓	
7.	A partnership is owned by not less than four individuals		✓
8.	A business transaction is the occurrence of an event or of a condition that must be recorded...	✓	
9.	A summary of the changes in the owner's equity of a business entity that have occurred during a specific period of time, such as a month or a year, is called a statement of cash flows		✓
10.	A claim against a customer for sales made on credit is an account payable..........		✓

MULTIPLE CHOICE

Instructions: Circle the best answer for each of the following questions.

1. Accountants employed by a particular business firm or not-for-profit organization, perhaps as chief accountant, controller, or financial vice-president, are said to be engaged in:
   a. general accounting
   b. public accounting
   c. independent accounting
   d. private accounting

2. Authoritative accounting pronouncements on accounting principles are issued by the:
   a. Accounting Principles Commission
   b. Accounting Procedures Committee
   c. Financial Accounting Standards Board
   d. General Accounting Principles Board

3. The records of properties and services purchased by a business are maintained in accordance with the:
   a. business entity concept
   b. cost principle
   c. matching principle
   d. proprietorship principle

4. Another way of writing the accounting equation is:
   a. Assets + Liabilities = Owner's Equity
   b. Owner's Equity + Assets = Liabilities
   c. Assets = Owner's Equity - Liabilities
   d. Assets - Liabilities = Owner's Equity

5. The form of balance sheet with the liability and owner's equity sections presented below the asset section is called the:
   a. report form
   b. balancing form
   c. account form
   d. systematic form

Name _____

EXERCISE 1-1

Instructions: Some typical transactions of Clem's Laundry Service are presented below. For each transaction, indicate the increase (+), the decrease (-), or no change (o) in the assets (A), liabilities (L), and owner's equity (OE) by placing the appropriate sign(s) in the appropriate column(s). More than one sign may have to be placed in the A, L, or OE column for a given transaction.

	A	L	OE
1. Received cash from owner as an additional investment	+	o	+
2. Purchased supplies on account	+	+	o
3. Charged customers for services sold on account	+	o	+
4. Received cash from cash customers	+	o	+
5. Paid cash for rent on building	-	o	-
6. Collected an account receivable in full	+,-	o	+
7. Paid cash for supplies	-,+	o	o
8. Returned supplies purchased on account and not yet paid for	-	-	o
9. Paid cash to creditors on account	-	-	o
10. Paid cash to owner for personal use	-	o	-

PROBLEM 1-1

Instructions: The assets, liabilities, and owner's equity of Ed Casey, who operates a small repair shop, are expressed in equation form below. Following the equation are ten transactions completed by Casey. On each of the numbered lines, show by addition or subtraction the effect of each of the transactions on the equation. For each transaction, identify the changes in owner's equity by placing the letter R (revenue), E (expense), D (drawing), or I (investment) at the right of each increase or decrease in owner's equity. On the lines labeled "Bal.," show the new equation resulting from the transaction.

	Assets			=	Liabilities	+	Owner's Equity
	Cash +	Supplies +	Land ·	=	Accounts Payable	+	Ed Casey, Capital

1. Casey started a repair shop and deposited $40,000 cash in the bank for use by the business.

(1) 40,000   40,000 I

2. Casey purchased $2,000 of supplies on account.

(2)   2,000   2,000
Bal. 40,000 2,000   2,000   40,000

3. Casey purchased land for a future building site for $14,000 cash.

(3) −14,000   14,000
Bal. 26,000 2,000 14,000   2,000   40,000

4. Casey paid creditors $1,800 on account.

(4) −1,800   −1,800
Bal. 24,000 2,000 14,000   200   40,000

5. Casey withdrew $2,000 for personal use.

(5) 2,000
Bal. 22,000 2,000 14,000   200   38,000 D

6. Casey paid $2,800 for building and equipment rent for the month.

(6) −2,800   −2,800 E
Bal. 19,400 2,000 14,000   200   35,200

7. During the month, another $900 of expenses were incurred on account by the business.

(7)   900   −900 E
Bal. 19,400 2,000 14,000   1,100   34,300

8. During the month, Casey deposited another $10,000 of personal funds in the business bank account.

(8) 10,000   10,000 I
Bal. 29,400 2,000 14,000   1,100   44,300

9. Casey received $500 for a cash service call.

(9)   500   500 R
Bal. 29,900 2,000 14,000   1,100   44,800

10. Casey used $600 worth of supplies.

(10)   −600   −600 E
Bal. 29,900 1,400 14,000   1,100   44,200

PROBLEM 1-2

The amounts of the assets and liabilities of Tom's Painting Service at December 31 of the current year, and the revenues and expenses for the year are as follows:

Cash	$10,050
Accounts receivable	8,950
Supplies	4,000
Accounts payable	4,450
Sales	27,450
Supplies expense	5,450
Advertising expense...........	4,825
Truck rental expense...........	1,525
Utilities expense...............	700
Miscellaneous expense..........	1,400

The capital of Tom Wallace, owner, was $4,000 at the beginning of the current year. During the year, Wallace withdrew $1,000, and made an additional investment of $2,000.

Instructions: Using the forms provided, prepare the following:

(1) An income statement for the year ended December 31, 19—.
(2) A statement of owner's equity for the year ended December 31, 19—.
(3) A balance sheet as of December 31, 19—.

(1)

Tom's Painting Service
Income Statement
For Year Ended December 31, 1994

12/31	Sales		$27,450
	Operating Expenses		
	Supplies Expense	$5,450	
	Advertising Expense	4,825	
	Truck Rental Expense	1,525	
	Utilities Expense	700	
	Misc. Expense	1,400	
	Total Oper. Exp		13,900
	Net Income		$13,550

(2)

Tom's Painting Service
Statement of Owner's Equity
For Year Ended December 31, 1994

Investment Jan. 1, 1994		$4,000
Addl Investment (owner)	$2,000	
Income for year	13,550	
Less Withdrawal	(1,000)	
Inc. in Owner's Equity		14,550
Tom Wallace, Capital Dec. 31, 1994		$18,550

Tom's Painting Service
Balance Sheet
December 31, 19~~94~~

Assets				
Cash			$	10050
Accounts Receivable				8950
Supplies				4000
Total Assets				23000
Liabilities				
Accounts Payable				4450
Owner's Equity				
Tom Wallace, Capital				18550
Total Liabilities & Owners Equity			$	23000

Chapter 2
Accounting Systems
for Recording
Business Transactions

QUIZ AND TEST HINTS

The following hints may be helpful to you in preparing for a quiz or a test over the material covered in Chapter 2.

1. Terminology is important in this chapter. Review the chapter Glossary of Key Terms. Pay special attention to major account classifications discussed on page 38 of the text.

2. Memorize the "Rules of Debit and Credit" and the "Normal Balances of Accounts." All instructors will ask questions to test your knowledge of these items.

3. Be able to prepare general journal entries for the types of transactions presented in this chapter. Review the illustration beginning on page 47, and be sure you understand each entry. Be especially careful not to confuse debits and credits.

Remember that a credit is indented slightly to the right when preparing a general journal entry. A good review is to rework the Illustrative Problem in the Chapter Review.

4. You should be familiar with the process of posting accounts for working assigned problems. However, you will probably not be required to post accounts on an examination.

5. Expect one or two questions on how to correct errors. These types of questions may require you to prepare a correcting journal entry. Review the section of the chapter and illustration containing this information.

CHAPTER OUTLINE

I. Purpose of an Account.
   A. The record of the increases and decreases in individual financial statement items is called an account.
   B. A group of accounts for a business entity is a ledger.
II. Chart of Accounts.
   A. The system of accounts that make up a ledger is called a chart of accounts. The accounts are normally listed in the order in which they appear in the financial statements.
   B. Assets are physical items (tangible) or rights (intangible) that have value and that are owned by the business entity.
   C. Liabilities are debts owed to outsiders (creditors) and are often identified by account titles that include the word "payable."

   D. Owner's equity is the claim against the assets of the business after the total liabilities are deducted.
      1. Owner's equity on the balance sheet is represented by the owner's capital account.
      2. A drawing account represents the amount of withdrawals made by the owner.
   E. Revenues are increases in the owner's equity as a result of the rendering of services or the selling of products to customers.
   F. Assets used up or services consumed in the process of generating revenues are expenses.
III. Characteristics of an Account.
   Accounts have the following characteristics:
   A. A title, which is the name of the item recorded in the account.

B. A space for recording increases in the amount of the item, in terms of money.
C. A space for recording decreases in the amount of the item, in terms of money.
D. The simplest form of the account is known as the T account.
E. The left side of an account is called the debit side.
F. The right side of an account is called the credit side.
G. Amounts entered on the left side of the account are called debits to the account.
H. Amounts entered on the right side of the account are called credits to the account.
I. Subtraction of the smaller of the total debits or credits from the larger amount yields the balance of the account.

IV. Recording Transactions in Accounts.
A. Recording transactions in balance sheet accounts (asset, liability, and owner's equity accounts) includes the following considerations:
1. Every business transaction affects a minimum of two accounts.
2. Transaction data are initially entered in a record called a journal.
3. The process of recording a transaction in the journal is called journalizing and the form of presentation is called a journal entry.
4. The data in the journal entry are transferred to the proper accounts by a process known as posting.
5. The rules of debit and credit for balance sheet accounts may be stated as follows:

    Debit may signify:
    Increase in asset accounts
    Decrease in liability accounts
    Decrease in owner's equity accounts
    Credit may signify:
    Decrease in asset accounts
    Increase in liability accounts
    Increase in owner's equity accounts

6. The rules of debit and credit for balance sheet accounts may also be stated in relationship to the accounting equation as follows:

Asset Accounts		=
Debit for increases	Credit for decreases	

Liability Accounts		+
Debit for decreases	Credit for increases	

Owner's Equity Accounts	
Debit for decreases	Credit for increases

B. Transactions in income statement accounts (revenue and expense accounts) are recorded in the following manner:
1. Increases in revenue accounts are recorded as credits. Decreases are recorded as debits.
2. Increases in expense accounts are recorded as debits. Decreases are recorded as credits.
3. An entry composed of two or more debits or two or more credits is called a compound journal entry.
4. The equality of debits and credits for each transaction is inherent in the accounting equation, and the system is known as double-entry accounting.
5. The rules for debit and credit for income statement accounts are summarized below:

Debit for decreases in owner's equity

Expense Accounts	
Debit for increases	Credit for decreases

Credit for increases in owner's equity

Revenue Accounts	
Debit for decreases	Credit for increases

C. Withdrawals by an owner are recorded as debits to a drawing account.

D. Normal balances of accounts.

1. The sum of the increases in an account is usually equal to or greater than the decreases in an account; therefore, an account is said to have a normal balance.

2. The rules of debit and credit and the normal balances of balance sheet and income statement accounts are summarized as follows:

	Increase	Decrease
	(Normal Balance)	
Balance sheet accounts:		
Asset	Debit	Credit
Liability	Credit	Debit
Owner's Equity		
Capital	Credit	Debit
Drawing	Debit	Credit
Income statement accounts:		
Revenue	Credit	Debit
Expense	Debit	Credit

V. Journals and Accounts.

A. The flow of accounting data may be diagrammed as follows:

		Entry recorded in	Entry posted to
Business TRANSACTION occurs	→ Business DOCUMENT prepared	→ JOURNAL	→ LEDGER

1. The initial record of each transaction is a business document.

2. Transactions are entered in chronological order in the journal.

3. The amounts of the debits and credits in the journal are posted to the accounts in the ledger.

B. Before a transaction is entered in the two-column journal, it should be analyzed according to the following steps:

1. Determine whether an asset, liability, owner's equity, revenue, or expense is affected.

2. Determine whether the affected asset, liability, owner's equity, revenue, or expense increases or decreases.

3. Determine whether the effect of the transaction should be recorded as a debit or as a credit in an asset, liability, owner's equity, revenue, or expense account.

C. The recording of a transaction in a two-column journal is summarized as follows:

1. Record the date:

a. Insert the year at the top only of the Date column of each page, except when the year date changes.

b. Insert the month on the first line only of the Date column of each page, except when the month date changes.

c. Insert the day in the Date column on the first line used for each transaction.

2. Record the debit:

Insert the title of the account to be debited at the extreme left of the Description column and enter the amount in the Debit column.

3. Record the credit:

Insert the title of the account to be credited below the account debited, moderately indented, and enter the amount in the Credit column.

4. Write an explanation:

Brief explanations may be written below each entry, moderately indented.

D. The four-column account form is normally used in accounting. This four-column form contains two columns for debit and credit postings and two additional columns to show the debit or credit balance of the account.

E. The posting of a debit journal entry or a credit journal entry to an account in the ledger is performed in the following manner:

1. Record the date and the amount of the entry in the account.

2. Insert the number of the journal page in the Posting Reference column of the account.

3. Insert the ledger account number in the Posting Reference column of the journal.

F. The journalizing and posting process for a month's transactions is illustrated on pages 47-54 of the text. To reduce repetition, some of the transactions are stated in summary form.

VI. Trial Balance.

A. The equality of debits and credits in the ledger should be verified at the end of each accounting period through the preparation of a trial balance.

B. The trial balance does not provide complete proof of the accuracy of the ledger. It indicates only that the debits and credits are equal.

VII. Discovery and Correction of Errors.
A. If the two totals of a trial balance are not equal, it is probably due to one or more of the following types of errors:
   1. Error in preparing the trial balance, such as:
      a. One of the columns of the trial balance was incorrectly added.
      b. The amount of an account balance was incorrectly recorded on the trial balance.
      c. A debit balance was recorded on the trial balance as a credit, or vice versa, or a balance was omitted entirely.
   2. Error in determining the account balances, such as:
      a. A balance was incorrectly computed.
      b. A balance was entered in the wrong balance column.
   3. Error in recording a transaction in the ledger, such as:
      a. An erroneous amount was posted to the account.
      b. A debit entry was posted as a credit, or vice versa.
      c. A debit or a credit posting was omitted.
B. Among the types of errors that will not cause inequality in the trial balance totals are the following:
   1. Failure to record a transaction or to post a transaction.
   2. Recording the same erroneous amount for both the debit and the credit parts of a transaction.
   3. Recording the same transaction more than once.
   4. Posting a part of a transaction correctly as a debit or credit but to the wrong account.
C. Two common types of errors are known as transpositions (an erroneous arrangement of digits) and slides (the movement of an entire number erroneously one or more spaces to the right or left).
D. The discovery of an error usually involves the retracing of the various steps in the accounting process.
E. Occasional errors in journalizing and posting transactions are unavoidable. Procedures used to correct errors in the journal and ledger vary according to the nature of the error and the phase of the accounting cycle in which it is discovered.
F. The procedures for correction of errors are summarized in the following table:

Error	Correction Procedure
Journal entry incorrect, but not posted.	Draw line through the error and insert correct title or amount.
Journal entry correct, but posted incorrectly.	Draw line through the error and post correctly.
Journal entry incorrect and posted.	Journalize and post a correcting entry.

MATCHING

Instructions: A list of terms and related statements appear below. From the list of terms, select the one that relates to each statement. Print its identifying letter in the space provided.

A. Account   F. Expenses   J. Owner's equity
B. Assets   G. Journalizing   K. Posting
C. Chart of accounts H. Ledger   L. Revenues
D. Double-entry accounting I. Liabilities M. Trial balance
E. Drawings

_H_ 1. A group of related accounts that comprise a complete unit, such as all of the accounts of a specific business enterprise.

_G_ 2. The process of recording a transaction in the journal.

_K_ 3. The process by which the data in the journal entry is transferred to the appropriate accounts.

_C_ 4. The system of accounts that make up the ledger for a business enterprise.

_B_ 5. Physical items (tangibles) or rights (intangibles) that have value and that are owned by the business entity.

_F_ 6. Assets or services consumed in the process of generating revenue.

_I_ 7. Debts owed to outsiders.

_D_ 8. A system for recording transactions, based on recording increases and decreases in accounts so that debits always equal credits.

_E_ 9. The amount of withdrawals made by the owner of a sole proprietorship.

_J_ 10. The residual claim against the assets of the business after the total liabilities are deducted.

_L_ 11. Increase in owner's equity as a result of providing services or selling products to customers.

_A_ 12. The form used to record additions and deductions for each individual asset, liability, owner's equity, revenue, and expense.

TRUE / FALSE

Instructions: Indicate whether each of the following statements is true or false by placing a check mark in the appropriate column.

		True	False
1.	Amounts entered on the left side of an account, regardless of the account title, are called credits or charges to the account.	✓	
2.	The difference between the total debits and the total credits posted to an account yields a figure called the balance of the account.	✓	
3.	Accounting systems provide information on business transactions for use by management in directing operations and preparing financial statements.	✓	
4.	Accounts receivable are claims against debtors evidenced by a written promise to pay a certain sum of money at a definite time to the order of a specified person or to bearer.		✓
5.	The residual claim against the assets of a business after the total liabilities are deducted is called owner's equity.	✓	
6.	Every business transaction affects a minimum of one account.		✓
7.	The process of recording a transaction in a journal is called posting.		✓
8.	A group of accounts for a business entity is called a journal.		✓
9.	A listing of the accounts in a ledger is called a chart of accounts.	✓	
10.	A recording error caused by the erroneous rearrangement of digits, such as writing $627 as $672, is called a slide.		✓

MULTIPLE CHOICE

Instructions: Circle the best answer for each of the following questions.

1. A journal entry composed of two or more debits or two or more credits is called a(n):
   a. multiple journal entry
   b. compound journal entry
   c. complex journal entry
   d. double journal entry

2. The first step in recording a transaction in a two-column journal is to:
   a. write an explanation
   b. record the debit
   c. record the credit
   d. record the date

3. The drawing account of a sole proprietorship is debited when:
   a. the owner invests cash
   b. the owner withdraws cash
   c. a liability is paid
   d. an expense is paid

4. The equality of debits and credits in the ledger should be verified at the end of each accounting period by preparing a(n):
   a. accounting statement
   b. balance report
   c. trial balance
   d. account verification report

5. Of the following errors, the one that will cause an inequality in the trial balance totals is:
   a. incorrectly computing an account balance
   b. failure to record a transaction
   c. recording the same transaction more than once
   d. posting a transaction to the wrong account

6. Credits to cash result in:
   a. an increase in owner's equity
   b. a decrease in assets
   c. an increase in liabilities
   d. an increase in revenue

7. Debits to expense accounts signify:
   a. increases in capital
   b. decreases in capital
   c. increases in assets
   d. increases in liabilities

8. When rent is prepaid for several months in advance, the debit is to:
   a. an expense account
   b. a capital account
   c. a liability account
   d. an asset account

9. When an asset is purchased on account, the credit is to:
   a. a capital account
   b. a revenue account
   c. a liability account
   d. an expense account

10. When a payment is made to a supplier for goods previously purchased on account, the debit is to:
   a. an asset account
   b. a liability account
   c. a capital account
   d. an expense account

Name _____

EXERCISE 2-1

Eight transactions are recorded in the following T accounts:

Cash				Machinery			Alan Moran, Drawing	
(1)	20,000	(5)	2,500	(2)	6,300		(8)	3,500
(7)	2,000	(8)	3,500					

Accounts Receivable				Accounts Payable				Service Revenue		
(4)	5,000	(7)	2,000	(5)	2,500	(2)	6,300		(4)	5,000
						(3)	820			
						(6)	1,600			

Supplies			Alan Moran, Capital			Operating Expenses	
(3)	820			(1)	20,000	(6)	1,600

Instructions: For each debit and each credit, indicate in the following form the type of account affected (asset, liability, owner's equity, revenue, or expense) and whether the account was increased (+) or decreased (-).

Transaction	Account Debited		Account Credited	
	Type	Effect	Type	Effect
(1)	asset	+	capital	+
(2)	asset	+	liability	+
(3)	asset	+	liability	+
(4)	asset	+	revenue	+
(5)	liability	−	asset	−
(6)	expense	+	liability	+
(7)	asset	+	asset	−
(8)	drawing	+	asset	−

19

PROBLEM 2-1

During June of the current year, Joan Star started Star Service Company.

Instructions:

(1) Record the following transactions in the two-column journal given below.

June 1. Invested $5,000 in cash, equipment valued at $14,500, and a van worth $21,000.

June 16. Purchased additional equipment on account, $5,500.

June 28. Purchased supplies on account, $500.

June 30. Paid $2,100 to creditors on account.

(2) Post to the appropriate ledger accounts on the next page.

(3) Prepare a trial balance of the ledger accounts of Star Service Company as of June 30 of the current year, using the form below.

(1) **JOURNAL** PAGE 1

	DATE		DESCRIPTION	POST. REF.	DEBIT	CREDIT	
1	June	1	Cash	11	5000		1
2			Equipment	18	14500		2
3			Vehicles	19	21000		3
4			Joan Star, Capital	31		40500	4
5		16	Equipment	18	5500		5
6			Accts Payable	21		5500	6
7		28	Supplies	12	500		7
8			Accts Payable	21		500	8
9		30	Accts Payable	21	2100		9
10			Cash	11		2100	10

(3)

Star Service Company
Trial Balance
June 30, 19—

Cash		2900	
Supplies		500	
Equipment		20000	
Vehicles		21000	
Accounts Payable			3900
Joan Star, Capital			40500
		44400	44400

(2)   LEDGER ACCOUNTS

ACCOUNT Cash   **ACCOUNT NO.** 11

DATE	ITEM	POST. REF.	DEBIT	CREDIT	BALANCE DEBIT	BALANCE CREDIT
1994						
June 1		1	5000		5000	
30		1		2100	2900	

ACCOUNT Supplies   **ACCOUNT NO.** 12

DATE	ITEM	POST. REF.	DEBIT	CREDIT	BALANCE DEBIT	BALANCE CREDIT
1994						
June 28		1	500		500	

ACCOUNT Equipment   **ACCOUNT NO.** 18

DATE	ITEM	POST. REF.	DEBIT	CREDIT	BALANCE DEBIT	BALANCE CREDIT
1994						
June 1		1	14500		14500	
16		1	5500		20000	

ACCOUNT Vehicles   **ACCOUNT NO.** 19

DATE	ITEM	POST. REF.	DEBIT	CREDIT	BALANCE DEBIT	BALANCE CREDIT
1994						
June 1		1	21000		21000	

ACCOUNT Accounts Payable   **ACCOUNT NO.** 21

DATE	ITEM	POST. REF.	DEBIT	CREDIT	BALANCE DEBIT	BALANCE CREDIT
1994 June 16		1		5500		5500
28		1		500		6000
30		1	2100			3900

ACCOUNT Joan Star, Capital   **ACCOUNT NO.** 31

DATE	ITEM	POST. REF.	DEBIT	CREDIT	BALANCE DEBIT	BALANCE CREDIT
1994						
June 1		1		40500		40500

PROBLEM 2-2

On January 2, 19—, Judy Turner, an attorney, opened a law office. The following transactions were completed during the month.

    a. Invested $20,000 cash and $13,200 worth of office equipment in the business.
    b. Paid a month's rent of $2,500.
    c. Paid $1,000 for office supplies.
    d. Collected legal fees of $19,600.
    e. Paid secretary a salary of $1,100.
    f. Purchased $200 worth of office supplies on account.
    g. Bought an auto for business use. It cost $13,000. Turner paid $2,600 down and charged the balance.
    h. Withdrew $5,000 from the firm for personal use.
    i. Paid $800 for auto repairs and maintenance.
    j. Received a $240 telephone bill.
    k. Paid the $240 telephone bill.
    l. Paid premiums of $1,700 on property insurance.
    m. Paid $2,000 on accounts payable.
    n. Paid $5,000 cash for books for the law library.
    o. Paid $500 cash for janitor service.

Instructions:
    (1) Record the transactions in the T accounts that follow.
    (2) Prepare a trial balance, using the form on the following page.

(1)

Cash	
(1) 20,000	(2) 2,500
(4) 19,600	(3) 1,000
	(5) 1,100
	(7) 2,600
	(8) 5,000
	(9) 800
	(11) 240
	(12) 1,700
	(13) 2,000
	(14) 5,000
	(15) 500

Library	
(14) 5,000	

Judy Turner, Capital	
	(1) 33,200

Office Equipment	
(1) 13,200	

Judy Turner, Drawing	
(8) 5,000	

Office Supplies	
(3) 1,000	
(6) 200	

Auto	
(7) 13,000	

Prepaid Insurance	
(12) 1,700	

Accounts Payable	
(11) 240	(6) 200
(13) 2,000	(7) 10,400
	(10) 240

22

Name _____

Legal Fees	Rent Expense	Telephone Expense
(4) 19,600	(2) 2,500	(10) 240

Salary Expense	Auto Repairs & Maintenance Expense
(5) 1,100	(9) 800

Janitor Expense
(8) 500

(2)

Judy Turner
Trial Balance
January 31, 19—

Cash	17160	
Office Supplies	1200	
Prepaid Insurance	1700	
Library	5000	
Office Equipment	13200	
Auto	13000	
Accounts Payable		8600
Judy Turner, Capital		33200
Judy Turner, Drawing	5000	
Legal Fees		19600
Rent Expense	2500	
Salary Expense	1100	
Telephone Expense	240	
Auto Reps & Mntnc Expense	800	
Janitor Expense	500	
	61400	61400

PROBLEM 2-3

The following errors were made in journalizing and posting transactions:

a. A $1,000 premium paid for insurance was debited to Prepaid Rent and credited to Cash.
b. A $200 purchase of supplies on account was recorded as a debit to Supplies and a credit to Accounts Receivable.
c. A withdrawal by the owner of $1,500 was debited to Cash and credited to the drawing account.

Instructions: Prepare entries in the two-column journal provided below to correct these errors.

JOURNAL

PAGE

	DATE	DESCRIPTION	POST. REF.	DEBIT	CREDIT	
1						1
2						2
3						3
4						4
5						5
6						6
7						7
8						8
9						9
10						10
11						11
12						12
13						13
14						14
15						15
16						16
17						17
18						18
19						19
20						20
21						21
22						22
23						23
24						24
25						25
26						26
27						27
28						28
29						29
30						30

Chapter 3
The Matching Concept and the Adjusting Process

QUIZ AND TEST HINTS

The following hints may be helpful to you in preparing for a quiz or a test over the material covered in Chapter 3.

1. Terminology is important in this chapter. Review the Glossary of Key Terms in the text.
2. The major focus of this chapter is the adjusting process. You should be able to prepare adjusting entries for each of the four types of adjustments: deferred expenses, deferred revenues, accrued expenses, and accrued revenues. Review the illustrations in the chapter and the adjusting entries required in the Illustrative Problem in the Chapter Review.
3. Most instructors will not require you to prepare a work sheet from scratch. However, some instructors may give you a partially completed work sheet and ask you to complete it. Or, you may be given a work sheet that has a Trial Balance and Adjusted Trial Balance columns completed, but has no data entered in the Adjustments columns. You would then be asked to figure out what the adjusting entries must have been. Practice working this type of problem by covering up the Adjustments columns with a sheet of paper and attempting to figure out the adjusting entries using Exhibit 6 on page 95 of the text or the Illustrative Problem in the Chapter Review.

CHAPTER OUTLINE

I. Matching Concept.
   A. Revenues and expenses may be reported on the income statement by the cash basis or the accrual basis of accounting.
   B. Most enterprises use the accrual basis of accounting.
   C. The accrual basis of accounting requires the use of the adjusting process at the end of the accounting period to properly match revenues and expenses for the period.
II. Nature of the Adjusting Process.
   A. The entries required at the end of the accounting period to bring the accounts up to date and to ensure the proper matching of revenues and expenses are called adjusting entries.
   B. Two basic classifications of items give rise to adjusting entries: deferrals and accruals.
   C. Deferrals are created by recording a transaction in a way that delays or defers the recognition of an expense or revenue.
      1. Deferred expenses are items that have been initially recorded as assets, but which are expected to become expenses over time or through the normal operations of the enterprise. Examples include supplies and prepaid insurance. Deferred expenses are often called prepaid expenses.
      2. Deferred revenues are items that have been initially recorded as liabilities, but which are expected to become revenues over time or through the normal operations of the enterprise. Examples include tuition and subscriptions received in advance. Deferred revenues are often called unearned revenues.

D. Accruals are created by the failure to record an expense that has been incurred or a revenue that has been earned.
  1. Accrued expenses are expenses that have been incurred, but which have not been recorded in the accounts. Examples include wages and interest.
  2. Accrued revenues are revenues that have been earned, but which have not be recorded in the accounts. Examples include unrecorded fees earned by an attorney or real estate agent.
E. The primary difference between deferrals and accruals is that deferrals have been recorded while accruals have not been recorded.

III. Recording Adjusting Entries.
A. An adjusting entry always affects a balance sheet account and an income statement account.
B. If an adjusting entry is omitted or erroneously recorded, both the balance sheet and the income statement will be affected.
C. The adjusting entry for deferred (prepaid) expenses debits an expense account and credits the deferred (prepaid) expense account.
D. The adjusting entry for deferred (unearned) revenue debits a deferred (unearned) revenue account and credits a revenue account.
E. The adjusting entry for accrued expenses (liabilities) debits an expense account and credits a liability account.
F. The adjusting entry for accrued revenues (assets) debits an asset account and credits a revenue account.
G. Tangible assets that are permanent or have a long life and are used in the business are called plant assets or fixed assets. The decrease in usefulness of a plant asset is generally referred to as depreciation.
  1. Depreciation, in an accounting sense, refers to the systematic allocation of the cost of a plant asset to expense.
  2. The adjusting entry to record depreciation debits a depreciation expense account and credits a contra asset account, accumulated depreciation.
  3. An accumulated depreciation account is normally maintained for each plant asset except land, which does not depreciate.
  4. The difference between the balance of a plant asset and its related accumulated depreciation (contra asset) account is called the book value of the asset.

IV. Work Sheet for Financial Statements.
A. At the end of an accounting period, a work sheet may be prepared by the accountant to facilitate the preparation of the financial statements and the necessary adjusting journal entries.
B. The Trial Balance columns of the work sheet are taken directly from the balances of the various ledger accounts at the end of the accounting period.
C. The necessary debit and credit portions of the adjusting entries are entered on the work sheet in the Adjustments columns.
D. After the adjusting entries have been entered on the work sheet, the account balances are extended to the Adjusted Trial Balance columns. The debit and credit columns are then totaled and compared to prove that no arithmetical errors have been made up to this point.
E. The completion of the work sheet, including the preparation of financial statements, is discussed in the next chapter.

MATCHING

Instructions: A list of terms and related statements appear below. From the list of terms, select the one that relates to each statement. Print its identifying letter in the space provided.

A. Accrual basis
B. Accrued expense
C. Adjusting entries
D. Book value of the asset
E. Cash Basis

F. Closing entries
G. Contra account
H. Deferral
I. Depreciation

J. General ledger
K. Matching principle
L. Plant assets
M. Work sheet

_A_ **1.** An accounting method in which revenues are reported in the period in which they are earned, and expenses are reported in the period in which they are incurred in an attempt to produce revenues.

_C_ **2.** The entries required at the end of an accounting period to bring the accounts up to date and to assure the proper matching of revenues and expenses.

_I_ **3.** The allocation of the cost of a plant asset to expense over the accounting periods making up its useful life.

_G_ **4.** An account which is "offset against" another account.

_B_ **5.** An accumulated expense that is unpaid and unrecorded.

_H_ **6.** A delay of the recognition of an expense already paid, or of a revenue already received.

_L_ **7.** Tangible assets that are permanent or have a long life and are used in the business.

_M_ **8.** A working paper often used by accountants to summarize adjusting entries.

_K_ **9.** The process of matching revenues and expenses.

_D_ **10.** The difference between the accumulated depreciation account and the related plant asset account.

TRUE / FALSE

Instructions: Indicate whether each of the following statements is true or false by placing a check mark in the appropriate column.

		True	False
1.	Most businesses use the accrual basis of accounting	✓	___
2.	When the reduction in prepaid expenses is not properly recorded, this causes the asset accounts and expense accounts to be overstated.	✓	✓
3.	Accumulated depreciation accounts may be referred to as contra asset accounts.	___	___
4.	When the Income Statement columns of the work sheet are totaled, if the debit column total is greater than the credit column total, the excess is the net income.	✓	___
5.	After all necessary adjustments are entered on the work sheet, the two Adjustments columns are totaled to prove the equality of debits and credits.	✓	
6.	The adjusting entry to record depreciation of plant assets consists of a debit to a depreciation expense account and a credit to an accumulated depreciation account. .	✓	___
7.	When services are not paid for until after they have been performed, the accrued expense is recorded in the accounts by an adjusting entry at the end of the accounting period.	✓	___
8.	A deferral is an expense that has not been paid or a revenue that has not been received.	___	✓
9.	Accrued expenses may be described on the balance sheet as accrued liabilities.	✓	___
10.	The amount of accrued revenue is recorded by debiting a liability account and crediting a revenue account.	___	___

MULTIPLE CHOICE

Instructions: Circle the best answer for each of the following questions.

1. Entries required at the end of an accounting period to bring the accounts up to date and to assure the proper matching of revenues and expenses are called:
   a. matching entries
   b. adjusting entries
   c. contra entries
   d. correcting entries

2. The decrease in usefulness of plant assets as time passes is called:
   a. consumption
   b. deterioration
   c. depreciation
   d. contra asset

3. The difference between the plant asset account and the related accumulated depreciation account is called the:
   a. book value of the asset
   b. fair market value of the asset
   c. net cost of the asset
   d. contra account balance of the asset

4. If a $250 adjustment for depreciation is not recorded, which of the following financial statement errors will occur?
   a. expenses will be overstated
   b. net income will be understated
   c. assets will be understated
   d. owner's equity will be overstated

5. The amount of accrued but unpaid expenses at the end of the fiscal period is both an expense and a(n):
   a. liability
   b. asset
   c. deferral
   d. revenue

This page is blank.

EXERCISE 3-1

Don Taylor closes his books at the end of each year (December 31). On May 1 of the current year, Don insured the business assets for three years at a premium of $5,400.

Instructions:

(1) Using the T accounts below, enter the adjusting entry that should be made by Taylor as of December 31 to record the amount of insurance expired as of that date. The May 1 premium payment is recorded in the T accounts.

Cash	Prepaid Insurance		Insurance Expense
May 1 5,400	May 1 5,400	Dec. 31 1,200	Dec. 31 1,200

(2) Taylor's balance sheet as of December 31 should show the asset value of the unexpired insurance as... $ 4,200

(3) Taylor's income statement for the year ended December 31 should show insurance expense of .... $ 1,200

EXERCISE 3-2

Jan Olin closes her books at the end of each month. Olin has only one employee, who is paid at the rate of $50 per day. The employee is paid every Friday at the end of the day. Each workweek is composed of five days, starting on Monday. Assume that the Fridays of this month (October) fall on the 7th, 14th, 21st, and 28th.

Instructions:

(1) Using the T accounts below, enter the four weekly wage payments for October. Then enter the adjusting entry that should be made by Olin as of October 31, to record the salary owed the employee but unpaid as of that date.

Cash		Salary Expense		Salaries Payable	
Oct. 7 250		Oct. 7 250		Oct. 31 50	
Oct. 14 250		Oct. 14 250			
Oct. 21 250		Oct. 21 250			
Oct. 28 250		Oct. 28 250			
		Oct. 31 50			

(2) Olin's income statement for October should show total salary expense of... $ 1,050

(3) Olin's balance sheet as of October 31 should show a liability for salaries payable of.. $ 50

50

EXERCISE 3-3

Keller Co.'s unearned rent account has a balance of $6,000 as of December 31 of the current year. This amount represents the rental of an apartment for a period of one year. The lease began on December 1 of the current year.

Instructions: Using the T accounts below, record the adjusting entry as of December 31 to recognize the rent income for the appropriate portion of the year. Then journalize the entry.

Unearned Rent		Rent Income	
Dec 31 500	Dec. 1 6,000		Dec 31 500

JOURNAL   PAGE _____

	DATE	DESCRIPTION	POST. REF.	DEBIT	CREDIT	
1	Dec 31	Unearned Rent		500		1
2		Rent Income			500	2
3						3
4						4
5						5
6						6
7						7
8						8
9						9
10						10
11						11
12						12
13						13
14						14
15						15
16						16
17						17
18						18
19						19
20						20
21						21
22						22
23						23
24						24
25						25
26						26
27						27
28						28
29						29
30						30

EXERCISE 3-4

Garret Co. has accrued but uncollected interest of $320 as of December 31 on a note receivable.

Instructions: Using the T accounts below, record the adjusting entry for accrued interest income as of December 31. Then journalize the entry.

Interest Receivable		Interest Income	
Dec 31 320			320 Dec. 31

JOURNAL

PAGE

	DATE		DESCRIPTION	POST. REF.	DEBIT	CREDIT	
1	1994 Dec	31	Interest Receivable		320		1
2			Interest Income			320	2
3							3
4							4
5							5
6							6
7							7
8							8
9							9
10							10
11							11
12							12
13							13
14							14
15							15
16							16
17							17
18							18
19							19
20							20
21							21
22							22
23							23
24							24
25							25
26							26
27							27
28							28
29							29
30							30

Name _____

PROBLEM 3-1

A partial work sheet with the trial balance portion completed is shown on the next page for Bob's Service Company for July.

Instructions:
 (1) Record the following adjustments in the Adjustments columns:
    (a) Salaries accrued but not paid at the end of the month amount to $2,000.
    (b) The $8,712 debit in the prepaid rent account is the payment of one year's rent on July 1.
    (c) The supplies on hand as of July 31 cost $1,000.
    (d) Depreciation of the tools and equipment for July is estimated at $400.
    (e) Fees for service rendered in July but collected in August amount to $2,100.
 (2) Complete the Adjusted Trial Balance columns of the work sheet.

Bob's Service Company
Partial Work Sheet
For Month Ended July 31, 19—

ACCOUNT TITLE	TRIAL BALANCE		ADJUSTMENTS		ADJUSTED TRIAL BALANCE	
	Dr.	Cr.	Dr.	Cr.	Dr.	Cr.
Cash	9 2 1 8					
Accounts Receivable	7 2 7 7					
Supplies	2 7 5 0					
Prepaid Rent	8 7 1 2					
Tools & Equipment	2 1 8 2 9					
Accumulated Depreciation		1 5 3 5				
Accounts Payable		7 1 1 7				
Bob Jones, Capital		3 7 4 1 7				
Bob Jones, Drawing	3 2 3 4					
Service Fees		2 8 6 9 9				
Salary Expense	1 5 9 2 9					
Miscellaneous Expense	5 8 1 9					
	7 4 7 6 8	7 4 7 6 8				

CONTINUING PROBLEM

The trial balance for Egor the Magician at the end of 1993 is shown in the partial work sheet on the next page.

Instructions:
   (4) Enter the following adjustments in the Adjustments columns:
   - (a) Office supplies on hand as of December 31, $210.
   - (b) Supplies and props on hand as of December 31, $365.
   - (c) The November 30 balance of prepaid insurance was used up as of December 31. The new policy purchased on December 2 must be adjusted for the amount used as of December 31.
   - (d) The notes payable account contains two notes. The first note is for $1,500 at 7% and was issued January 2. Interest accrued on this note is $105. The second note is for $5,000 at 6% and was issued December 24. No interest has accrued on this note.
   - (e) Mr. Gribbet owes the theater $850 for its services, which have not been recorded.
   - (f) Mr. Gribbet owes J. P. Magic $600 for a performance in November.
   - (g) Depreciation on the furniture and fixtures for the year, $2,680.
   - (h) Depreciation on the equipment, $2,400.

   (5) Complete the Adjusted Trial Balance columns of the work sheet.

(4) and (5)

Egor the Magician
Partial Work Sheet
For the Year Ended December 31, 1993

ACCOUNT TITLE	TRIAL BALANCE Dr.				TRIAL BALANCE Cr.				ADJUSTMENTS Dr.				ADJUSTMENTS Cr.			
Cash	9 9 5 6															
Fees Receivable	6 0 8 6															
Supplies & Props	1 2 6 8															
Office Supplies	7 8 9															
Prepaid Insurance	2 0 0 0															
Furniture & Fixtures	1 3 4 0 0															
Equipment - Stage	1 2 0 0 0															
Accounts Payable					1 5 8 0											
Theater Services Payable																
Subcontractors Payable																
Notes Payable					6 5 0 0											
E.J. Gribbet, Capital					2 1 8 5 2											
E.J. Gribbet, Drawing	4 0 0															
Fees Earned					3 1 3 0 0											
Theater Services Expense	4 0 0 0															
Subcontractor Expense	2 4 6 0															
Auto Expense	3 2 5 0															
Cosmetics Expense	4 2 8															
Rent Expense	4 8 0 0															
Telephone Expense	3 9 5															
	6 1 2 3 2				6 1 2 3 2											

ADJUSTED TRIAL BALANCE						
Dr.				Cr.		

This page is blank.

Chapter 4
Completion of the Accounting Cycle

QUIZ AND TEST HINTS

The following hints may be helpful to you in preparing for a quiz or a test over the material covered in Chapter 4.

1. The completion of the work sheet is an important part of this chapter. Although most instructors will not require you to prepare a work sheet from scratch, a test question might include a partially completed work sheet that you would be asked to complete.

2. Be thoroughly familiar with the financial statements presented in Exhibit 5 in the text. Know the financial statement captions and how the statements tie together. In a test situation, you may be provided with partially completed financial statements that you would be asked to complete.

3. You should be able to prepare the formal adjusting entries and closing entries in general journal form. You may have to prepare these entries from a completed work sheet.

4. The accounting cycle is an essential part of accounting. Expect multiple-choice or other types of short answer questions related to the accounting cycle.

5. Your instructor may or may not have discussed the material in the end-of-chapter appendix on reversing entries. If your instructor covered the appendix, you should know what adjusting entries normally require reversing entries, and be able to prepare reversing entries.

CHAPTER OUTLINE

I. Work Sheet for Financial Statements.
   A. At the end of an accounting period, a work sheet may be prepared by the accountant to facilitate the preparation of the financial statements and the necessary adjusting journal entries.
   B. The Trial Balance columns of the work sheet are taken directly from the balances of the various ledger accounts at the end of the accounting period.
   C. The necessary debit and credit portions of the adjusting entries are entered on the work sheet in the Adjustments columns.
   D. After the adjusting entries have been entered on the work sheet, the account balances are extended to the Adjusted Trial Balance columns. The debit and credit columns are then totaled and compared to prove that no arithmetical errors have been made up to this point.
   E. The data in the Adjusted Trial Balance columns are extended to the Income Statement and Balance Sheet columns of the work sheet. After all of the balances have been extended, each of the four columns is totaled. The net income or the net loss for the period is the amount of the difference between the totals of the two Income Statement columns. This net income or net loss is entered on the work sheet so that the Income Statement debit and credit columns and the Balance Sheet debit and credit columns balance.

II. Financial Statements.
   A. The Income Statement columns of the work sheet are the source for all of the data reported on the income statement.
   B. The work sheet is the source for all the data reported on the statement of owner's equity, with the exception of any in-

creases in the capital of a sole proprietorship which have occurred during the period. It is necessary to refer to the capital account in the ledger to determine the beginning balance and any such additional investments.

C. The work sheet is the source of all the data reported on the balance sheet, with the exception of the amount of a sole proprietor's capital, which can be obtained from the statement of owner's equity.

D. The balance sheet may be expanded to include additional subsections for current assets, plant assets, and current liabilities. Such a balance sheet is sometimes called a classified balance sheet.

1. Cash and other assets that are expected to be converted to cash or sold or used up within one year or less, through the normal operations of the business, are called current assets.

2. Plant assets include equipment, machinery, buildings, and land. The cost, accumulated depreciation, and book value of each major category of plant asset is normally reported on the balance sheet.

3. Liabilities that will be due within a short time (usually one year or less) and that are to be paid out of current assets are called current liabilities. Examples of current liabilities include short-term notes payable and accounts payable.

4. Liabilities that will not be due for a long time (usually more than one year) are called long-term liabilities or fixed liabilities. As they come due within one year and are to be paid, such liabilities become current. Examples include long-term notes payable and mortgage notes payable.

5. Owner's equity is the owner's claim against the assets of the business entity after the total liabilities have been deducted. The total liabilities of the enterprise plus the owner's equity must equal total assets.

III. Journalizing and Posting Adjusting Entries.

A. At the end of the accounting period, the adjusting entries appearing in the work sheet are recorded in the journal and posted to the ledger.

B. The process of journalizing and posting adjusting journal entries at the end of the accounting period brings the ledger into agreement with the data reported on the financial statements.

IV. Nature of the Closing Process.

A. The balances of all revenue and expense accounts should be zero at the beginning of each period.

B. To zero out the balances of the revenue and expense accounts at the end of the period, the balances of these accounts are transferred to a summarizing account and are said to be closed.

C. Because they are periodically closed, revenue and expense accounts are sometimes called temporary accounts or nominal accounts. Balance sheet accounts are sometimes called real accounts.

D. The owner's drawing account is also closed at the end of the period to the owner's capital account.

E. Revenue, expense, and drawing account balances are transferred to the owner's capital account by a series of entries called closing entries. The process of transferring these balances to the owner's capital account is called the closing process.

F. An account titled Income Summary is used for transferring the revenue and expense account balances to the owner's capital account at the end of the period. Because Income Summary has the effect of clearing the revenue and expense accounts of their balances, it is sometimes referred to as a clearing account. Income Summary is only used at the end of the period and is both opened and closed during the closing process.

G. The following four entries are required in order to close the temporary accounts of a sole proprietorship at the end of the period.

1. Each revenue account is debited for the amount of its balance, and Income Summary is credited for the total revenue.

2. Each expense account is credited for the amount of its balance, and Income Summary is debited for the total expense.

3. Income Summary is debited for the amount of its balance (net income), and

the capital account is credited for the same amount. (Debit and credit are reversed if there is a net loss.)

4. The drawing account is credited for the amount of its balance, and the capital account is debited for the same amount.

H. After the closing entries have been journalized, the balance in the capital account will correspond to the amounts reported on the statement of owner's equity and the balance sheet. In addition, the revenue, expense, and drawing accounts will have zero balances.

I. The last procedure for a period is the preparation of a post-closing trial balance after all of the temporary accounts have been closed.

J. The purpose of the post-closing trial balance is to make sure the ledger is in balance at the beginning of the new accounting period. The accounts and amounts should agree exactly with the accounts and amounts listed on the balance sheet at the end of the period.

V. Fiscal Year.

A. The maximum length of an accounting period is usually one year, which includes a complete cycle of the seasons of business activities.

B. The annual accounting period adopted by an enterprise is known as its fiscal year.

C. An accounting period ending when a business's activities have reached the lowest point in its annual operating cycle is termed the natural business year.

D. The long-term financial history of a business enterprise may be shown by a succession of balance sheets, prepared every year. The history of operations for the intervening periods is represented in a series of income statements.

VI. Accounting Cycle.

A. The sequence of accounting procedures of a fiscal period is called the accounting cycle.

B. The basic steps of the accounting cycle are as follows:

1. Transactions are analyzed and recorded in a journal.
2. Transactions are posted to the ledger.
3. A trial balance is prepared, data needed to adjust the accounts are assembled, and the work sheet is completed.
4. Financial statements are prepared.
5. Adjusting and closing entries are journalized.
6. Adjusting and closing entries are posted to the ledger.
7. A post-closing trial balance is prepared.

C. The most important output of the accounting cycle is the financial statements.

MATCHING

Instructions: A list of terms and related statements appear below. From the list of terms, select the one that relates to each statement. Print its identifying letter in the space provided.

A. Accounting cycle
B. Accounts receivable
C. Adjusting entries
D. Adjusting process
E. Capital account

F. Closing entries
G. Closing process
H. Current asset
I. Fiscal year
J. Income summary

K. Long-term liability
L. Natural business year
M. Notes receivable
N. Post-closing trial balance
O. Unadjusted trial balance

_K_ **1.** A liability that is not due within one year.

_A_ **2.** The sequence of accounting procedures for processing transactions during a fiscal period.

_H_ **3.** Cash or another asset that is expected to be converted to cash or sold or consumed within one year or less, through the normal operation of a business.

_M_ **4.** Written claims against debtors who promise to pay the amount and possibly interest, at an agreed date, to a specified person or bearer.

_G_ **5.** The process of transferring revenue, expenses, and drawing account balances to the owner's capital account by a series of entries.

_F_ **6.** The balances are removed from the temporary accounts so that they will be ready for use in accumulating data for the following accounting period by means of (?).

_J_ **7.** An account that is used for summarizing the data in the revenue and expense accounts at the end of the accounting period.

_N_ **8.** A listing prepared in order to make sure that the ledger is in balance at the beginning of the new accounting period.

_I_ **9.** The annual accounting period adopted by an enterprise.

_L_ **10.** A period ending when a business's activities have reached the lowest point in its annual operating cycle.

Name _____

TRUE / FALSE

Instructions: Indicate whether each of the following statements is true or false by placing a check mark in the appropriate column.

		True	False
1.	The balance of Accumulated Depreciation—Equipment is extended to the Income Statement columns of the work sheet.		✓
2.	The difference between the debit and credit columns of the Income Statement section of the work sheet is normally larger than the difference between the debit and credit columns of the Balance Sheet section.		✓
3.	The first item normally presented in the statement of owner's equity is the balance of the proprietor's capital account at the beginning of the period.	✓	
4.	The balance that is transferred from the income summary account to the capital account is the net income or net loss for the period.	✓	
5.	The balances of the accounts reported in the balance sheet are carried from year to year and are called temporary accounts.		✓
6.	An account titled Income Summary is normally used for transferring the revenue and expense account balances to the owner's capital account at the end of the period.	✓	
7.	If the Income Statement debit column is greater than the Income Statement credit column, the difference is net income.		✓
8.	A type of working paper frequently used by accountants prior to the preparation of financial statements is called a post-closing trial balance.		✓
9.	At the end of the period, the balances are removed from the temporary accounts and the net effect is recorded in the permanent account by means of closing entries.	✓	
10.	The annual accounting period adopted by an enterprise is known as its fiscal year.	✓	

MULTIPLE CHOICE

Instructions: Circle the best answer for each of the following questions.

1. A work sheet is completed by:
   a. extending the adjusted trial balance amounts to the Income Statement and Balance Sheet columns
   b. totaling the Adjustment columns
   c. extending the work sheet adjustments to the Adjusted Trial Balance columns
   d. footing the trial balance

2. If the Income Statement credit column is greater than the Income Statement debit column:
   a. a net income exists
   b. a net loss exists
   c. an asset account is debited
   d. a liability account is credited

3. Notes receivable are written claims against:
   a. creditors
   b. owner's equity
   c. debtors
   d. assets

4. The maximum length of an accounting period is normally:
   a. 6 months
   b. 1 year
   c. 2 years
   d. 3 years

5. The complete sequence of accounting procedures for a fiscal period is frequently called the:
   a. work sheet process
   b. opening and closing cycle
   c. accounting cycle
   d. fiscal cycle

EXERCISE 4-1

Instructions: The account titles and Adjustments columns of the work sheet for Sally's Small Engine Repair are listed below.

Sally's Small Engine Repair
Work Sheet
For Month Ended August 31, 19—

	Adjustments	
	Dr.	Cr.
Cash		
Accounts Receivable...........	(e) 3,200	
Supplies......................		(c) 700
Prepaid Rent..................		(b) 560
Tools/Equipment		
Accumulated Depreciation......		(d) 1,000
Accounts Payable		
Sally Sand, Capital		
Sally Sand, Drawing............		
Repair Fees		(e) 3,200
Salary Expense................	(a) 1,500	
Miscellaneous Expense		
Salaries Payable................		(a) 1,500
Rent Expense	(b) 560	
Supplies Expense..............	(c) 700	
Depreciation Expense..........	(d) 1,000	

Instructions: Prepare journal entries for the adjustments indicated for Sally's Small Engine Repair.

JOURNAL   PAGE

	DATE	DESCRIPTION	POST. REF.	DEBIT	CREDIT	
1	Aug. 31	Salaries exp	a	1500		1
2		Sal Payable			1500	2
3						3
4	31	Rent Exp	b	560		4
5		Prepaid Rent			560	5
6						6
7	31	Supplies Expense	c	700		7
8		Supplies			700	8
9						9
10	31	Depreciation Expense	d	1000		10
11		Accum. Dep.			1000	11
12						12
13	31	Accnts Rec	e	3200		13
14		Repair Fees			3200	14
15						15
16						16

EXERCISE 4-2

Instructions: The journal, the income summary account, the service fees account, the salary expense account, and the supplies expense account of Tony Brown as of March 31, the first month of the current fiscal year, appear below. In the journal, prepare the entries to close Brown's revenue and expense accounts into the income summary account. Then post to the ledger.

JOURNAL

PAGE 1

	DATE	DESCRIPTION	POST. REF.	DEBIT	CREDIT	
1	March 31	Service Fees	50	19225		1
2		Income Summary	45		19225	2
3	31	Income Summary	45	13980		3
4		Salary Expense	58		8550	4
5		Supplies Expense	67		5430	5

ACCOUNT Income Summary   **ACCOUNT NO.** 45

DATE	ITEM	POST. REF.	DEBIT	CREDIT	BALANCE DEBIT	BALANCE CREDIT
Mar 31		1		19225		19225
31		1	13980			5245

ACCOUNT Service Fees   **ACCOUNT NO.** 50

DATE	ITEM	POST. REF.	DEBIT	CREDIT	BALANCE DEBIT	BALANCE CREDIT
19— Mar. 15		5		4850		4850
31		6		14375		19225
31		1	19225			—

ACCOUNT Salary Expense   **ACCOUNT NO.** 58

DATE	ITEM	POST. REF.	DEBIT	CREDIT	BALANCE DEBIT	BALANCE CREDIT
19— Mar. 31		5	8550		8550	
31		1		8550	—	—

ACCOUNT Supplies Expense   **ACCOUNT NO.** 67

DATE	ITEM	POST. REF.	DEBIT	CREDIT	BALANCE DEBIT	BALANCE CREDIT
19— Mar. 15		5	2430		2430	
25		6	1720		4150	
31		6	1280		5430	
31		1		5430	—	—

66

PROBLEM 4-1

The partially completed ten-column work sheet of Castle Shop for the fiscal year ended April 30, 19—, appears on the following page. The following adjustment data have been entered in the Adjustments columns of the work sheet:

        (a) Supplies on hand as of April 30, 19—, 1,800.
        (b) Rent prepaid for 12 months on April 1, $9,504.
        (c) Depreciation on tools and equipment during the year, $1,000.
        (d) Wages accrued but not paid as of April 30, 19—, $2,000.
        (e) Accrued fees earned but not recorded as of April 30, 19—, $3,000.
        (f) Unearned fees as of April 30, 19—, $1,500.

Instructions:
    (1) Complete the ten-column work sheet.
    (2) Prepare an income statement, statement of owner's equity, and a balance sheet.

Castle Shop
Work Sheet
For the Year Ended April 30, 19—

ACCOUNT TITLE	TRIAL BALANCE Dr.	TRIAL BALANCE Cr.	ADJUSTMENTS Dr.	ADJUSTMENTS Cr.
Cash	1 0 0 5 6			
Accounts Receivable	7 9 3 8		(e) 3 0 0 0	
Supplies	3 0 0 0			(a) 1 2 0 0
Prepaid Rent	9 5 0 4			(b) 7 9 2
Tools & Equipment	2 3 8 1 4			
Accumulated Depreciation		1 6 7 4		(c) 1 0 0 0
Accounts Payable		7 7 6 4		
Unearned Fees		2 0 0 0	(f) 1 5 0 0	
Castle, Capital		3 8 8 1 8		
Castle, Drawing	3 5 2 8			
Service Fees		3 1 3 0 8		(e) 3 0 0 0
				(f) 1 5 0 0
Wages Expense	1 7 3 7 6		(d) 2 0 0 0	
Miscellaneous Expense	6 3 4 8			
	8 1 5 6 4	8 1 5 6 4		
Wages Payable				(d) 2 0 0 0
Rent Expense			(b) 7 9 2	
Supplies Expense			(a) 1 2 0 0	
Depreciation Expense			(c) 1 0 0 0	
			8 4 9 2	8 4 9 2

68

| ADJUSTED TRIAL BALANCE | | INCOME STATEMENT | | BALANCE SHEET | |
Dr.	Cr.	Dr.	Cr.	Dr.	Cr.
10056				10056	
10938				10938	
1800				1800	
8712				8712	
23814				23814	
	2674				2674
	7764				7764
	3500				3500
	38818				38818
3528				3528	
	34308		34308		
19376		19376			
6348		6348			
	2000				2000
792		792			
1200		1200			
1000		1000			
87564	87564	28716	34308	58848	54756
		6092			
		34308	34308		

Castle Shop
Income Statement
For the Year Ended April 30, 19—

Service Fees						3 4 8 0 8
Operating expenses			1 9 3 7 6			
Total Oper Expenses						1 9 3 7 6
Net Income						6 0 9 2

Castle Shop
Statement of Owner's Equity
For the Year Ended April 30, 19—

Capital, May 1, 1993						3 8 8 1 8
Income for year			6 0 9 2			
Less Drawing			3 5 2 8			
Inc. in Owner's Eq						
Cap, April 30, 99						

Name _____

Castle Shop
Balance Sheet
April 30, 19—

Assets											

PROBLEM 4-2

Instructions:
  (1) On the basis of the data in the Adjustments columns of the work sheet in Problem 4-1, journalize the adjusting entries.
  (2) On the basis of the data in the Income Statement and Balance Sheet columns of the work sheet in Problem 4-1, journalize the closing entries.

JOURNAL

PAGE

	DATE	DESCRIPTION	POST. REF.	DEBIT	CREDIT	
1						1
2						2
3						3
4						4
5						5
6						6
7						7
8						8
9						9
10						10
11						11
12						12
13						13
14						14
15						15
16						16
17						17
18						18
19						19
20						20
21						21
22						22
23						23
24						24
25						25
26						26
27						27
28						28
29						29

CONTINUING PROBLEM

The work sheet for Egor the Magician at the end of 1993, on the next two pages, shows the trial balance, adjustments, and adjusted trial balance.

Instructions:
- (6) Complete the work sheet.
- (7) Prepare an income statement, a statement of owner's equity, and a balance sheet.
- (8) Journalize the adjusting entries and post them to the ledger on pages 30-41.
- (9) Journalize the closing entries and post them to the ledger on pages 30-41.

Egor the Magician
Work Sheet
For the Year Ended December 31, 1993

ACCOUNT TITLE	TRIAL BALANCE Dr.	TRIAL BALANCE Cr.	ADJUSTMENTS Dr.	ADJUSTMENTS Cr.
Cash	9 9 5 6			
Fees Receivable	6 0 8 6			
Supplies & Props	1 2 6 8			(b) 9 0 3
Office Supplies	7 8 9			(a) 5 7 9
Prepaid Insurance	2 0 0 0			(c) 1 4 5 0
Furniture & Fixtures	1 3 4 0 0			
Equipment - Stage	1 2 0 0 0			
Accounts Payable		1 5 8 0		
Theater Services Payable				(e) 8 5 0
Subcontractors Payable				(f) 6 0 0
Notes Payable		6 5 0 0		
E.J. Gribbet, Capital		2 1 8 5 2		
E.J. Gribbet, Drawing	4 0 0			
Fees Earned		3 1 3 0 0		
Theater Services Expense	4 0 0 0		(e) 8 5 0	
Subcontractor Expense	2 4 6 0		(f) 6 0 0	
Auto Expense	3 2 5 0			
Cosmetics Expense	4 2 8			
Rent Expense	4 8 0 0			
Telephone Expense	3 9 5			
	6 1 2 3 2	6 1 2 3 2		
Office Supplies Expense			(a) 5 7 9	
Supplies & Props Expense			(b) 9 0 3	
Insurance Expense			(c) 1 4 5 0	
Interest Expense			(d) 2 5 5	
Interest Payable				(d) 2 5 5
Depr. Exp.—Furn. & Fix.			(g) 2 6 8 0	
Accum. Depr.—Furn. & Fix.				(g) 2 6 8 0
Depr. Exp.—Equip.			(h) 2 4 0 0	
Accum. Depr.—Equip.				(h) 2 4 0 0
			9 7 1 7	9 7 1 7

ADJUSTED TRIAL BALANCE		INCOME STATEMENT		BALANCE SHEET	
Dr.	Cr.	Dr.	Cr.	Dr.	Cr.
9 9 5 6					
6 0 8 6					
3 6 5					
2 1 0					
5 5 0					
1 3 4 0 0					
1 2 0 0 0					
	1 5 8 0				
	8 5 0				
	6 0 0				
	6 5 0 0				
	2 1 8 5 2				
4 0 0					
	3 1 3 0 0				
4 8 5 0					
3 0 6 0					
3 2 5 0					
4 2 8					
4 8 0 0					
3 9 5					
5 7 9					
9 0 3					
1 4 5 0					
2 5 5					
	2 5 5				
2 6 8 0					
	2 6 8 0				
2 4 0 0					
	2 4 0 0				
6 8 0 1 7	6 8 0 1 7				

Egor the Magician
Income Statement
For the Year Ended December 31, 1993

Name _____

Egor the Magician
Statement of Owner's Equity
For the Year Ended December 31, 1993

Egor the Magician
Balance Sheet
December 31, 1993

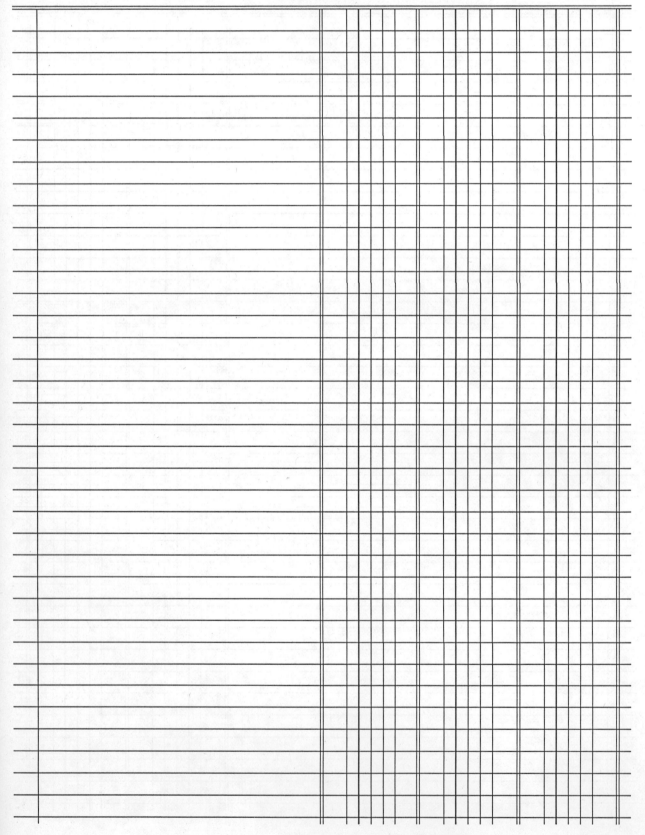

(8)   **JOURNAL**   PAGE

	DATE		DESCRIPTION	POST. REF.	DEBIT	CREDIT	
1							1
2							2
3							3
4							4
5							5
6							6
7							7
8							8
9							9
10							10
11							11
12							12
13							13
14							14
15							15
16							16
17							17
18							18
19							19
20							20
21							21
22							22
23							23
24							24
25							25
26							26
27							27
28							28
29							29
30							30
31							31
32							32
33							33
34							34
35							35

JOURNAL

	DATE	DESCRIPTION	POST. REF.	DEBIT	CREDIT	
1						1
2						2
3						3
4						4
5						5
6						6
7						7
8						8
9						9
10						10
11						11
12						12
13						13
14						14
15						15
16						16
17						17
18						18
19						19
20						20
21						21
22						22
23						23
24						24
25						25
26						26
27						27
28						28
29						29
30						30
31						31
32						32
33						33
34						34
35						35

Chapter 5
Merchandising Transactions—Periodic Inventory Systems

QUIZ AND TEST HINTS

The following hints may be helpful to you in preparing for a quiz or a test over the material covered in Chapter 5.

1. This chapter introduces merchandising enterprise terminology that you should know. Review the Glossary of Key Terms.

2. You should be able to prepare general journal entries for the types of transactions illustrated in the chapter. Be sure you can compute purchases discounts and sales discounts. Review the chapter illustrations. The Illustrative Problem in the Chapter Review is an excellent review of the types of entries you might have to prepare.

3. Expect a multiple-choice question that requires you to compute the net savings on borrowings to take a purchases discount. You can review this computation on page 157 of the chapter.

4. The accounting for transportation costs can be confusing, but you will probably be required to prepare one or more journal entries, or answer one or more multiple-choice questions, involving such costs. Review the chapter discussion and illustration related to such costs.

5. The illustration of the journal entries for both the buyer and seller of merchandise on page 161 of the chapter provides an excellent review. Often, instructors will require students to prepare journal entries based upon the same data for both the buyer and the seller.

6. Be able to prepare the cost of merchandise sold section of the income statement. A common test question is to provide students with a partially completed cost of merchandise sold section that requires completion. Be careful not to confuse the beginning and ending merchandise inventories. The beginning merchandise inventory is added and the ending merchandise inventory is subtracted in computing cost of merchandise sold.

7. The chart of accounts for a merchandising enterprise will be useful in Chapter 6. However, you will probably not be tested on this listing in Chapter 5.

CHAPTER OUTLINE

I. Income Statement for Merchandising Enterprise.
   A. The primary difference between service and merchandise enterprises relates to the revenue activities of the enterprises. The revenue generating activities of a service enterprise involve the rendering of services to clients. The revenue generating activities of a merchandise enterprise involve the purchasing and selling of merchandise to customers.
   B. The income statement of a merchandising enterprise reports sales, cost of merchandise sold, and gross profit.
   C. Merchandise that is not sold at the end of an accounting period is called merchandise inventory, which is reported as a current asset on the balance sheet.

II. Accounting for Sales.
   A. Merchandise sales are recorded by the seller by a credit to a sales account.
      1. Cash sales are recorded by a debit to Cash and a credit to Sales.
      2. Sales to customers who use bank credit cards are recorded as cash sales.
      3. Sales of merchandise on account are recorded by a debit to Accounts Receivable and a credit to Sales.

81

4. Sales made by use of nonbank credit cards are recorded as sales on account.

5. Any service charges for handling bank or nonbank credit cards are debited to an expense account, Bank (Nonbank) Credit Card Expense.

B. The terms agreed upon by the buyer and the seller are normally indicated on the invoice or bill that the seller sends to the buyer. The terms agreed upon as to when payments for merchandise are to be made are called the credit terms.

1. The credit period, during which the buyer is allowed to pay, begins with the date of the sale as shown by the date of the invoice or bill.

2. If the payment is due within a stated number of days after the date of invoice, for example, 30 days, the terms may be expressed as n/30. If payment is due at the end of the month, the terms may be expressed as n/eom.

3. The terms 2/10, n/30 mean that, although the credit period is thirty days, the buyer may deduct 2% of the amount of the invoice if payment is made within ten days of the invoice date.

C. The seller refers to the discounts taken by the buyer for early payment of an invoice as sales discounts. These discounts are recorded by debiting the sales discount account, which is viewed as a reduction in the amount initially recorded as Sales. In this sense, sales discounts can be thought of as a contra (or offsetting) account to Sales.

D. Merchandise sold that is returned by the buyer, or for which a price adjustment is made, is recorded by the seller by debiting Sales Returns and Allowances and crediting Accounts Receivable.

1. A sales return and allowance is granted by the seller by issuing a credit memorandum.

2. Sales returns and allowances are viewed as a reduction of the amount initially recorded as sales. The sales returns and allowances account is a contra (or offsetting) account to Sales.

E. Almost all states and many other taxing units levy a tax on sales of merchandise (referred to as a sales tax) which becomes a liability at the time the sale is made.

1. At the time of a cash sale, the seller collects the sales tax and credits a liability account, Sales Tax Payable.

2. Periodically, the sales tax liability is paid to the taxing unit.

III. Accounting for Purchases.

A. Purchases of merchandise for resale are identified in the ledger as (debited to) Purchases.

B. Discounts taken by the buyer for early payment of an invoice are called purchases discounts. They are recorded by debiting Purchases Discounts.

1. Purchases discounts are usually reported as a deduction from the amount initially recorded in Purchases. In this sense, the purchases discounts account is a contra (or offsetting) account to Purchases.

2. It is normally best for a buyer to take all available discounts. This is true even if the buyer must borrow the money to make the payment.

C. If merchandise is returned or a price adjustment is requested by the buyer, the transaction is recorded by a credit to a purchases returns and allowances account.

1. The details of the merchandise returned or the price adjustment requested are set forth by the buyer in a debit memorandum.

2. A confirmation from the seller of the amount of the merchandise returned or the price adjustment requested is set forth in a credit memorandum.

3. The purchases returns and allowances account can be viewed as a deduction from the amount initially recorded as Purchases. In this sense, purchases returns and allowances can be thought of as a contra (or offsetting) account to Purchases.

4. When a buyer returns merchandise or has been granted an allowance prior to the payment of the invoice, the amount of the debit memorandum is deducted from the invoice amount before the purchases discount is computed.

D. Trade discounts are special discounts from prices listed in catalogs or offered to certain classes of buyers such as government agencies. Trade discounts are not normally entered into the accounts, but are recorded at the actual purchase price by the buyer.

IV. Transportation Costs.

   A. If the ownership of merchandise passes to the buyer when the seller delivers the merchandise to the shipper, the buyer is to absorb the transportation cost, and the terms are said to be FOB shipping point.

     1. Transportation costs paid by the buyer should be debited to Transportation In or Freight In and credited to Cash.

     2. The balance of the transportation in or freight in account should be added to net purchases in determining the total cost of merchandise purchased.

     3. Sellers may prepay the transportation costs and add them to the invoice, as an accommodation to the buyer. In this case, the buyer should debit Transportation In for the transportation costs and compute any purchases discounts on the amount of the sale rather than on the invoice total. The seller records the prepayment of transportation costs by adding the amount of the total invoice and debiting Accounts Receivable.

   B. If ownership of the merchandise passes to the buyer when the merchandise is received by the buyer, the seller is to assume the costs of transportation, and the terms are said to be FOB destination.

     1. The amounts paid by the seller for delivery of merchandise are debited to Transportation Out, or Delivery Expense, or a similarly titled account.

     2. The total of such costs incurred during a period is reported on the seller's income statement as a selling expense.

   C. Shipping terms, the passage of title, and whether the buyer or seller is to pay transportation costs is summarized as follows:

	FOB Shipping Point	FOB Destination
Ownership (title) passes to buyer when merchandise is	delivered to freight carrier	delivered to buyer
Transportation costs are paid by	buyer	seller

V. Illustration of Accounting for Merchandising Transactions.

   A. Each merchandising transaction affects both a buyer and a seller.

   B. Review the illustration on page 161 of the text where the entries that both the seller and buyer would record are shown for each transaction.

VI. Merchandise Inventory Systems.

   A. In a periodic inventory system, the revenues from sales are recorded when sales are made, but no attempt is made on the sales date to record the cost of merchandise sold.

     1. A detailed listing of merchandise on hand (called a physical inventory) is made at the end of the accounting period.

     2. The physical inventory at the end of the accounting period is used to determine the cost of merchandise sold during the period and the cost of inventory on hand at the end of the period.

   B. Under the perpetual inventory system, both the sales amount and the cost of merchandise sold amount are recorded when each item of merchandise is sold. In this manner, the accounting records continuously (perpetually) disclose the inventory on hand.

VII. Cost of Merchandise Sold.

   A. In a periodic inventory system, the cost of merchandise sold during a period is reported in a separate section of the income statement.

   B. Net purchases are determined by subtracting the purchases returns and allowances and purchases discounts from the total purchases.

   C. The cost of merchandise purchased during the period is determined by adding to the net purchases the amount of transportation in incurred during the period.

   D. Merchandise available for sale is determined by adding the beginning merchandise inventory for the period to the cost of merchandise purchased during the period.

E. The cost of merchandise sold for the period is determined by subtracting the ending merchandise inventory for the period from the merchandise available for sale.

VIII. Chart of Accounts for Merchandising Enterprises.

A. The chart of accounts for a merchandising enterprise will differ from that of a service enterprise.

B. The chart of accounts for Computer King, which uses three-digit account numbers, is shown on page 163. The accounts related to merchandising transactions are shown in color.

Name _____

MATCHING

Instructions: A list of terms and related statements appear below. From the list of terms, select the one that relates to each statement. Print its identifying letter in the space provided.

A. Cash discount   E. FOB shipping point   I. Perpetual inventory system
B. Credit memorandum   F. Invoice   J. Purchases discounts
C. Debit memorandum   G. Merchandise inventory   K. Sales discounts
D. FOB destination   H. Periodic inventory system L. Trade discounts

A K **1.** As a means of encouraging payment before the end of the credit period, the seller may offer a discount for the early payment of cash, known as a (?).

J **2.** Discounts taken by the buyer for early payment of an invoice are called (?).

C **3.** When merchandise is returned or a price adjustment is requested, the buyer may inform the seller through the use of a (?).

B **4.** The document issued by the seller, allowing for returns of merchandise or a price reduction.

K **5.** The seller refers to the discounts taken by the buyer for early payment of an invoice as (?).

E **6.** If the ownership of the merchandise passes to the buyer when the seller delivers the merchandise to the shipper, the buyer is to absorb the transportation costs, and the terms are said to be (?).

D **7.** If ownership passes to the buyer when the merchandise is received by the buyer, the seller is to assume the costs of transportation, and the terms are said to be (?).

H **8.** Under this inventory system, the revenues from sales are recorded when sales are made, but no attempt is made on the sales date to record the cost of the merchandise sold.

I **9.** Under this inventory system, both the sales amount and the cost of merchandise sold amount are recorded when each item of merchandise is sold.

F **10.** The bill provided by the seller to a buyer for items purchased.

G **11.** Merchandise on hand and available for sale to customers.

L **12.** Special discounts from published list prices, offered by sellers to certain classes of buyers.

TRUE / FALSE

Instructions: Indicate whether each of the following statements is true or false by placing a check mark in the appropriate column.

		True	False
1.	A discount offered the purchaser of goods as a means of encouraging payment before the end of the credit period is known as a bank discount....................		✓
2.	Credit terms of "2/10, n/30" mean that the buyer may deduct 2% of the amount of the invoice if payment is made within 10 days of the invoice date..................	✓	
3.	If the seller is to absorb the cost of delivering the goods, the terms are stated FOB (free on board) shipping point.		✓
4.	The two main systems for accounting for merchandise held for sale are called periodic and perpetual.	✓	
5.	The debit balance of the merchandise inventory account appearing in the trial balance represents the amount of the inventory at the end of the current year.......		✓
6.	The balance in the merchandise inventory account at the beginning of the period represents the cost of the merchandise on hand at that time.	✓	
7.	The liability for the sales tax is incurred at the time the seller receives payment from the buyer...	✓	✓
8.	The purchases returns and allowances account can be viewed as a deduction from the amount initially recorded as Purchases....................................	✓	
9.	The cost of merchandise purchased during the period is determined by subtracting from the net purchases the amount of transportation costs incurred during the period...	✓	✓
10.	The chart of accounts for a merchandising enterprise will differ from that of a service enterprise	✓	

MULTIPLE CHOICE

Instructions: Circle the best answer for each of the following questions.

1. A buyer receives an invoice for $60 dated June 10. If the terms are 2/10, n/30, and the buyer pays the invoice within the discount period, what amount will the seller receive?
   a. $60
   b. $58.80
   c. $48
   d. $1.20

2. The purchases discount account is a contra account to:
   a. Accounts Payable
   b. Sales Discounts
   c. Sales
   d. Purchases

3. When a seller of merchandise allows a customer a reduction from the original price for defective goods, the seller usually issues to the customer a(n):
   a. debit memorandum
   b. credit memorandum
   c. sales invoice
   d. inventory slip

4. When the seller prepays the transportation costs and the terms of sale are FOB shipping point, the seller records the payment of the transportation costs by debiting:
   a. Accounts Receivable
   b. Sales
   c. Transportation In
   d. Accounts Payable

5. If the seller collects sales tax at the time of sale, the seller credits the tax to:
   a. Sales
   b. Accounts Receivable
   c. Sales Tax Payable
   d. Sales Tax Receivable

6. The account that appears in the chart of accounts for a merchandising enterprise but not for a service enterprise is:
   a. Accounts Receivable
   b. Advertising Expense
   c. Sales Returns and Allowances
   d. Accumulated Depreciation

EXERCISE 5-1

Instructions: Prepare entries for each of the following related transactions of Foley Co. in the general journal given below.

(1) Purchased $5,000 of merchandise from Phillips Co. on account, terms 2/10, n/30.
(2) Paid Phillips Co. on account for purchases, less discount.
(3) Purchased $3,500 of merchandise from Farris Co. on account, terms FOB shipping point, 2/10, n/30, with prepaid shipping costs of $80 added to the invoice.
(4) Returned merchandise from Farris Co., $900.
(5) Paid Farris Co. on account for purchases, less returns and discount.

JOURNAL   PAGE

	DATE	DESCRIPTION	POST. REF.	DEBIT	CREDIT	
1						1
2						2
3						3
4						4
5						5
6						6
7						7
8						8
9						9
10						10
11						11
12						12
13						13
14						14
15						15
16						16
17						17
18						18
19						19
20						20
21						21
22						22
23						23
24						24
25						25
26						26

EXERCISE 5-2

Instructions: Prepare entries for each of the following related transactions of Wilson Co. in the general journal given below.

   (1) Sold merchandise on nonbank credit cards and reported accounts to the card company, $3,150.
   (2) Sold merchandise for cash, $2,850.
   (3) Received cash from card company for nonbank credit card sales, less $100 service fee.
   (4) Sold merchandise on account to Rask Co., $4,500, terms 2/10, n/30, FOB shipping point. Prepaid transportation costs of $150 at the customer's request.
   (5) Received merchandise returned by Rask Co., $400.
   (6) Received cash on account from Rask Co. for sale and transportation costs, less returns and discount.

JOURNAL   PAGE _____

	DATE		DESCRIPTION	POST. REF.	DEBIT	CREDIT	
1							1
2							2
3							3
4							4
5							5
6							6
7							7
8							8
9							9
10							10
11							11
12							12
13							13
14							14
15							15
16							16
17							17
18							18
19							19
20							20
21							21
22							22
23							23
24							24

PROBLEM 5-1

The following transactions were selected from among those completed by the Bowman Company during September of the current year:

Sept. 3.   Purchased merchandise on account from Axel Co., list price $10,000, trade discount 15%, terms FOB destination, 1/10, n/30.

4.   Purchased office supplies for cash, $800.

6.   Sold merchandise on account to Hart Co., list price $5,000, trade discount 20%, terms 2/10, n/30.

7.   Returned merchandise purchased on September 3 from Axel Co., $2,000.

10.   Purchased merchandise for cash, $5,000.

12.   Sold merchandise on nonbank credit cards and reported accounts to the card company, $5,500.

13.   Paid Axel Co. on account for purchase of September 3, less return of September 7 and discount.

16.   Received cash on account from sale of September 6 to Hart Co., less discount.

20.   Received cash from card company for nonbank credit sales of September 12, less $300 service fee.

24.   Sold merchandise to Wilcox Co., $3,000, terms 1/10, n/30.

26.   Sold merchandise for cash, $2,200.

30.   Received merchandise returned by Wilcox Co. from sale on September 24, $1,000.

Instructions: Journalize the transactions for the Bowman Co., using the journal provided on the following page.

Name _____

JOURNAL

PAGE _____

	DATE		DESCRIPTION	POST. REF.	DEBIT	CREDIT	
1							1
2							2
3							3
4							4
5							5
6							6
7							7
8							8
9							9
10							10
11							11
12							12
13							13
14							14
15							15
16							16
17							17
18							18
19							19
20							20
21							21
22							22
23							23
24							24
25							25
26							26
27							27
28							28
29							29
30							30
31							31
32							32
33							33

PROBLEM 5-2

Instructions: On the basis of the following data, prepare the cost of merchandise sold section of the income statement for the fiscal year ended June 30, 1994, for Stillman Co.

Merchandise Inventory, June 30, 1994	$155,000
Merchandise Inventory, July 1, 1993	130,000
Purchases	415,000
Purchases Returns and Allowances	3,780
Purchases Discounts	4,590
Transportation In	2,970

CONTINUING PROBLEM

Things have been going very well for Egor J. Gribbet. Egor has invented a line of magic tricks that he will begin selling to toy stores and magic shops. His performance schedule is heavy, however, so he has hired Sam Delisle to manage the retail part of the business on a part-time basis. Further, Egor has contracted with a factory, Magical Enterprises, to manufacture the tricks.

The following transactions were completed by Egor the Magician during the second year of operations (1994):

Jan   2. Paid office rent for January through June, $2,400.
        2. Paid auto lease for January through December, $2,400.
        2. Paid off the $1,500 note payable plus the $105 of interest that was accrued and recorded at the end of 1993.
      22. Received payment for performances billed in November of the previous year, $2,486.
Feb   11. Paid for theater services recorded at the end of 1993, $850.
      24. Paid J. P. Magic, $600.
Mar   15. Paid cash for props, $840.
      15. Paid Sam Delisle's salary for two months, $800.
      31. Received cash for performances, $9,400.
Apr   11. Purchased merchandise on account from Magical Enterprises, $4,800, terms FOB destination, 2/10, n/30.
      20. Paid Magical Enterprises for merchandise purchased, less discount.
May   15. Paid Sam Delisle's salary for two months, $800.
June   5. Sold merchandise on account to Jerome's Toys, $2,200, terms FOB destination, 2/10, n/30.
       5. Paid transportation costs on the merchandise sold, $45.
      30. Received check from Jerome's Toys for purchase on June 5.
July   1. Paid office rent for July through December, $2,400.
       1. Paid six months' interest on $5,000, 6% note, $150.
       2. Paid telephone expense, $120.
      10. Paid creditors on account, $500.
      15. Sold merchandise on account to Evan's Magic, $2,850, terms FOB destination, 2/10, n/30.
      15. Paid Sam Delisle's salary for two months, $800.
      18. Purchased merchandise from Magical Enterprises, $5,600, terms FOB shipping point, 2/10, n/eom. Prepaid transportation costs of $200 were added to the invoice.
      20. Returned to Magical Enterprises $400 of merchandise purchased.
      24. Received check due from Evan's Magic.
      28. Paid Magical Enterprises (less debit memorandum) for the July 18 purchase, less discount.
      31. Sold merchandise on account to Toy Depot, $4,600, terms FOB destination, n/30.
Aug   1. Paid transportation costs for merchandise shipped, $75.
       3. Billed clients for performances during the last two months, $9,200.
      16. Issued a credit memorandum for $500 to Toy Depot for merchandise returned from sale of July 31.
      30. Received check due from Toy Depot less credit memorandum of August 16.
Sep   1. Collected cash from August 3 billings, $9,200.
      15. Paid cash for cosmetics, $100.
      15. Paid Sam Delisle's salary for two months, $800.
Oct   8. Paid Jane the Fantastic for a performance, $400.
Nov   13. Paid cash to the Apollo Theater for its use, $600.
      15. Paid Sam Delisle's salary for two months, $800.
Dec   2. Paid cash for renewal of property insurance policy for another year, $600.
       2. Billed clients for work done for the last two months, $8,100.
      11. Sold merchandise on account to Mystic Emporium, $3,400, terms FOB shipping point, 2/10, n/30.
      30. Paid telephone expense, $135.

Instructions:
    (10) Journalize the transactions for Egor the Magician.
    (11) Post the journal to the ledger on pages 30-41.

	DATE		DESCRIPTION	POST. REF.	DEBIT	CREDIT	
1							1
2							2
3							3
4							4
5							5
6							6
7							7
8							8
9							9
10							10
11							11
12							12
13							13
14							14
15							15
16							16
17							17
18							18
19							19
20							20
21							21
22							22
23							23
24							24
25							25
26							26
27							27
28							28
29							29
30							30
31							31
32							32

Name _____

JOURNAL

PAGE _____

	DATE		DESCRIPTION	POST. REF.	DEBIT	CREDIT	
1							1
2							2
3							3
4							4
5							5
6							6
7							7
8							8
9							9
10							10
11							11
12							12
13							13
14							14
15							15
16							16
17							17
18							18
19							19
20							20
21							21
22							22
23							23
24							24
25							25
26							26
27							27
28							28
29							29
30							30
31							31
32							32

JOURNAL

PAGE

	DATE	DESCRIPTION	POST. REF.	DEBIT	CREDIT	
1						1
2						2
3						3
4						4
5						5
6						6
7						7
8						8
9						9
10						10
11						11
12						12
13						13
14						14
15						15
16						16
17						17
18						18
19						19
20						20
21						21
22						22
23						23
24						24
25						25
26						26
27						27
28						28
29						29
30						30
31						31
32						32

Name _____

JOURNAL

PAGE

	DATE		DESCRIPTION	POST. REF.	DEBIT	CREDIT	
1							1
2							2
3							3
4							4
5							5
6							6
7							7
8							8
9							9
10							10
11							11
12							12
13							13
14							14
15							15
16							16
17							17
18							18
19							19
20							20
21							21
22							22
23							23
24							24
25							25
26							26
27							27
28							28
29							29
30							30
31							31
32							32

JOURNAL

PAGE

	DATE		DESCRIPTION	POST. REF.	DEBIT	CREDIT	
1							1
2							2
3							3
4							4
5							5
6							6
7							7
8							8
9							9
10							10
11							11
12							12
13							13
14							14
15							15
16							16
17							17
18							18
19							19
20							20
21							21
22							22
23							23
24							24
25							25
26							26
27							27
28							28
29							29
30							30
31							31
32							32

Name _____

JOURNAL

PAGE _____

	DATE		DESCRIPTION	POST. REF.	DEBIT	CREDIT	
1							1
2							2
3							3
4							4
5							5
6							6
7							7
8							8
9							9
10							10
11							11
12							12
13							13
14							14
15							15
16							16
17							17
18							18
19							19
20							20
21							21
22							22
23							23
24							24
25							25
26							26
27							27
28							28
29							29
30							30
31							31
32							32

JOURNAL

PAGE

	DATE		DESCRIPTION	POST. REF.	DEBIT	CREDIT	
1							1
2							2
3							3
4							4
5							5
6							6
7							7
8							8
9							9
10							10
11							11
12							12
13							13
14							14
15							15
16							16
17							17
18							18
19							19
20							20
21							21
22							22
23							23
24							24
25							25
26							26
27							27
28							28
29							29
30							30
31							31
32							32

Chapter 6
Financial Statements;
Perpetual Inventory
Systems

QUIZ AND TEST HINTS

The following hints may be helpful to you in preparing for a quiz or a test over the material covered in Chapter 6.

1. You should be able to prepare a merchandising work sheet such as the one illustrated in Exhibit 1 on page 183. Except for the treatment of merchandising inventory, this work sheet is similar to others you have prepared. Under the periodic inventory method (illustrated first in the chapter), two adjusting entries are required for merchandise inventory. You may find it a helpful exercise to cover up portions of Exhibit 1, and see if you know how to complete the covered sections.

2. A major portion of this chapter describes the preparation of financial statements for a merchandising enterprise. Particular emphasis is placed on preparing the income statement. Practice preparing the financial statements for Computer King using Exhibit 1. Your instructor may provide partially completed financial statements, and you will be required to complete the statements.

3. Pay special attention to the new terminology introduced in the chapter. Most of these new terms relate to the income statement for a merchandising enterprise. Review the Glossary of Key Terms.

4. If your instructor lectures on the perpetual inventory system, you may have to prepare journal entries using this system. You should also be able to prepare journal entries for both the periodic system (described in Chapter 5) and the perpetual inventory system, using the same data for each system. An excellent study aid for this purpose is Exhibit 6 on page 194.

5. Be familiar with the impact of the perpetual inventory system on the work sheet, income statement, adjusting entries, and closing entries. You will probably not have to prepare a work sheet using the perpetual method. Instead, emphasize preparing the work sheet using the periodic method as shown in Exhibit 1.

CHAPTER OUTLINE

I. Periodic Reporting for Merchandising Enterprises.
  A. The sequence of year-end procedures for a merchandising enterprise is as follows:
    1. Prepare a trial balance of the ledger on a work sheet form.
    2. Review the accounts and gather the data required for the adjustments.
    3. Insert the adjustments and complete the work sheet.
    4. Prepare financial statements from the data in the work sheet.
    5. Journalize the adjusting entries and post to the ledger.
    6. Journalize the closing entries and post to the ledger.
    7. Prepare a post-closing trial balance of the ledger.
  B. The summarizing and reporting procedures for a merchandising enterprise are

similar to those of a service enterprise except for merchandise inventory.

II. Work Sheet for Merchandising Enterprises.

A. After year-end posting of the journal has been completed, a work sheet is used to assist in preparing the adjusting entries, closing entries, and financial statements.

B. Except for merchandise inventory, all the adjustments have been discussed in earlier chapters.

C. At the end of the period, it is necessary to remove from Merchandise Inventory the amount representing the inventory at the beginning of the period and to replace it with the amount representing the inventory at the end of the period. This is accomplished by two adjusting entries.

1. The first adjusting entry transfers the beginning inventory to Income Summary by debiting Income Summary and crediting Merchandise Inventory for the beginning inventory.

2. The second adjusting entry debits the cost of merchandise inventory at the end of the period to Merchandise Inventory and credits the amount to Income Summary.

D. The effect of the two inventory adjustments is to transfer the beginning inventory amount to Income Summary as part of the cost of merchandise available for sale and to transfer the ending inventory amount to Income Summary as a deduction from the cost of merchandise available for sale.

E. After all the necessary adjustments are entered on the work sheet, the two Adjustments columns are totaled to prove the equality of the debits and credits, and the adjusted balances are then extended to the Adjusted Trial Balance columns, which are totaled to prove the equality of the debits and credits.

F. The balances of the Adjusted Trial Balance columns are then extended to the statement columns in a manner similar to that for a service enterprise, except that both the debit and credit amounts for Income Summary are extended to the Income Statement columns.

G. After all items have been extended to the statement sections of the work sheet, the four columns are totaled and the net income or net loss is determined in the normal manner.

H. The year-end accounting procedures that are necessary for a merchandising enterprise include the preparation of financial statements, adjusting entries, and closing entries. These items are prepared from the work sheet.

III. Financial Statements for Merchandising Enterprises.

A. The basic financial statements for a merchandising enterprise are similar to those of a service enterprise, except for the following:

1. As described in Chapter 5, the income statement differs in the reporting of revenue, cost of merchandise sold, and gross profit.

2. For a merchandising enterprise, the balance sheet includes merchandise inventory as a current asset.

B. The multiple-step income statement contains many sections, subsections, and intermediate balances.

1. The total of all charges to customers for merchandise sold, both for cash and on account, is reported as revenue from sales. Sales returns and allowances and sales discounts are deducted from the gross sales amount to yield net sales.

2. The cost of merchandise sold section appears next, as described and illustrated in Chapter 5.

3. The excess of the net revenue from sales over the cost of merchandise sold is called gross profit.

4. Operating expenses are generally grouped into selling expenses and administrative expenses.

5. The excess of gross profit over total operating expenses is called income from operations, or operating income. If operating expenses are greater than gross profit, the excess is loss from operations.

6. Revenue from sources other than the principal activity of a business is classified as other income. In a merchandising enterprise, this category often includes income from interest, rent, dividends, and gains resulting from the sale of plant assets.

7. Expenses that cannot be associated definitely with operations are identified as other expense, or nonoperating expense. Interest expense and losses incurred in the disposal of plant assets are examples of items that are reported in this section.

8. The final figure on the income statement is labeled net income (or net loss).

C. The single-step form of income statement derives its name from the fact that the total of all expenses is deducted from all revenues.

D. The balance sheet can be presented in two different forms.

1. The arrangement of the balance sheet in downward sequence with total assets equaling the combined totals of liabilities and owner's equity is referred to as the report form.

2. The arrangement of the balance sheet with the assets on the left-hand side and the liabilities and owner's equity on the right-hand side is referred to as the account form.

IV. Adjusting Entries.

A. The analyses necessary to prepare the adjusting entries are completed during the process of preparing the work sheet. Therefore, it is only necessary to refer to the work sheet when recording the adjusting entries in the journal.

B. After the adjusting entries are posted, the balances of all asset, liability, revenue, and expense accounts should equal the amounts reported in the financial statements.

V. Closing Entries.

A. Closing entries are recorded in the journal immediately following the adjusting entries and reduce all temporary owner's equity accounts to zero balances. The final effect of closing out such balances is a net increase or net decrease in the owner's capital account.

B. The four entries required to close the accounts are as follows:

1. The first entry closes all income statement accounts with credit balances by transferring the total to the credit side of Income Summary.

2. The second entry closes all income statement accounts with debit balances by transferring the total to the debit side of Income Summary.

3. The third entry closes Income Summary by transferring its balance, the net income or net loss for the year, to the owner's capital account.

4. The fourth entry closes the owner's drawing account by transferring its balance to the owner's capital account.

C. After all temporary owner's equity accounts have been closed, the only accounts with balances are the owner's capital account and the asset, contra asset, and liability accounts. It is advisable to take a post-closing trial balance to verify the debit-credit equality of the balances of these accounts, which should correspond exactly with the amounts reported on the balance sheet.

VI. Use of Perpetual Inventory Systems.

A. The perpetual inventory system uses accounting records that always (perpetually) disclose the amount of merchandise on hand.

B. Large retailers often use perpetual inventory systems with the aid of computers.

C. Perpetual inventory systems are also often used by business enterprises that sell a relatively small number of high-unit-cost items.

VII. Recording Merchandise Transactions Using a Perpetual Inventory System.

A. In a perpetual inventory system, all increases and decreases related to merchandise are recorded directly in the merchandise inventory account.

1. Purchases of merchandise are debited to the merchandise inventory account.

2. When merchandise is sold, the cost of merchandise sold account is debited and the merchandise inventory account is credited.

B. Accounts for purchases, purchases returns and allowances, purchases discounts, and transportation in are not used in a perpetual inventory system.

C. An illustration of entries for both the periodic and perpetual inventory systems is presented in the chapter in Exhibit 6.

VIII. End-of-Period Procedures for a Perpetual Inventory System.

A. The end-of-period procedures are generally the same for the periodic and perpetual inventory systems except for the work sheet, the income statement, adjusting entries, and closing entries.

B. On the work sheet, no adjusting entry is required for beginning and ending merchandise inventory at the end of the period.

   1. The merchandise inventory balance shown in the trial balance is extended directly to the Adjusted Trial Balance debit column and the Balance Sheet debit column of the work sheet.

   2. The balance in the cost of merchandise sold account in the trial balance is extended directly to the Adjusted Trial Balance debit column and the Income Statement debit column of the work sheet.

C. The cost of merchandise sold is normally reported as a single amount on the income statement when the perpetual inventory system is used.

D. The adjusting entries are the same under both the perpetual and periodic inventory systems except that no adjusting entries are necessary for merchandise inventory in a perpetual inventory system.

E. Under the perpetual inventory system, the balance of the cost of merchandise sold account is closed to Income Summary.

MATCHING

Instructions: A list of terms and related statements appear below. From the list of terms, select the one that relates to each statement. Print its identifying letter in the space provided.

A. Account form
B. Administrative expenses
C. Gross profit
D. Income from operations

E. Multiple-step
F. Other expenses
G. Other income

H. Report form
I. Selling expenses
J. Single-step

____ 1. The form of income statement that has many sections, subsections, and intermediate balances.

____ 2. The form of income statement in which the total of all expenses is deducted from the total of all revenues.

____ 3. The excess of the net revenue from sales over the cost of merchandise sold.

____ 4. Expenses that are incurred directly and entirely in connection with the sale of merchandise are classified as (?).

____ 5. Expenses incurred in the general operations of the business are classified as (?).

____ 6. The excess of gross profit over total operating expenses is called (?).

____ 7. Expenses that cannot be associated definitely with operations are identified as (?).

____ 8. The form of balance sheet with the assets on the left-hand side and the liabilities and owner's equity on the right-hand side is referred to as the (?).

____ 9. The form of balance sheet in which the liabilities and owner's equity sections are listed below rather than to the right of the asset section is referred to as the (?).

____ 10. Revenue from sources other than the primary operating activity of a business.

TRUE / FALSE

Instructions: Indicate whether each of the following statements is true or false by placing a check mark in the appropriate column.

		True	False
1.	Expenses incurred directly and entirely in connection with the sale of merchandise are called administrative expenses..	____	____
2.	Revenue from sources such as income from interest, rent, dividends, and gains resulting from the sale of plant assets is classified as income from operations.	____	____
3.	The single-step form of income statement has the advantage of being simple, and it emphasizes total revenues and total expenses as the factors that determine net income.	____	____
4.	Gross profit is not calculated in the single-step form of income statement.	____	____
5.	The excess of gross profit over total operating expenses is called income from operations.	____	____
6.	The traditional balance sheet arrangement of assets on the left-hand side with the liabilities and owner's equity on the right-hand side is called the report form.	____	____
7.	After the adjusting and closing entries have been recorded and posted, the general ledger accounts that appear on the balance sheet have no balances.	____	____
8.	The closing entries are recorded in the journal immediately following the adjusting entries.	____	____
9.	In a perpetual inventory system, purchases of merchandise are recorded in the purchases account.	____	____
10.	In a periodic inventory system, no attempt is made to record the cost of merchandise sold at the date of the sale.	____	____

MULTIPLE CHOICE

Instructions: Circle the best answer for each of the following questions.

1. The basic differences between the financial statements of a merchandising enterprise and a service enterprise include the cost of merchandise sold section of the income statement and the:
   a. owner's equity section of the balance sheet
   b. other income section of the income statement
   c. inclusion of merchandise inventory on the balance sheet as a current asset
   d. inclusion of a retained earnings statement

2. The excess of net revenue from sales over the cost of merchandise sold is called:
   a. gross profit
   b. operating profit
   c. net profit from operations
   d. merchandising income

3. Income from operations is computed by subtracting from gross profit the:
   a. selling expenses
   b. general expenses
   c. total administrative expenses
   d. total operating expenses

4. After all adjusting entries are posted, the balances of all asset, liability, revenue, and expense accounts correspond exactly to the amounts in the:
   a. work sheet trial balance
   b. general journal
   c. post-closing trial balance
   d. financial statements

5. In a multiple-step income statement of a merchandising enterprise, which of the following would appear as "other income"?
   a. sales
   b. interest income
   c. sales discounts
   d. sales returns and allowances

EXERCISE 6-1

The beginning and ending merchandise inventories for Mabel Co. for the fiscal year ended December 31, 19—, are as follows:

Merchandise inventory as of January 1, 19—............................... 150,000
Merchandise inventory as of December 31, 19—.......................... 115,000

Instructions: Journalize the two adjusting entries to update the merchandise inventory account as of December 31, 19—, assuming that the periodic inventory system is used.

JOURNAL

PAGE

	DATE		DESCRIPTION	POST. REF.	DEBIT	CREDIT	
1							1
2							2
3							3
4							4
5							5
6							6
7							7
8							8
9							9
10							10
11							11
12							12
13							13
14							14
15							15
16							16
17							17
18							18
19							19
20							20
21							21
22							22
23							23
24							24
25							25
26							26

EXERCISE 6-2

Baker Co. had the following purchases and sales transactions during the month of January.

Jan. 3.	Purchased $25,000 of merchandise on account from Zeff Co., terms 2/10, n/30.
5.	Returned merchandise purchased on account from Zeff Co. on January 3, $5,000.
12.	Sold merchandise on account to Smith Co., $50,000, terms 1/10, n/30. The cost of the merchandise sold was $35,000.
13.	Paid Zeff Co. for purchase on January 3, on account, less return and discount.
15.	Received merchandise return on account from Smith Co., $8,000. The cost of the merchandise returned was $5,600.
22.	Received payment in full on account from Smith Co., less return and discount.

Instructions:
(1) Prepare journal entries for these transactions, assuming that a periodic inventory system is used.
(2) Prepare journal entries for these transactions, assuming that a perpetual inventory system is used.

JOURNAL

PAGE _____

	DATE	DESCRIPTION	POST. REF.	DEBIT	CREDIT	
1						1
2						2
3						3
4						4
5						5
6						6
7						7
8						8
9						9
10						10
11						11
12						12
13						13
14						14
15						15
16						16
17						17
18						18
19						19
20						20
21						21
22						22

	DATE		DESCRIPTION	POST. REF.	DEBIT	CREDIT	
1							1
2							2
3							3
4							4
5							5
6							6
7							7
8							8
9							9
10							10
11							11
12							12
13							13
14							14
15							15
16							16
17							17
18							18
19							19
20							20
21							21
22							22
23							23
24							24
25							25
26							26
27							27
28							28
29							29
30							30
31							31
32							32
33							33

PROBLEM 6-1

Instructions: Record the following adjustments in the Adjustments columns and complete the work sheet for Miller Company for the fiscal year ended March 31.

    (a) Interest earned but not received on notes receivable, $520.
    (b) Transfer the beginning inventory to Income Summary.
    (c) The merchandise inventory on March 31 is $115,800.
    (d) The office supplies on hand March 31 are $1,250.
    (e) The insurance expense for the year is $16,000.
    (f) Depreciation on delivery equipment for the year is $9,050.
    (g) Salaries accrued but not paid, $2,000 (sales salaries, $1,130; office salaries, $870).

Miller Company
Work Sheet
For the Year Ended March 31, 19—

ACCOUNT TITLE	TRIAL BALANCE Dr.	TRIAL BALANCE Cr.	ADJUSTMENTS Dr.	ADJUSTMENTS Cr.
Cash	4 3 1 0 0			
Notes Receivable	6 0 0 0			
Accounts Receivable	10 7 7 8 0			
Interest Receivable				
Merchandise Inventory	16 0 3 9 0			
Office Supplies	1 0 3 5 0			
Prepaid Insurance	2 4 7 4 0			
Delivery Equipment	6 0 1 5 0			
Accum. Depr.—Del. Equip.		1 3 9 0 0		
Accounts Payable		7 5 3 0 0		
Salaries Payable				
Miller, Capital		19 3 6 5 0		
Miller, Drawing	3 0 0 0 0			
Income Summary				
Sales		101 6 7 0 0		
Sales Returns & Allow.	1 3 0 1 0			
Purchases	64 2 9 0 0			
Purchases Discounts		6 4 3 0		
Sales Salaries Expense	7 7 1 2 0			
Advertising Expense	1 3 0 9 0			
Delivery Expense	4 2 1 0 0			
Depr. Exp.—Del. Equip.				
Misc. Selling Expense	1 3 9 5 0			
Office Salaries Expense	5 4 9 3 0			
Office Supplies Expense				
Insurance Expense				
Misc. Administrative Exp.	6 8 7 0			
Interest Income		5 0 0		
	130 6 4 8 0	130 6 4 8 0		
Net Income				

ADJUSTED TRIAL BALANCE		INCOME STATEMENT		BALANCE SHEET	
Dr.	Cr.	Dr.	Cr.	Dr.	Cr.

Instructions: Using the Income Statement columns of the work sheet in Problem 6-1, prepare a multiple-step income statement with a cost of merchandise sold section for the year ended March 31, 19—.

Miller Company
Income Statement
For Year Ended March 31, 19—

Name _____

PROBLEM 6-2B

Instructions: Using the Income Statement and Balance Sheet columns of the work sheet in Problem 6-1, prepare a statement of owner's equity.

Miller Company
Statement of Owner's Equity
For the Year Ended March 31, 19—

PROBLEM 6-2C

Instructions: Using the Balance Sheet columns of the work sheet in Problem 6-1, prepare a balance sheet in report form as of March 31, 19—.

Miller Company
Balance Sheet
March 31, 19—

Name _____

PROBLEM 6-3

Instructions: Use the work sheet in Problem 6-1 for this problem.
    (1) Record the adjusting entries in the general journal below.

JOURNAL

PAGE

	DATE	DESCRIPTION	POST. REF.	DEBIT	CREDIT	
1						1
2						2
3						3
4						4
5						5
6						6
7						7
8						8
9						9
10						10
11						11
12						12
13						13
14						14
15						15
16						16
17						17
18						18
19						19
20						20
21						21
22						22
23						23
24						24
25						25
26						26
27						27
28						28
29						29

(2) Record the closing entries in the general journal below.

JOURNAL

	DATE	DESCRIPTION	POST. REF.	DEBIT	CREDIT	
1						1
2						2
3						3
4						4
5						5
6						6
7						7
8						8
9						9
10						10
11						11
12						12
13						13
14						14
15						15
16						16
17						17
18						18
19						19
20						20
21						21
22						22
23						23
24						24
25						25
26						26
27						27
28						28
29						29
30						30
31						31

Name _____

PROBLEM 6-4

A partially completed work sheet for Zesta Company, including all adjustments, is presented on the next 2 pages.

Instructions: Complete the work sheet for Zesta Company.

PROBLEM 6-5

Instructions: Prepare a condensed, single-step income statement from the work sheet in Problem 6-4.

Zesta Company
Income Statement
For Year Ended December 31, 19—

Zesta Company
Work Sheet
For the Year Ended December 31, 19—

ACCOUNT TITLE	TRIAL BALANCE Dr.	TRIAL BALANCE Cr.	ADJUSTMENTS Dr.	ADJUSTMENTS Cr.
Cash	3 5 8 0 0			
Accounts Receivable	8 8 3 0 0			
Merchandise Inventory	8 0 5 0 0			
Prepaid Insurance	1 1 5 0 0			(a) 7 2 0 0
Store Supplies	2 3 0 0			(b) 1 4 0 0
Office Supplies	1 5 0 0			(c) 1 0 0 0
Store Equipment	16 6 6 0 0			
Accum. Depr.—Store Equip.		4 8 5 0 0		(d) 8 1 0 0
Accounts Payable		1 5 0 0 0		
Salaries Payable				(f) 4 7 0 0
Unearned Rent		2 4 0 0	(e) 1 6 0 0	
Note Payable		10 0 0 0 0		
Zesta, Capital		13 6 1 0 0		
Zesta, Drawing	3 0 0 0 0			
Sales		77 7 0 0 0		
Sales Returns & Allow.	1 2 0 0 0			
Sales Discounts	7 5 0 0			
Cost of Merchandise Sold	48 1 0 0 0			
Sales Salaries Expense	6 4 0 0 0		(f) 3 5 0 0	
Advertising Expense	2 0 0 0 0			
Depr. Exp.—Store Equip.			(d) 8 1 0 0	
Store Supplies Expense			(b) 1 4 0 0	
Misc. Selling Expense	4 4 0 0			
Office Salaries Expense	3 1 0 0 0		(f) 1 2 0 0	
Rent Expense	3 0 0 0 0			
Insurance Expense			(a) 7 2 0 0	
Office Supplies Expense			(c) 1 0 0 0	
Misc. Administrative Exp.	1 1 0 0			
Rent Income				(e) 1 6 0 0
Interest Expense	1 1 5 0 0			
	107 9 0 0 0	107 9 0 0 0	2 4 0 0 0	2 4 0 0 0
Net Income				

ADJUSTED TRIAL BALANCE		INCOME STATEMENT		BALANCE SHEET	
Dr.	Cr.	Dr.	Cr.	Dr.	Cr.

PROBLEM 6-6

Instructions: Prepare closing entries from the work sheet in Problem 6-4.

JOURNAL

	DATE		DESCRIPTION	POST. REF.	DEBIT	CREDIT	
1							1
2							2
3							3
4							4
5							5
6							6
7							7
8							8
9							9
10							10
11							11
12							12
13							13
14							14
15							15
16							16
17							17
18							18
19							19
20							20
21							21
22							22
23							23
24							24
25							25
26							26
27							27
28							28
29							29
30							30
31							31

CONTINUING PROBLEM

Instructions:

(12) On the work sheet for Egor the Magician, shown on the next two pages, prepare a trial balance as of December 31, 1994.

(13) Enter the following adjustments in the Adjustments columns:
   (a) Office supplies on hand at December 31, $100.
   (b) Supplies and props on hand as of December 31, $260.
   (c) Merchandise inventory on December 31, $2,370.
   (d) The January 1 balance of prepaid insurance was used up as of December 31. The new policy purchased on December 2 must be adjusted for the amount used as of December 31.
   (e) Interest accrued on note payable, $300.
   (f) Egor owes Sam two months' salary, $800.
   (g) Depreciation on the furniture and fixtures, $2,680.
   (h) Depreciation on equipment, $2,400.

(14) Complete the work sheet.
(15) Prepare an income statement, a statement of owner's equity, and a balance sheet.
(16) Journalize the adjusting entries and post them to the ledger on pages 30-41.
(17) Journalize the closing entries and post them to the ledger.

ACCOUNT TITLE	TRIAL BALANCE		ADJUSTMENTS	
	Dr.	Cr.	Dr.	Cr.

Name _____

_____

_____

ADJUSTED TRIAL BALANCE		INCOME STATEMENT		BALANCE SHEET	
Dr.	Cr.	Dr.	Cr.	Dr.	Cr.

Name _____

Name _____

JOURNAL

PAGE _____

	DATE		DESCRIPTION	POST. REF.	DEBIT	CREDIT	
1							1
2							2
3							3
4							4
5							5
6							6
7							7
8							8
9							9
10							10
11							11
12							12
13							13
14							14
15							15
16							16
17							17
18							18
19							19
20							20
21							21
22							22
23							23
24							24
25							25
26							26
27							27
28							28
29							29
30							30
31							31
32							32

	DATE		DESCRIPTION	POST. REF.	DEBIT	CREDIT	
1							1
2							2
3							3
4							4
5							5
6							6
7							7
8							8
9							9
10							10
11							11
12							12
13							13
14							14
15							15
16							16
17							17
18							18
19							19
20							20
21							21
22							22
23							23
24							24
25							25
26							26
27							27
28							28
29							29
30							30
31							31
32							32

Chapter 7
Accounting Systems and Special Journals

QUIZ AND TEST HINTS

The following hints may be helpful to you in preparing for a quiz or a test over the material covered in Chapter 7.

1. You should be familiar with the terminology related to the principles of accounting systems. Pay close attention to the terms related to an enterprise's internal control structure. Review the Glossary of Key Terms.

2. Chapter 7 focuses on the recording of transactions using subsidiary ledgers and special journals. Carefully review the content and format of the various special journals illustrated throughout the chapter.

3. Your instructor may provide a list of transactions and ask you to identify the journal in which each transaction would be recorded. Re-member, if a transaction does not fit into any of the special journals, it would be recorded in the general journal. In addition, any time the accounts receivable or accounts payable accounts are debited or credited, their related subsidiary ledgers must also be posted.

The diagram at the bottom of page 236 is especially helpful in indicating the types of transactions recorded in each special journal. In addition, the Illustrative Problem in the Chapter Review is typical of the problems that commonly appear on quizzes and tests.

CHAPTER OUTLINE

I. Principles of Accounting Systems.
   A. Although accounting systems vary from business to business, a number of broad principles apply to all systems.
   B. Cost-benefit balance is a major consideration. Information should not be produced if the cost of the information is more than the benefit received by those who use it.
   C. An accounting system must be flexible enough to be adapted to the future needs of the business as the environment in which it operates changes.
   D. The accounting system should aid management in planning and controlling operations and provide strong internal controls.

II. Accounting System Installation and Revision.
   A. The job of installing or changing an accounting system is made up of three phases: (1) analysis, (2) design, and (3) implementation.
   B. The goal of systems analysis is to determine information needs, the sources of such information, and the weaknesses in procedures and data processing methods being used.
   C. Systems design requires the ability to evaluate alternative data processing methods.
   D. The final phase of the creation or revision of an accounting system is to carry out, or implement, the proposals. In the systems implementation phase, all personnel responsible for operating the system must be carefully trained and closely supervised until the system is fully operational.

III. Internal Control Structure.
   A. The objective of an internal control structure is to provide reasonable assurance that an enterprise's goals and objectives are achieved.
   B. The internal control structure consists of three elements: (1) the control environ-

ment, (2) the control procedures, and (3) the accounting system.

C. The control environment of an enterprise is an overall attitude toward and awareness of the importance of controls by both management and other employees.

D. The accounting system generates the information management needs to plan and direct the operations of the enterprise.

E. The control procedures are the policies and procedures management has established to provide reasonable assurance that enterprise goals will be achieved. General control procedures which apply to all enterprises include:

1. The successful operation of an accounting system requires competent personnel who are able to perform the duties to which they are assigned. It is also advisable to rotate clerical personnel periodically from job to job and require vacations.

2. If employees are to work efficiently, their responsibilities must be clearly defined.

3. To decrease the possibility of errors, inefficiency, and fraud, responsibility for a sequence of related operations should be divided among two or more persons.

4. Responsibility for maintaining the accounting records should be separated from the responsibility for engaging in business transactions and for the custody of a firm's assets.

5. Proofs and security measures, such as the use of cash registers and fidelity bonds, safeguard business assets and assure reliable accounting data.

6. To determine whether the other internal control principles are being effectively applied, the system should be periodically reviewed and evaluated.

IV. Subsidiary Ledgers and Special Journals.

A. The entire amount of data collected, stored, and used by an enterprise is called its data base.

B. Depending upon the variety and the amount of data included in the data base, either a manual or computerized processing method may be used.

C. When there are a large number of accounts with a common characteristic, it is

common to place them in a separate ledger called a subsidiary ledger. The principal ledger, which contains all the balance sheet and income statement accounts, is then called the general ledger.

D. Each subsidiary ledger is represented by a summarizing account in the general ledger called a controlling account. The sum of the balances of the accounts in a subsidiary ledger must agree with the balance of the related controlling account.

E. The subsidiary ledger containing the individual accounts for credit customers is called the accounts receivable ledger or customers ledger. The related controlling account in the general ledger is Accounts Receivable.

F. The individual accounts with creditors are arranged in alphabetical order in a subsidiary ledger called the accounts payable ledger or creditors ledger. The related controlling account in the general ledger is Accounts Payable.

G. One method of processing data more efficiently in a manual accounting system is to expand the two-column journal to a multicolumn journal. Each amount column included in a multicolumn journal is used only for recording transactions that affect a certain account. Such journals are known as special journals. The two-column journal form used in previous chapters is known as the general journal or simply the journal.

H. The special journals most commonly found in business are as follows:

1. The sales journal is used to record all sales of merchandise on account. The sales journal normally has one column for debiting Accounts Receivable and crediting Sales.

a. As sales on account occur and are entered in the sales journal, the debits to Accounts Receivable are posted to the subsidiary ledger.

b. Periodically the column of the sales journal is totaled and posted to the general ledger accounts for Accounts Receivable and Sales.

c. Sales returns and allowances are recorded in the general journal as illustrated in Chapter 5.

2. All transactions involving cash receipts are recorded in a cash receipts journal. The special columns of the cash receipts journal normally include an Other (or Miscellaneous) Accounts Credit column, a Sales Credit column, an Accounts Receivable Credit column, a Sales Discounts Debit column, and a Cash Debit column.

   a. Amounts in the Other Accounts Credit column are posted to the appropriate general ledger accounts at frequent intervals during the month.

   b. Individual credits in the Accounts Receivable Credit column are posted to the accounts receivable ledger at frequent intervals.

   c. At the end of the month, the special columns are totaled and posted to the accounts in the general ledger.

   d. After all posting has been completed for the month, the sum of the accounts receivable ledger balances and the general ledger accounts receivable balance should be compared and any errors should be corrected.

3. The purchases journal is designed to record all purchases on account. The purchases journal has an Accounts Payable Credit column and various debit columns such as a Purchases Debit column, Store Supplies Debit column, Office Supplies Debit column, and an Other (or Miscellaneous) Accounts Debit column.

   a. The individual credits to accounts payable in the purchases journal are posted to the accounts payable ledger as the transactions occur.

   b. The individual amounts in the Other Accounts Debit column are posted to the appropriate general ledger accounts at frequent intervals during the month.

   c. The totals of the special columns are posted to the general ledger accounts on a periodic basis, usually at the end of each month.

   d. Purchases returns and allowances are recorded in the general journal, as illustrated in Chapter 5.

4. The cash payments journal is designed to record all cash payments. The special columns of the cash payments journal normally include an Other (or Miscellaneous) Accounts Debit column, Accounts Payable Debit column, Purchases Discounts Credit column, and Cash Credit column.

   a. Individual debits to accounts payable are posted to the accounts payable ledger at frequent intervals during the month.

   b. Amounts in the Other Accounts Debit column are also posted to appropriate general ledger accounts at frequent intervals.

   c. At the end of the month, the special columns are totaled and posted to the accounts in the general ledger.

   d. After all posting has been completed for the month, the sum of the balances in the accounts payable ledger should be compared with the balance in the general ledger accounts payable account, and any errors should be corrected.

V. Adapting Accounting Systems.

   A. Subsidiary ledgers, in addition to Accounts Receivable and Accounts Payable, may be used by a business enterprise.

      1. Subsidiary ledgers are used for accounts that consist of a large number of individual items, each of which has unique characteristics.

      2. Examples of other subsidiary ledgers include an inventory subsidiary ledger, a notes receivable (or payable) subsidiary ledger, and a plant and equipment subsidiary ledger.

   B. Businesses may modify special journals by adding one or more columns for recording transactions that occur frequently.

      1. A sales journal is often modified for the collection of sales tax payable.

      2. Regardless of the modifications, the basic principles and procedures discussed in this chapter apply.

   C. Computerized accounting systems are used by many businesses. The concepts, methods, and procedures that apply to a manual system also apply to computerized systems.

MATCHING

Instructions: A list of terms and related statements appear below. From the list of terms, select the one that relates to each statement. Print its identifying letter in the space provided.

A. Accounts payable ledger
B. Accounts receivable ledger
C. Accounting system
D. Cash payments journal

E. Cash receipts journal
F. Controlling account
G. General ledger
H. Internal controls

I. Internal control structure
J. Purchases journal
K. Sales journal
L. Subsidiary ledger

_____ 1. The detailed procedures used by management to control operations.

_____ 2. A special journal used for recording all items purchased on account.

_____ 3. A special journal used for recording all cash payments.

_____ 4. A supplementary record used to provide detailed information for a control account in the general ledger.

_____ 5. The principal ledger, containing all of the balance sheet and income statement accounts.

_____ 6. A general ledger account which is supported by information in a subsidiary ledger.

_____ 7. A subsidiary ledger containing an account with each creditor.

_____ 8. A subsidiary ledger containing an account with each credit customer.

_____ 9. A special journal used exclusively for recording sales of merchandise on account.

_____ 10. A special journal used to record all cash receipts.

_____ 11. The system that provides the information for use in conducting the affairs of the business and reporting to owners, creditors, and other interested parties.

_____ 12. Consists of the following three elements: The accounting system, the control environment, and the control procedures.

TRUE / FALSE

Instructions: Indicate whether each of the following statements is true or false by placing a check mark in the appropriate column.

	True	False

1. The goal of systems design is to determine information needs, the sources of such information, and the deficiencies in procedures and data processing methods presently used. . . . . _____ _____

2. Responsibility for maintaining the accounting records should be separated from the responsibility for custody of the firm's assets. . . . . _____ _____

3. Transactions involving the payment of cash for any purpose usually are recorded in a cash journal. . . . . _____ _____

4. When there are a large number of individual accounts with a common characteristic, it is common to place them in a separate ledger called a detail ledger. _____ _____

5. For each transaction recorded in the purchases journal, the credit is entered in the "Accounts Payable Cr." column. . . . . _____ _____

6. Acquisitions on account which are not provided for in special debit columns are recorded in the purchases journal in the final set of columns called "Misc." . . . . _____ _____

7. Debits to creditors accounts for invoices paid are recorded in the "Accounts Payable Dr." column of the cash payments journal. . . . . _____ _____

8. At the end of each month, the total of the amount column of the sales journal is posted as a debit to Cash and a credit to Sales. . . . . _____ _____

9. Each amount in the "Other Accounts Cr." column of the cash receipts journal must be posted individually to an appropriate general ledger account. . . . . _____ _____

10. Accounting systems must be continually reviewed for possible revisions in order to keep pace with the changing information needs of enterprises. _____ _____

11. Many special journals are modified in practice to adapt them to meet the specific needs of an enterprise. . . . . _____ _____

12. The high cost of microcomputers makes computerized processing of accounting data unaffordable to small- and medium-size businesses. . . . . _____ _____

13. After all posting has been completed for the month, if the sum of balances in the accounts receivable ledger does not agree with the balance of the accounts receivable account in the general ledger, the errors must be located and corrected. . _____ _____

14. The primary ledger that contains all of the balance sheet and income statement accounts is called the general ledger. . . . . _____ _____

15. If a business uses computers to process accounting data, the concepts and methods for a manual system are not relevant. . . . . _____ _____

MULTIPLE CHOICE

Instructions: Circle the best answer for each of the following questions.

1. The job of installing or changing an accounting system is made up of three phases: (1) analysis, (2) design, and (3):
   a. installation
   b. verification
   c. management
   d. implementation

2. To determine whether internal control principles are being effectively applied, the system should be periodically reviewed and evaluated by the:
   a. users of the system
   b. internal auditors
   c. employees responsible for operations
   d. EDP service center

3. The individual amounts in the "Accounts Payable Cr." column of the purchases journal are posted to the appropriate account in the:
   a. general ledger
   b. general journal
   c. accounts payable ledger
   d. accounts payable journal

4. When merchandise is returned or a price adjustment is granted, an entry is made in the:
   a. general journal
   b. cash receipts journal
   c. adjustments journal
   d. purchases journal

5. The controlling account in the general ledger that summarizes the individual accounts with creditors in a subsidiary ledger is titled:
   a. Accounts Payable
   b. Purchases
   c. Accounts Receivable
   d. Sales Returns and Allowances

6. Internal control policies and procedures provide reasonable assurance that:
   a. all liabilities will be paid
   b. a net income will be earned
   c. they are being effectively applied
   d. enterprise goals will be achieved

Name _____

EXERCISE 7-1

Wilco Co. maintains a cash receipts journal, cash payments journal, sales journal, purchases journal, and general journal. Selected transactions of Wilco Co. for the month of February are listed below.

Instructions: Indicate the journal in which each of the transactions would be recorded.

Transaction	Journal

Feb. 1. Purchased merchandise on account from Winkler's
         Wholesale....................................... _____

      6. Sold merchandise to Phil's Grocery Store for cash..... _____

      8. Received a credit memorandum from Winkler's
         Wholesale for merchandise returned................ _____

     11. Issued check no. 1099 for payment of merchandise
         purchased on February 1, less return on February 8,
         to Winkler's Wholesale........................... _____

     18. Sold merchandise on account to Sally's Shop-N-Save.. _____

     28. Received full payment, less discount, from Tony's
         Grocery Store.................................... _____

EXERCISE 7-2

The following transactions related to purchases and cash payments were completed by Kent Company during March of the current year.

Mar. 2. Purchased merchandise on account from Eastside Co., $15,250, terms n/30.
8. Purchased merchandise on account from Bench Co., $3,500, terms 2/10, n/30.
9. Received a credit memorandum from Eastside Co., $620 for defective merchandise.
16. Issued Check No. 230 to Bench Co. in payment of the balance due, less 2% discount.
20. Issued Check No. 231 for a cash purchase of merchandise, $1,500.
27. Issued Check No. 232 to Eastside Co. in payment of the balance due.
28. Purchased the following on account from James & Co.: store supplies, $800; office supplies, $100.

Instructions: Record the above transactions in the purchases journal, cash payments journal, or two-column general journal given below:

PURCHASES JOURNAL   PAGE

	DATE	ACCOUNT CREDITED	POST. REF.	ACCOUNTS PAYABLE CR.	PURCHASES DR.	STORE SUPPLIES DR.	OFFICE SUPPLIES DR.	
1								1
2								2
3								3
4								4

CASH PAYMENTS JOURNAL   PAGE

	DATE	CK. NO.	ACCOUNT DEBITED	POST. REF.	OTHER ACCOUNTS DR.	ACCOUNTS PAYABLE DR.	PURCHASES DISCOUNTS CR.	CASH CR.	
1									1
2									2
3									3
4									4

JOURNAL   PAGE

	DATE	DESCRIPTION	POST. REF.	DEBIT	CREDIT	
1						1
2						2
3						3
4						4
5						5
6						6
7						7

EXERCISE 7-3

The following transactions related to sales and cash receipts were completed by Mezza Co. during October of the current year. The terms of all sales on account are 2/10, n/30, FOB destination.

Oct. 3. Sold merchandise on account to Blanders Co., Invoice No. 2883, $8,250.
4. Sold merchandise on account to Montana Co., Invoice No. 2884, $5,000.
8. Issued to Blanders Co. a credit memorandum for merchandise returned, Credit Memo No. 396, $1,000.
13. Received cash from Blanders Co. in payment of the $7,250 due on Invoice No. 2883, less discount.
14. Received cash from Montana Co. in payment of Invoice No. 2884, less discount.
25. Received cash for office supplies returned to the manufacturer, $300.
31. Cash sales for October, $39,600.

Instructions: Record the above transactions in the sales journal, cash receipts journal, or general journal given below.

SALES JOURNAL

	DATE	INVOICE No.	ACCOUNT DEBITED	POST. REF.	ACCTS. REC. DR. SALES CR.	
1						1
2						2
3						3
4						4

CASH RECEIPTS JOURNAL   PAGE

	DATE	ACCOUNT DEBITED	POST. REF.	OTHER ACCOUNTS CR.	SALES CR.	ACCOUNTS RECEIVABLE CR.	SALES DISCOUNTS DR.	CASH DR.	
1									1
2									2
3									3
4									4

JOURNAL   PAGE

	DATE	DESCRIPTION	POST. REF.	DEBIT	CREDIT	
1						1
2						2
3						3
4						4
5						5
6						6
7						7

PROBLEM 7-1

Willbury's, a retail store, completed the following transactions with creditors on account during April of the current year.

Apr. 2. Purchased merchandise on account from Gudorf Co., $7,010.
      14. Purchased store supplies on account from Mills Co., $300.
      16. Purchased office supplies on account from Quick Co., $175.
      22. Purchased store equipment on account from Mills Co., $5,250.
      26. Purchased merchandise on account from Gudorf Co., $6,925.
      30. Purchased store supplies on account from Mills Co., $280.

Instructions:
  (1) Record the above transactions in the purchases journal below.
  (2) Post the individual items from the purchases journal to the T accounts in the general and accounts payable ledgers. Indicate that each item has been posted by placing a check mark (✓) or an account number in the appropriate Post. Ref. column of the purchases journal.
  (3) Post the totals of the purchases journal to the general ledger T accounts. Insert the appropriate account numbers in the journal under the amount posted.

(1)   **PURCHASES JOURNAL**   PAGE

	DATE	ACCOUNT CREDITED	POST. REF.	ACCOUNTS PAYABLE CR.	PURCHASES DR.	STORE SUPPLIES DR.	OFFICE SUPPLIES DR.	OTHER ACCOUNTS DR. ACCOUNT	POST. REF.	AMOUNT	
1											1
2											2
3											3
4											4
5											5
6											6
7											7
8											8

(2) and (3)   GENERAL LEDGER   ACCTS. PAYABLE LEDGER

Store Supplies 115   Office Supplies 116   Gudorf Co.

Store Equipment 121   Accounts Payable 211   Mills Co.

Purchases 511   Quick Co.

  (4) Determine that the sum of the balances of the individual accounts in the subsidiary accounts payable ledger agrees with the balance of the accounts payable controlling account in the general ledger by completing the following summary form:

Gudorf Co. . . . . $ _____
Mills Co. . . . . _____
Quick Co. . . . . _____
Total accounts payable . . . . $ _____

140

Name _____

PROBLEM 7-2

The "Totals" line and one other line of the purchases journal of Hamilton Surplus Store for the month of October are shown below. Also shown are selected T accounts taken from Hamilton's general ledger.

Instructions:
   (1) Verify the equality of the debits and the credits in the Hamilton's Surplus Store purchases journal for October by completing the following schedule:

DEBIT TOTALS		CREDIT TOTALS	
Purchases.................	_____	Accounts Payable.........	_____
Store Supplies	_____		
Office Supplies	_____		
Other Accounts...........	_____		
Total.....................	_____	Total.....................	_____

   (2) Post all amounts that require posting to the T accounts provided. Show the appropriate posting references in the purchases journal.

PURCHASES JOURNAL   PAGE

DATE	POST. REF.	ACCOUNTS PAYABLE CR.	PURCHASES DR.	STORE SUPPLIES DR.	OFFICE SUPPLIES DR.	OTHER ACCOUNTS DR. ACCOUNT	POST. REF.	AMOUNT
31	✓	620				Store Equipment		620
31	✓	8,430	6,000	640	800			990

GENERAL LEDGER

Store Supplies 115	Office Supplies 116	Store Equipment 121

Accounts Payable 211	Purchases 511

Kleco Co., a sporting goods store, completed the following transactions with customers on account during September of the current year.

Sept. 8. Invoice No. 210 to Robert Poon, $220.
      12. Invoice No. 225 to Jeff Lucas, $50.
      24. Invoice No. 260 to Pamela Stark, $70.
      30. Invoice No. 290 to Steve Kocan, $400.

Instructions:
  (1) Record the above transactions in the sales journal below.
  (2) Post the individual items from the sales journal to the T accounts for customers. Indicate that each item has been posted by placing a check mark (✓) in the Post. Ref. column of the sales journal.
  (3) Post the total of the sales journal to the T accounts for Accounts Receivable and Sales. Indicate that the posting is completed by inserting the appropriate account numbers in the journal under the amount posted.

SALES JOURNAL

	DATE	INVOICE No.	ACCOUNT DEBITED	POST. REF.	ACCTS. REC. DR. SALES CR.	
1						1
2						2
3						3
4						4

GENERAL LEDGER   ACCOUNTS RECEIVABLE LEDGER

Accounts Receivable 113   Steve Kocan   Jeff Lucas

Sales 411   Robert Poon   Pamela Stark

  (4) Determine that the sum of the balances of the individual accounts in the subsidiary accounts receivable ledger agrees with the balance of the accounts receivable controlling account in the general ledger by completing the following summary form.

            Steve Kocan .... $ _____
            Jeff Lucas...................... _____
            Robert Poon .... _____
            Pamela Stark.................... _____
            Total accounts receivable .... $ _____

Chapter 8
Cash

The following hints may be helpful to you in preparing for a quiz or a test over the material covered in Chapter 8.

1. You should be able to prepare a bank reconciliation of the type illustrated in the chapter. Instructors often include short bank reconciliations of the type shown in the Illustrative Problem in the Chapter Review and in Problem 8-1 of this Study Guide. Attempt to work the Illustrative Problem and the Study Guide Problem 8-1 without looking at the solution.

2. Be able to identify in which section of the bank reconciliation different types of reconciling items would be included. The form of the reconciliation illustrated on page 281 may be a helpful study aid. Have a friend read off the reconciling items from the chapter illustration of the bank reconciliation on page 282, and identify whether the item would appear in the section of the reconciliation beginning with "Cash balance according to bank statement" or the section beginning with "Cash balance according to depositor's records."

Note that sometimes instructors may refer to the "Cash balance according to bank statement" as the "Balance per bank" and "Cash balance according to depositor's records" as "Balance per books."

3. You may expect some general terminology questions (usually true/false or multiple-choice) related to internal control over cash receipts and cash payments. Although you should be familiar with the five components of the voucher system, most instructors will not include a problem on an exam requiring the entering of data in a voucher system. Remember, a general journal entry using a voucher system initially credits Vouchers Payable rather than Accounts Payable.

4. You should be able to prepare journal entries to establish and replenish cash funds including cash change funds and petty cash. In replenishing such funds, the cash short and over account may need to be debited (short) or credited (over).

5. Finally, many instructors like to include short problems or multiple-choice questions related to use of the purchases discounts lost account. Be able to record general journal entries for purchases recorded at their gross amount and net amount.

CHAPTER OUTLINE

I. Bank Reconciliation as a Control over Cash.
  A. Because of the ease with which money can be transferred, cash is the asset most likely to be diverted and used improperly by employees. Therefore, cash must be effectively safeguarded by special controls.
  B. One of the major devices for maintaining control over cash is the bank account.

1. To get the most benefit from a bank account, all cash received must be deposited in the bank, and all payments must be made by checks drawn on the bank or from special cash funds.
2. The forms used by business in connection with a bank account are a signature card, deposit ticket, check, and a record of checks drawn.

3. The three parties to a check are the drawer, the one who signs the check; the drawee, the bank on which the check is drawn; and the payee, the one to whose order the check is drawn.
4. A remittance advice is a notification which indicates to a creditor which specific invoice is being paid.

C. Banks usually mail to each depositor a statement of account once a month which shows the beginning balance, checks and other debits (deductions by the bank), deposits and other credits (additions by the bank), and the balance at the end of the period.

D. The balance shown on the depositor's records as cash in bank and the ending balance on the bank statement are not likely to be equal on any specific date because of either or both of the following: (1) delay by either party in recording transactions and (2) errors by either party in recording transactions.

E. To determine the reasons for any difference between the balance according to the bank statement and the bank balance according to the depositor's records, a bank reconciliation is prepared. The bank reconciliation is divided into two sections: one section begins with the balance according to the bank statement and ends with the adjusted balance; the other section begins with the balance according to the depositor's records and also ends with the adjusted balance. The form and the content of the bank reconciliation are outlined as follows:

Bank balance according to bank statement
Add: Additions by depositor not on bank statement
       Bank errors
Deduct: Deductions by depositor not on bank statement
       Bank errors
Adjusted balance
Bank balance according to depositor's records
Add: Additions by bank not recorded by depositor
       Depositor errors
Deduct: Deductions by bank not recorded by depositor
       Depositor errors
Adjusted balance

F. The following procedures are used in finding reconciling items and determining the adjusted balance of cash in bank:
1. Individual deposits listed on the bank statement are compared with unrecorded deposits appearing in the preceding reconciliation and with deposit receipts or other records of deposits. Deposits not recorded by the bank are added to the balance according to the bank statement.
2. Paid checks are compared with outstanding checks appearing on the preceding reconciliation and with checks listed in the cash payments journal. Checks issued that have not been paid by the bank are outstanding and are deducted from the balance according to the bank statement.
3. Bank credit memorandums are compared to entries in the cash receipts journal. Credit memorandums not recorded in the cash receipts journal are added to the balance according to the depositor's records.
4. Bank debit memorandums are compared to entries in the cash payments journal. Credit memorandums not recorded in the cash payments journal are deducted from the balance according to the depositor's records.
5. Errors discovered during the preceding steps are listed separately on the reconciliation. For example, if the amount for which a check was written had been recorded incorrectly by the depositor, the amount of the error should be added to or deducted from the Cash in Bank balance. Similarly, errors by the bank should be added to or deducted from the balance according to the bank statement.

G. Bank memorandums not recorded by the depositor and the depositor's errors shown by the bank reconciliation require that entries be made in the accounts.
1. The data needed for these adjustments are provided by the section of the bank reconciliation that begins with the balance per depositor's records.
2. After the adjusting entries are posted, the cash in bank account will have a balance which agrees with the adjusted

balance shown on the bank reconciliation.

H. The bank reconciliation is an important part of the system of internal controls, because it is a means of comparing recorded cash, as shown by the accounting records, with the amount of cash reported by the bank.

1. Better internal control is achieved when the bank reconciliation is prepared by an employee who does not take part in or record cash transactions with the bank.

2. Without a proper separation of duties, cash is more likely to be embezzled.

II. Internal Control of Cash Receipts.

A. Cash should be protected from theft or misuse from the time it is received until it is deposited in the bank.

1. Controls designed to protect cash from theft or misuse are called protective controls.

2. Controls designed to detect theft or misuse of cash are called detective controls.

B. Retail businesses normally receive cash from either over-the-counter sales to customers or mail from credit customers.

1. A cash register provides a record of cash received over the counter from cash customers. The amounts in the cash drawer are compared with the cash register tapes at the end of each business day. The cash is taken to the cashier's office and the tapes are sent to the accounting department for proper recording.

2. The employees who open incoming mail should compare the amount of cash received with the amount shown on the accompanying remittance advice to make sure the two amounts agree. The cash should then be forwarded to the cashier's department and the remittance advices should be delivered to the accounting department for proper recording.

3. After cash is deposited in the bank by an employee of the cashier's department, the duplicate deposit slip or bank receipt form is returned to the accounting department where an employee compares the deposit with the recorded cash receipts for the day. Any cash shortages are thus promptly detected.

C. Retail stores usually maintain cash change funds in order to make change for customers.

1. A cash change fund is established by writing a check for the desired amount and debiting Cash on Hand and crediting Cash in Bank.

2. The cash is divided up among the various cash registers and the amounts in each register are recorded for later use in reconciling cash sales for the day.

3. No additional debits or credits to Cash on Hand are made unless the fund is increased or decreased in amount.

D. When the amount of cash actually received during the day does not agree with the record of cash receipts, the difference should be debited or credited to a cash short and over account.

1. A debit balance in the cash short and over account at the end of the fiscal period is listed as an expense on the income statement. A credit balance is listed as a revenue.

2. If the balance of the cash short and over account becomes larger than may be accounted for by minor errors, management should take corrective measures.

III. Internal Control of Cash Payments.

A. It is common practice for business enterprises to require that all payments of cash be made by checks signed by an authorized individual. In a small business, an owner-manager may sign all checks based upon personal knowledge of all goods and services purchased.

B. In large business enterprises, the issuance of purchase orders, inspection of goods received, and verification of invoices is divided among the employees of several departments. One system used for this purpose is the voucher system.

C. A voucher system is a set of methods and procedures for authorizing and recording liabilities and cash payments. It normally uses (1) vouchers, (2) a voucher register, (3) a file for unpaid vouchers, (4) a check register, and (5) a file for paid vouchers.

1. A voucher is a special form on which is recorded relevant data about a liability and the details of its payment. Vouchers are customarily prepared by the accounting department on the basis of an invoice or a memorandum that serves as proof of an expenditure. A check may not be issued except in payment of an authorized voucher.

2. In a voucher system, the voucher register replaces the purchases journal and is the record in which all vouchers are entered in numerical order. Each voucher represents a credit to Accounts Payable (sometimes titled Vouchers Payable) and a debit to the account or accounts to be charged for the expenditure. When a voucher is paid, the date of payment and the number of the check are inserted in the proper columns in the voucher register.

3. After a voucher has been recorded in the voucher register, it is filed in an unpaid voucher file where it remains until it is paid. The amount due on each voucher represents the credit balance of an account payable, and the voucher itself is like an individual account in a subsidiary accounts payable ledger. A voucher is filed in the unpaid voucher file according to the earliest date that consideration should be given to its payment. When a voucher is paid, it is removed from the unpaid voucher file and a check is issued for payment. Paid vouchers and the supporting documents should be canceled to prevent accidental or intentional reuse.

4. The payment of a voucher is recorded in a check register. The check register is a modified form of the cash payments journal and is so called because it is a complete record of all checks.

5. After payment, vouchers are usually filed in numerical order in a paid voucher file.

D. The relationship of the voucher system and special journals and subsidiary ledgers discussed in the preceding chapters is summarized as follows:

Special Journal   *Voucher System*
Purchases Journal ———→ Voucher Register
Cash Payments Journal —→ Check Register

Subsidiary Ledger
Accounts Payable
  Subsidiary Ledger ———→ Unpaid Voucher File

E. The voucher system not only provides effective accounting controls but it also aids management in making the best use of cash resources and in planning cash disbursements.

F. Discounts on the purchase of merchandise may be accounted for either as deductions from purchases or as other income.

1. A major disadvantage of recording purchases at the invoice price and recognizing purchases discounts at the time of payment as a deduction from purchases is that this method does not measure the cost of failing to take purchases discounts.

2. By recording purchases at the net amount (assuming that all discounts will be taken) and using a discounts lost account, better control can be maintained over the taking of cash discounts.

3. When the net method of recording purchases is used, all vouchers are prepared and recorded at the net amount. Any discount lost is noted on the related voucher and recorded in a special column in the check register when the voucher is paid.

G. A petty cash fund is commonly used by businesses for which there is a frequent need for the payment of relatively small amounts, such as for postage due, etc.

1. In establishing a petty cash fund, the account Petty Cash is debited. If a voucher system is used, Accounts Payable (or Vouchers Payable) is credited. When the check is drawn to pay the voucher, Accounts Payable (Vouchers Payable) is debited and Cash in Bank is credited.

2. The petty cash fund is replenished by a general journal entry debiting the vari-

ous expense and asset accounts and crediting Accounts Payable (Vouchers Payable). The check in payment of the voucher is recorded in the usual manner.

    3. Because disbursements are not recorded in the accounts until the fund is replenished, petty cash funds and other special funds that operate in a like manner should be replenished at the end of an accounting period.

  H. Other cash funds may also be established to meet other special needs of a business. These funds are accounted for in a manner similar to that for a petty cash fund.

IV. Presentation of Cash on the Balance Sheet.

  A. Cash is listed as the first asset in the Current Assets section of the balance sheet. Most companies combine all their cash accounts and present only a single cash amount on the balance sheet.

  B. A company may invest in short-term, highly liquid investments in order to earn interest. Such investments, which can be readily converted to cash, are called cash equivalents. In such cases, "cash and cash equivalents" are usually reported as one amount on the balance sheet.

  C. Restrictions on the ability to withdraw cash and any compensating balance requirements should be disclosed in the notes to the financial statements.

V. Cash Transactions and Electronic Funds Transfer.

  A. Electronic funds transfer is a payment system which uses computerized electronic impulses rather than paper (money, checks, etc.) to effect cash transactions. Payroll checks and social security checks are often transmitted in this manner.

  B. EFT is beginning to play an important role in retail sales through point-of-sale (POS) systems.

MATCHING

Instructions: A list of terms and related statements appear below. From the list of terms, select the one that relates to each statement. Print its identifying letter in the space provided.

A. Bank reconciliation
B. Check register
C. Compensating balance
D. Electronic funds transfer

E. Payee
F. Petty cash fund
G. Remittance advice

H. Unpaid voucher file
I. Voucher
J. Voucher register

____ 1. The party to whom payment is made.

____ 2. A required minimum cash balance maintained in a bank account, generally imposed by the bank as part of a loan agreement.

____ 3. A notification which accompanies checks issued to a creditor that indicates the specific invoice that is being paid.

____ 4. An accounting record in which the bank balance according to the bank statement is reconciled with the bank balance according to the depositor's records.

____ 5. A special form on which is recorded relevant data about a liability and the details of its payment.

____ 6. After a voucher has been recorded in the voucher register, it is filed in a(n) (?).

____ 7. After approval by the designated official, each voucher is recorded in the (?).

____ 8. A modified form of the cash payments journal used for recording cash payments when a voucher system is in use.

____ 9. A special cash fund set aside for the payment of relatively small amounts for which payment by check is not efficient.

____ 10. A payment system using computerized electronic impulses rather than paper to effect a cash transaction.

Name _____

TRUE / FALSE

Instructions: Indicate whether each of the following statements is true or false by placing a check mark in the appropriate column.

		True	False
1.	There are four parties to a check.	___	___
2.	The drawer is the one to whose order the check is drawn.	___	___
3.	In a bank reconciliation, checks issued that have not been paid by the bank are added to the balance according to the bank statement.	___	___
4.	Bank memorandums not recorded by the depositor require entries in the depositor's accounts.	___	___
5.	For a greater degree of internal control, the bank reconciliation should be prepared by an employee who does not engage in or record cash transactions with the bank.	___	___
6.	If there is a debit balance in the cash short and over account at the end of the fiscal period, this represents income to be included in "Miscellaneous general income" in the income statement.	___	___
7.	It is common practice for business enterprises to require that every payment of cash be evidenced by a check signed by the owner.	___	___
8.	After vouchers are paid, it is customary to file them in numerical sequence in the paid voucher file.	___	___
9.	It is a widely accepted view that purchases discounts should be reported as deductions from purchases.	___	___
10.	If a voucher is used, Vouchers Payable should be debited when the petty cash fund is replenished.	___	___
11.	A voucher system is a set of methods and procedures for authorizing and recording liabilities and cash payments.	___	___
12.	When the net method of recording purchases is used with the voucher system, all vouchers are prepared and recorded at the invoice price.	___	___

MULTIPLE CHOICE

Instructions: Circle the best answer for each of the following questions.

1. The bank on which a check is drawn is known as the:
   a. drawer
   b. drawee
   c. payee
   d. creditor

2. In a bank reconciliation, deposits not recorded by the bank are:
   a. added to the balance according to the bank statement
   b. deducted from the balance according to the bank statement
   c. added to the balance according to the depositor's records
   d. deducted from the balance according to the depositor's records

3. For good internal control over cash receipts, remittance advices should be separated from cash received by mail and sent directly to the:
   a. treasurer
   b. cashier's department
   c. accounting department
   d. voucher clerk

4. An important characteristic of the voucher system is the requirement that:
   a. vouchers be prepared by the treasurer
   b. vouchers be paid immediately after they are prepared
   c. the face of the voucher show the account distribution
   d. a voucher be prepared for each expenditure

5. The entry to record the replenishment of the petty cash fund includes a debit to various expense and asset accounts and a credit to:
   a. Cash in Bank
   b. Petty Cash
   c. Accounts Payable
   d. various liability accounts

EXERCISE 8-1

A comparison of the bank statement and the accompanying canceled checks and memorandums with the records of Pearl Co. for the month of September of the current year revealed the following reconciling items:

    (1) A check drawn for $25 had been erroneously charged by the bank for $250.
    (2) The bank collected $1,920 on a note left for collection. The face of the note was $1,800.
    (3) Bank service charges for September totaled $28.
    (4) Check No. 231, written to Stanley Optical Warehouse for $2,500, and Check No. 236, written to Stella's Janitorial Service for $100, were outstanding.
    (5) A deposit of $5,250 made on September 30 was not recorded on the bank statement.
    (6) A canceled check for $1,100, returned with the bank statement, had been recorded erroneously in the check register as $1,000. The check was a payment on account to Charlie's Optical Supply.

    Instructions: In the following general journal, prepare the entries that Pearl Co. should make as a result of these reconciling items. The accounts have not been closed.

JOURNAL   PAGE

	DATE	DESCRIPTION	POST. REF.	DEBIT	CREDIT	
1						1
2						2
3						3
4						4
5						5
6						6
7						7
8						8
9						9
10						10
11						11
12						12
13						13
14						14
15						15
16						16
17						17
18						18
19						19
20						20
21						21
22						22
23						23
24						24

EXERCISE 8-2

Instructions: Record the following transactions in the general journal provided below, assuming that invoices for commodities purchased are recorded at their net price after deducting the allowable discount.

Jan. 8. Voucher No. 2710 is prepared for merchandise purchased from Hanks Co., $5,000, terms 2/10, n/60.
 10. Voucher No. 2711 is prepared for merchandise purchased from Murphy Co., $12,000, terms 1/10, n/30.
 20. Check No. 3210 is issued, payable to Murphy Co., in payment of Voucher No. 2711.
Feb. 9. Check No. 3217 is issued, payable to Hanks Co., in payment of Voucher No. 2710.

JOURNAL   PAGE

	DATE	DESCRIPTION	POST. REF.	DEBIT	CREDIT	
1						1
2						2
3						3
4						4
5						5
6						6
7						7
8						8
9						9
10						10
11						11
12						12
13						13
14						14
15						15
16						16
17						17
18						18
19						19
20						20
21						21
22						22
23						23
24						24
25						25
26						26
27						27
28						28
29						29
30						30
31						31
32						32

Name _____

EXERCISE 8-3

Instructions: In the general journal provided below, prepare the entries to record the following transactions:

(1) Voucher No. 312 is prepared to establish a petty cash fund of $400.

(2) Check No. 805 is issued in payment of Voucher No. 312.

(3) The amount of cash in the petty cash fund is now $128.34. Voucher No. 443 is prepared to replenish the fund, based on the following summary of petty cash receipts:

  Office supplies, $80.25
  Miscellaneous selling expense, $115.33
  Miscellaneous administrative expense, $78.05

(4) Check No. 844 is issued by the disbursing officer in payment of Voucher No. 443. The check is cashed and the money is placed in the fund.

JOURNAL   PAGE _____

	DATE	DESCRIPTION	POST. REF.	DEBIT	CREDIT	
1						1
2						2
3						3
4						4
5						5
6						6
7						7
8						8
9						9
10						10
11						11
12						12
13						13
14						14
15						15
16						16
17						17
18						18
19						19
20						20
21						21
22						22
23						23
24						24
25						25
26						26
27						27
28						28
29						29

PROBLEM 8-1

On September 30 of the current year, Dumont Co.'s checkbook showed a balance of $7,540 and the bank statement showed a balance of $8,510. A comparison of the bank statement and Dumont's records as of September 30 revealed the following:

(a) A deposit of $1,900, mailed to the bank by Dumont on September 29, was not included in the bank statement of September 30.
(b) The following checks were outstanding:
Check No. 255 for $325
Check No. 280 for $100
Check No. 295 for $700
(c) Check No. 289 in payment of a voucher had been written for $140 and had been recorded at that amount by the bank. However, Dumont had recorded it in the check register as $410.
(d) A check for $910 received from a customer was deposited in the bank. The bank recorded it at the correct amount, but Dumont recorded it at $190.
(e) Included with the bank statement was a credit memorandum for $780, representing the proceeds of a $700 note receivable left at the bank for collection. This had not been recorded on Dumont's books.
(f) Included with the bank statement was a debit memorandum for $25 for service charges which had not been recorded on Dumont's books.

Instructions:
(1) Complete the following bank reconciliation:

Dumont Co.
Bank Reconciliation
September 30, 19—

Balance according to bank statement .... $
Add:

Deduct:

Adjusted balance .... $

Balance according to depositor's records................................ $
Add:

Deduct:
Adjusted balance .... $

(2) In the following general journal, prepare the entry or entries that Dumont should make as a result of the bank reconciliation.

(1)   **JOURNAL**   PAGE

	DATE	DESCRIPTION	POST. REF.	DEBIT	CREDIT	
1						1
2						2
3						3
4						4
5						5
6						6
7						7
8						8
9						9
10						10
11						11
12						12
13						13
14						14
15						15
16						16
17						17
18						18
19						19
20						20
21						21
22						22
23						23
24						24
25						25
26						26
27						27
28						28
29						29
30						30
31						31
32						32
33						33
34						34
35						35
36						36
37						37

PROBLEM 8-2

Gretta Gift Shop uses a voucher system. On April 1 of the current year, Gretta issued Voucher No. 325 to record the purchase of $700 of novelty items from Sillo Co., terms 2/10, n/30. Also on April 1, Gretta issued Voucher No. 326 to record the purchase of $525 of leather goods from Cross Inc., terms 2/10, n/30, and Voucher No. 327 to record the purchase of $1,000 of stuffed animals from Leo's Co., terms 1/10, n/30.

Gretta issued the following checks: April 5, Check No. 810 in payment of Voucher No. 325; April 8, Check No. 811 in payment of Voucher No. 327; April 15, Check No. 812 in payment of Voucher No. 326.

Instructions:
(1) Record the vouchers in the partial voucher register below.

PAGE

VOUCHER REGISTER

	DATE	VOU. NO.	PAYEE	DATE PAID	CK. NO.	ACCOUNTS PAYABLE CR.	PURCHASES DR.	
1								1
2								2
3								3
4								4
5								5
6								6
7								7

(2) Record the checks in the check register below. (Bank Deposits and Balance columns are omitted.) Also make the appropriate notations in the voucher register above.

CHECK REGISTER

PAGE

	DATE	CK. NO.	PAYEE	VOU. NO.	ACCOUNTS PAYABLE DEBIT	PURCHASES DISCOUNTS CREDIT	CASH CREDIT	
1								1
2								2
3								3
4								4
5								5
6								6
7								7
8								8
9								9
10								10
11								11
12								12
13								13
14								14
15								15
16								16

Chapter 9
Receivables and
Temporary
Investments

The following hints may be helpful to you in preparing for a quiz or test over the material in Chapter 9.

1. You should be able to determine the due date, interest, and maturity value of a note receivable and to compute the proceeds for a note receivable that has been discounted.

2. You should be able to determine the amount of the adjusting entry for uncollectible receivables (the allowance method) for both estimation methods presented in the chapter (percentage of sales and aging of receivables). Note that the percentage of sales method is the easiest to use since the amount of the entry is the same as the estimate of the uncollectible sales. The aging method requires the entry to be made for an amount that will result in the estimated balance of the allowance account.

3. You may be tested on a problem requiring a series of general journal entries that encompass both notes receivable and entries for uncollectible accounts receivable. The materials presented in this Study Guide and the Illustrative Problem in the Chapter Review provide an excellent review.

CHAPTER OUTLINE

I. Classification of Receivables.
   A. The term receivables includes all money claims against people, organizations, or other debtors.
      1. A promissory note is a written promise to pay a sum of money on demand or at a definite time. The enterprise owning a note refers to it as a note receivable.
      2. Accounts and notes receivable originating from sales transactions are called trade receivables.
      3. Other receivables include interest receivable, loans to officers or employees, and loans to affiliated companies.
   B. All receivables that are expected to be realized in cash within a year are presented as current assets on the balance sheet. Those not currently collectible, such as long-term loans, are shown as investments.

II. Internal Control of Receivables.
   A. The broad principles of internal control should be used to establish procedures to safeguard receivables.
   B. The following controls are commonly used:
      1. Separation of the business operations and the accounting for receivables.
      2. The maintenance of subsidiary records and ledgers for accounts and notes receivable.
      3. Proper approval of all credit sales by an authorized company official.
      4. Proper authorization of all sales returns and allowances and sales discounts.
      5. Effective collection procedures to ensure timely collection and to minimize losses from uncollectible accounts.

III. Characteristics of Notes Receivable.
   A. The one to whose order the note is payable is called the payee, and the one

making the promise is called the maker. The face amount of the note is called the principal.

B. The date a note is to be paid is called the due date or maturity date.

1. The period of time between the issuance date and the maturity date of a short-term note may be stated either in days or months.

2. When the term of a note is stated in days, the due date is a specified number of days after its issuance.

3. When the term of a note is stated as a certain number of months after the issuance date, the due date is determined by counting the number of months from the issuance date. For example, a three-month note dated July 31 would be due on October 31.

C. A note that provides for payment of interest is called an interest-bearing note. If a note does not specify an interest rate, it is said to be non-interest-bearing.

1. Interest rates are usually stated in terms of a period of one year, regardless of the actual period of time involved.

2. The basic formula for computing interest is as follows: Principal × Rate × Time = Interest.

3. For purposes of computing interest, the commercial practice of using 1/12 of a year for a month and a 360-day year will be used.

D. The amount that is due at the maturity or due date of a note is called the maturity value.

IV. Accounting for Notes Receivable.

A. When a note is received from a customer to apply on account, Notes Receivable is debited and Accounts Receivable is credited for the face amount of the note.

B. At the time a note matures and payment is received, Cash is debited, Notes Receivable is credited for the face amount of the note, and Interest Income is credited for the amount of interest due, if any.

C. At the end of the fiscal year, an adjusting entry is necessary to record the accrued interest on any outstanding interest-bearing notes receivable.

D. Instead of retaining a note until maturity, notes receivable may be transferred to a bank by endorsement, a process known as discounting notes receivable.

1. The interest (discount) charged by the bank is computed on the maturity value of the note for the period of time the bank must hold the note, namely the time that will pass between the date of the transfer and the due date of the note. This period is called the discount period.

2. The amount of the proceeds paid to the endorser is the excess of the maturity value over the discount.

3. The entry to record the discounting of notes receivable is to debit Cash for the proceeds, credit Notes Receivable for the face value of the note, and either debit Interest Expense or credit Interest Income for the amount to balance the entry.

4. The endorser of a note that has been discounted has a contingent liability to the holder of the note for the face amount of the note plus accrued interest and any protest fee. Any significant contingent liabilities should be disclosed on the balance sheet or in an accompanying note.

E. If the maker of the note fails to pay the debt on the due date, the note is said to be dishonored. The entry for a dishonored note is to debit Accounts Receivable for the maturity amount of the note, credit Notes Receivable for the face value of the note, and credit Interest Income for the amount of interest due on the note at maturity. When a discounted note receivable is dishonored, the holder usually notifies the endorser and asks for payment. If request for payment and notification of dishonor are timely, the endorser is legally obligated to pay the amount due on the note, including any accrued interest and protest fee. The payment of a protest fee is debited to the account receivable of the maker.

V. Uncollectible Receivables.

A. When merchandise or services are sold on credit, a part of the claims against customers will normally not be collectible.

B. The operating expense incurred because of the failure to collect receivables is called uncollectible accounts expense, doubtful accounts expense, or bad debts expense.

C. The two methods of accounting for receivables believed to be uncollectible are the allowance method and the direct write-off method.

VI. Allowance Method of Accounting for Uncollectibles.

A. Under the allowance method of accounting for uncollectibles, advance provision for uncollectibility is made by an adjusting entry at the end of the fiscal period.

1. The adjusting entry to record the allowance for uncollectibles is to debit Uncollectible Accounts Expense and credit Allowance for Doubtful Accounts. The account Allowance for Doubtful Accounts is a contra asset account offsetting Accounts Receivable.

2. The balance of the accounts receivable account less the contra account, Allowance for Doubtful Accounts, determines the expected value of the receivables to be realized in the future, called the net realizable value.

3. Uncollectible accounts expense is reported on the income statement as an administrative expense.

B. When an account is believed to be uncollectible, it is written off against the allowance account by debiting Allowance for Doubtful Accounts and crediting the customer's account receivable.

C. An account receivable that has been written off against the allowance account may later be collected.

1. The account should be reinstated by an entry that is the exact reverse of the write-off entry—a debit to the customer's account receivable and a credit to Allowance for Doubtful Accounts.

2. The cash received in payment would be recorded in the usual manner as a debit to Cash and a credit to Accounts Receivable.

D. The estimate of uncollectibles at the end of the fiscal period is based on past experience and forecasts of future business activity. Two methods of estimating uncollectibles are as follows:

1. The amount of uncollectibles may be estimated based upon the percentage of sales.

a. Based upon past experience or industry averages, the percentage of sales which will prove to be uncollectible is estimated.

b. The estimated percentage of uncollectible sales is then multiplied by the credit sales for the period and the Uncollectible Accounts Expense is debited and Allowance for Doubtful Accounts is credited for this amount.

c. The estimated percentage should ideally be based upon credit sales, but total sales may be used if the ratio of credit sales to total sales does not change much from year to year.

2. Uncollectibles may be estimated by analyzing the individual account receivable accounts in terms of length of time past due.

a. An aging of accounts receivable is prepared which lists accounts by due date.

b. Percentages are applied to each category of past due accounts to estimate the balance of the allowance for doubtful accounts as of the end of the accounting period.

c. The amount of the adjusting entry at the end of the fiscal period for uncollectible accounts expense is that amount necessary to bring the allowance account to its estimated balance as of the end of the period.

E. Estimates of uncollectible accounts expense based on analysis of the receivables are less common than estimates based on sales.

VII. Direct Write-Off Method of Accounting for Uncollectibles.

A. Under the direct write-off method of accounting for uncollectibles, no entry is made for uncollectibility until an account is determined to be worthless. At that time, an entry is made debiting Uncollectible Accounts Expense and crediting the individual customer's account receivable.

B. If the account that has been written off is later collected, the account should be reinstated by reversing the earlier entry to write off the account.

C. The receipt of cash in payment of a reinstated account is recorded in the usual manner.

VIII. Temporary Investments.

A. Most businesses invest idle or excess cash in temporary investments or marketable securities. These securities can be quickly sold when cash is needed.

B. Temporary investments and securities include stocks and bonds. Stocks are equity securities issued by corporations and bonds are debt securities issued by corporations and various government agencies.

C. A temporary investment in a portfolio of debt securities is carried at cost.

D. A temporary investment in a portfolio of equity securities is carried at the lower of its total cost or market value determined at the date of the balance sheet.

1. The carrying amount is based upon the total cost and total market value of the portfolio, rather than the lower of cost or market price of each individual equity security.

2. If the total market value of the equity securities is less than cost, an unrealized loss is recorded and reported on the income statement as a separate item.

3. If the market value of the portfolio later rises, the unrealized loss is reversed and included in net income, but only to the extent that it does not exceed the original cost. In such cases, the increase is reported separately in the Other Income section of the income statement.

IX. Temporary Investments and Receivables in the Balance Sheet.

A. Temporary investments and all receivables that are expected to be realized in cash within a year are presented in the Current Assets section of the balance sheet.

B. It is customary to list the assets in the order of their liquidity, that is, in the order in which they can be converted to cash in normal operations.

C. Disclosures presented either on the face of the financial statements or in accompanying notes include the market value of the investments and receivables. In addition, any unusual credit risks related to the receivables should be disclosed.

MATCHING

Instructions: A list of terms and related statements appear below. From the list of terms, select the one that relates to each statement. Print its identifying letter in the space provided.

A. Aging the receivables	**E.** Direct write-off method	**I.** Maturity value
B. Allowance method	**F.** Discount	**J.** Proceeds
C. Carrying amount	**G.** Dishonored	**K.** Promissory note
D. Contingent liabilities	**H.** Expected realizable value	**L.** Temporary investments

_____ 1. A written promise to pay a certain sum of money on demand or at a definite time.

_____ 2. The interest charged by a bank for discounting a note receivable.

_____ 3. The amount received from selling a note receivable prior to its maturity.

_____ 4. Potential obligations that will become actual liabilities only if certain events occur in the future.

_____ 5. If the maker of a note fails to pay the debt on the due date, the note is said to be (?).

_____ 6. A method of accounting for receivables which provides in advance for uncollectible receivables through the use of an allowance for doubtful accounts.

_____ 7. A method of accounting for uncollectible receivables in which no expense is recognized until individual accounts are determined to be worthless.

_____ 8. The balance of the accounts receivable following the deduction of the allowance for doubtful accounts.

_____ 9. The process of analyzing the receivable accounts in terms of the length of time past due.

_____ 10. Securities that can be readily sold when cash is needed.

_____ 11. The amount at which a temporary investment is reported on the balance sheet; also called basis or book value.

_____ 12. The amount that is due at the due date of a note.

TRUE / FALSE

Instructions: Indicate whether each of the following statements is true or false by placing a check mark in the appropriate column.

	True	False
1. The term "notes" includes all money claims against people, organizations, or other debtors.	____	____
2. Accounts and notes receivable originating from sales transactions are sometimes called trade receivables.	____	____
3. For good internal control, an employee who handles the accounting for notes and accounts receivable should not be involved with credit approvals or collections of receivables.	____	____
4. When a note is received from a customer on account, this is recorded by debiting Notes Receivable and crediting Sales.	____	____
5. When the holder transfers a note to a bank by endorsement, the discount (interest) charged is computed on the face value of the note for the period of time the bank must hold the note.	____	____
6. When the proceeds from discounting a note receivable are less than the face value, the difference is recorded as interest income.	____	____
7. The endorser of a note that has been discounted has a contingent liability that is in effect until the due date.	____	____
8. The method of accounting which provides in advance for receivables deemed uncollectible is called the allowance method.	____	____
9. The process of analyzing the receivable accounts in order to estimate the uncollectibles is sometimes called aging the receivables.	____	____
10. The carrying amount of a temporary investment in equity securities is the higher of its total cost or market value.	____	____

MULTIPLE CHOICE

Instructions: Circle the best answer for each of the following questions.

1. On a promissory note, the one making the promise to pay is called the:
   a. payee
   b. creditor
   c. maker
   d. noter

2. The amount that is due on a note at the maturity or due date is called the:
   a. terminal value
   b. face value
   c. book value
   d. maturity value

3. When a note is discounted, the excess of the maturity value over the discount is called the:
   a. gain
   b. proceeds
   c. interest
   d. present value

4. When the allowance method is used in accounting for uncollectible accounts, any uncollectible account is written off against the:
   a. allowance account
   b. sales account
   c. accounts receivable account
   d. uncollectible accounts expense account

5. Assume that the allowance account has a credit balance at the end of the year of $170 before adjustment. If the estimate of uncollectible accounts based on aging the receivables is $3,010, the amount of the adjusting entry for uncollectible accounts would be:
   a. $170
   b. $2,840
   c. $3,010
   d. $3,180

6. Assume that the allowance account has a debit balance at the end of the year of $250 before adjustment. If the estimate of uncollectible accounts based on sales for the period is $2,200, the amount of the adjusting entry for uncollectible accounts would be:
   a. $250
   b. $1,950
   c. $2,200
   d. $2,450

EXERCISE 9-1

Instructions: Using the basic formula for interest and assuming a 360-day year, compute the interest on the following notes.

1. $8,000 at 12% for 30 days...................................... $_____

2. $3,500 at 6% for 60 days.. $_____

3. $2,000 at 12% for 90 days...................................... $_____

Instructions: Using the 60-day, 6% method, complete the following interest calculations. (Items 4 and 5 are the same as 1 and 2, so that the two methods of computing interest may be compared.)

4. The interest on $8,000 at 12% for 30 days is .... $_____

5. The interest on $3,500 at 6% for 60 days is .... $_____

6. The interest on $12,000 for 90 days at 9% is .... $_____

7. The interest on $5,250 for 120 days at 12% is .... $_____

EXERCISE 9-2

Instructions: Based on the information given, fill in the blanks below.

(1) A 12%, 90-day note receivable for $12,000 was discounted at 14%, 30 days after receiving the note.

Face value .... _____

Interest on face value .... _____

Maturity value .... _____

Discount on maturity value .... _____

Proceeds... _____

(2) An 8%,120-day note receivable for $15,000 was discounted at 10%, 50 days after receiving the note.

Face value .... _____

Interest on face value .... _____

Maturity value .... _____

Discount on maturity value .... _____

Proceeds... _____

EXERCISE 9-3

Coco Co. uses the direct write-off method of accounting for uncollectibles. On August 31, 19—, Coco deemed that an amount of $550 due from Don Shore was uncollectible and wrote it off. On October 8, 19—, Shore paid the $550.

Instructions:
    (1) Prepare the entry to write off the account on August 31.
    (2) Prepare the entry to reinstate the account on October 8, and to record the cash received.

JOURNAL   PAGE

	DATE	DESCRIPTION	POST. REF.	DEBIT	CREDIT	
1						1
2						2
3						3
4						4
5						5
6						6
7						7
8						8
9						9
10						10
11						11
12						12
13						13
14						14
15						15
16						16
17						17

EXERCISE 9-4

Wallace Co. had a temporary investment in a portfolio of equity securities as of December 31, 19—, as follows:

	Cost	Market
Security A	$11,000	$12,000
Security B..	$18,000	$16,600
Security C..	$21,000	$23,000
Security D	$18,800	$16,400

    Instructions: Compute the proper carrying amount of these securities on Wallace's December 31, 19— balance sheet.

Carrying amount, December 31 .... $ _____

EXERCISE 9-5

The following data regarding the current assets of Walton Company were selected from the accounting records after adjustment at the end of the current fiscal year:

Accounts Receivable	$35,000
Allowance for Decline to Market of Marketable Securities	2,000
Allowance for Doubtful Accounts	1,200
Cash	37,500
Interest Receivable	9,900
Marketable Equity Securities	55,000
Notes Receivable	20,000

Instructions: Prepare the Current Assets section of the balance sheet for Walton Company.

PROBLEM 9-1

Instructions: Prepare the general journal entries to record the following transactions. (Omit explanations.)

(1) Pequot Co. received a 60-day, 12% note for $8,000 from a customer, Dave Davidson, in settlement of Davidson's account.

JOURNAL   PAGE _____

	DATE	DESCRIPTION	POST. REF.	DEBIT	CREDIT	
1						1
2						2
3						3

(2) Thirty days after (1), Pequot discounted Davidson's note at the bank at 10%.

4						4
5						5
6						6
7						7
8						8

(3) Davidson failed to pay the note in (1) and (2) at maturity. Pequot paid the bank.

9						9
10						10
11						11
12						12

(4) Ten days after the maturity of the note in (1), (2), and (3), Davidson paid Pequot in full, including interest at 11% for this 10-day period.

13						13
14						14
15						15
16						16
17						17

(5) Pequot received a 90-day, 10% note for $3,000 from a customer, Sue Smith, in settlement of Smith's account.

18						18
19						19
20						20

(6) The note in (5) was dishonored at maturity.

21						21
22						22
23						23
24						24

PROBLEM 9-2

Instructions: Prepare the appropriate general journal entries for each of the following situations.

(1) Net sales for the year are $800,000, uncollectible accounts expense is estimated at 3% of net sales, and the allowance account has a $425 credit balance before adjustment. Prepare the adjusting entry at year end for the uncollectibles.

JOURNAL

PAGE

	DATE	DESCRIPTION	POST. REF.	DEBIT	CREDIT	
1						1
2						2
3						3

(2) Based on an analysis of accounts in the customers ledger, estimated uncollectible accounts total $6,280, and the allowance account has a $325 credit balance before adjustment. Prepare the adjusting entry at year end for the uncollectibles.

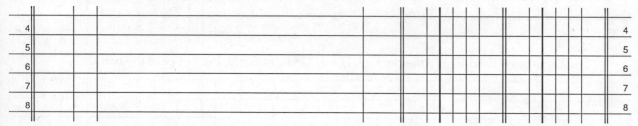

(3) A $3,500 account receivable from Bentley Co. is written off as uncollectible. The allowance method is used.

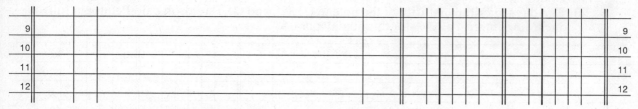

(4) A $1,235 account receivable from Apple Co., which was written off three months earlier, is collected in full. The allowance method is used.

Chapter 10
Inventories

QUIZ AND TEST HINTS

The following hints may be helpful to you in preparing for a quiz or a test over the material covered in Chapter 10.

1. Be prepared to answer multiple-choice or short answer questions regarding the effect of misstatements in beginning and ending inventory on the financial statements.
2. The chapter emphasizes determining the cost of inventory using the first-in, first-out (fifo), last-in, first-out (lifo), and average cost methods. Most instructors ask questions related to these cost flow assumptions using a periodic inventory system. The Illustrative Problem in the Chapter Review is an excellent study aid for this type of question.
3. The retail method and gross profit method of estimating inventory are also popular subjects for quiz and test questions with instructors. Be prepared to work each method.

CHAPTER OUTLINE

I. The Effects of Errors in Reporting Inventory.
  A. The term *inventories* is used to indicate (1) merchandise held for sale in the normal course of business and (2) materials in the process of production or held for production. Inventory of merchandise purchased for resale is commonly called merchandise inventory.
  B. Inventory is a significant item on the balance sheet and the income statement.
  C. Misstatements of inventory will affect the current period's financial statements.
    1. An overstatement of inventory at the end of the accounting period will cause an overstatement of gross profit and net income on the income statement and an overstatement of assets and owner's equity on the balance sheet.
    2. An understatement of inventory at the end of the accounting period will cause an understatement of gross profit and net income on the income statement, and an understatement of assets and owner's equity on the balance sheet.
  D. Misstatements of inventory will also affect the following period's financial statements.
    1. If the inventory is incorrectly stated at the end of the period, the net income of that period will be misstated and so will the net income for the following period.
    2. The amount of the two misstatements of net income will be equal and in opposite directions. Thus, the effect on net income of an incorrectly stated inventory, if not corrected, is limited to the period of the error and the following period. At the end of the following period, assuming no additional errors, the balance sheet will be properly stated. This is because the two misstatements of net income will offset each other and both assets and owner's equity will be correctly stated.
II. Internal Control of Inventories.
  A. The objective of internal controls over inventory is to assure that the inventory is

safeguarded and properly reported in the financial statements.

B. Internal controls for safeguarding of inventory begin with developing and using security measures to protect the inventory from theft or damage.

C. Other controls over inventory include using a voucher system. Prenumbered receiving reports should establish the initial accountability for inventory when it is received. These receiving reports are later reconciled to the initial purchase order and vendor's invoice before recording the purchase in the voucher register. Requisition forms authorizing withdrawals of inventory and a perpetual inventory system are also useful for control purposes.

D. A physical count of inventory, called a physical inventory, should be taken periodically and compared to the recorded inventory to detect any shortages or possible thefts.

III. Determining Actual Quantities in the Inventory.

A. The actual quantities of inventory at the end of an accounting period are determined by the process of "taking" an inventory.

B. All the merchandise owned by the business on the inventory date, and only such merchandise, should be included in the inventory.

C. It may be necessary to examine purchase and sales invoices of the last few days of the accounting period and the first few days of the following period to determine who has legal title to merchandise in transit on the inventory date.

1. When goods are purchased or sold FOB shipping point, title usually passes to the buyer when the goods are shipped. Therefore, these items should be included in inventory by the purchaser on the shipping date.

2. When goods are purchased or sold FOB destination, title usually does not pass to the buyer until the goods are delivered. Therefore, goods shipped under these terms should be included in inventory by the purchaser only when the goods have been received.

D. Special care should be taken in accounting for merchandise that has been shipped on a consignment basis to a retailer (the consignee). Even though the manufacturer does not have physical possession, consigned merchandise should be included in the manufacturer's (the consignor's) inventory.

IV. The Cost of Inventory.

A. The cost of merchandise inventory is made up of the purchase price and all costs incurred in acquiring such merchandise, including transportation, customs duties, and insurance.

B. Some costs of aquiring merchandise, such as the salaries of the Purchasing Department employees and other administrative costs, are not easily allocated to inventory. Such costs are treated as operating expenses of the period.

V. Inventory Costing Methods under a Periodic Inventory System.

A. A major accounting issue arises in the use of the periodic system when identical units of a commodity are acquired at different unit costs during a period. In such cases, it is necessary to determine the unit costs of the items on hand at the end of the period and the costs of the items sold during the period.

B. If a unit can be identified with a specific purchase, the specific identification method can be used.

C. If the specific identification method is not practical, an assumption must be made as to the flow of costs. The three most common cost flow assumptions are as follows:

1. Cost flow is in the order in which the expenditures were made—first-in, first-out.

2. Cost flow is in the reverse order in which the expenditures were made—last-in, first-out.

3. Cost flow is an average of the expenditures.

D. The first-in, first-out (fifo) method of costing inventory assumes that costs should be charged against revenue in the order in which they are incurred.

1. The inventory remaining at the end of the period is assumed to be made up of the most recent costs.

2. The fifo method is generally consistent with the physical movement of merchandise in an enterprise. To this extent, the fifo method approximates

the results that would be obtained by the specific identification of costs.

E. The last-in, first-out (lifo) method assumes that the most recent costs incurred should be charged against revenue.

1. The inventory remaining at the end of the period is assumed to be composed of the earliest costs.

2. Even though it does not represent the physical flow of the goods, the lifo method is widely used in business today.

F. The average cost method, sometimes called the weighted average method, assumes that costs should be charged against revenue according to the weighted average unit costs of the goods sold.

1. The same weighted average unit costs are used in determining the cost of the merchandise remaining in the inventory and the cost of merchandise sold.

2. For businesses in which various purchases of identical units of a commodity are mixed together, the average method approximates the physical flow of goods.

G. Each of the three alternative inventory costing methods is based on a different assumption as to the flow of costs.

1. If the cost of units and prices at which they are sold remain stable, all three methods yield the same results.

2. Prices do change, however, and as a result the three methods will yield different amounts for ending inventory, cost of merchandise sold, and gross profit for the period.

3. In periods of rising prices, the fifo method yields the lowest cost of merchandise sold, the highest net income, and the highest amount for ending inventory.

4. In periods of rising prices, the lifo method yields the highest cost of merchandise sold, the lowest net income, and the lowest ending inventory.

5. The average cost method yields results that are in between those of fifo and lifo.

H. During periods of rising prices, many companies prefer to use the last-in, first-out method to reduce the amount of income taxes.

I. Often, businesses apply different inventory costing methods to different types of inventory. The method used by a company for inventory costing purposes should be properly disclosed in the financial statements. Any changes in methods also should be disclosed.

VI. Inventory Costing Methods under a Perpetual Inventory System.

A. Under the perpetual inventory system, all merchandise increases and decreases are recorded in a manner similar to the recording of increases and decreases in cash. The merchandise inventory account at any point in time reflects the merchandise on hand at that date.

B. The basic accounting entries for a perpetual inventory system are as follows:

1. Purchases of merchandise are recorded by debiting Merchandise Inventory and crediting Accounts Payable or Cash.

2. Sales of merchandise are recorded by debiting Cost of Merchandise Sold and crediting Merchandise Inventory for the cost of the merchandise sold.

3. Unlike the periodic inventory system, no adjusting journal entries are necessary for beginning and ending inventory under the perpetual inventory system.

4. The balance in the merchandise inventory account as of the end of the accounting period would be the amount reported on the balance sheet on that date.

5. The balance of the cost of merchandise sold account would be the amount reported on the income statement for the period.

C. Details of inventory transactions are maintained in a subsidiary inventory ledger.

1. The balances of these accounts are called the book inventories of the items on hand.

2. Costs are normally assigned to units in the inventory ledger using one of the three costing methods (first-in, first-out; last-in, first-out; or average).

a. Under the first-in, first-out method of cost flow in a perpetual system, the cost of the units sold and cost of

171

units on hand after each transaction are accounted for on the fifo basis. The items received first are assumed to be the first sold.

b. Under the last-in, first-out method of cost flow in a perpetual system, the cost of units sold and the cost of units on hand after each transaction are accounted for on the last-in, first-out basis. The items received last are assumed to be the first sold.

c. When the average cost method is used in a perpetual inventory system, an average unit cost for each type of commodity is computed each time a purchase is made. This averaging technique is called a moving average.

D. If there is a large number of inventory items and/or transactions, businesses will often computerize the perpetual system for faster and more accurate processing of data. By computerizing a system, additional data may be entered into the inventory records so that inventory may be ordered and maintained at optimal levels.

VII. Valuation of Inventory at Other than Cost.

A. Although cost is the primary basis for the valuation of inventories, under certain circumstances inventory may be valued at other than cost.

B. If the market price of an inventory item is lower than its cost, the lower of cost or market method is used.

1. Market means the cost to replace the merchandise on the inventory date, based on quantities purchased from the usual source of supply.

2. The use of the lower of cost or market method provides two advantages: the gross profit is reduced for the period in which the decline occurred, and an approximately normal gross profit is realized during the period in which the item is sold.

3. It is possible to apply the lower of cost or market basis to each item in the inventory, major classes or categories, or the inventory as a whole.

C. Obsolete, spoiled, or damaged merchandise and other merchandise that can only be sold at prices below cost should be valued at net realizable value. Net realizable value is the estimated selling price less any direct cost of disposition, such as sales commissions.

VIII. Presentation of Merchandise Inventory on the Balance Sheet.

A. Merchandise inventory is usually presented in the Current Assets section of the balance sheet following receivables.

B. Both the method of determining the cost of the inventory (fifo, lifo, or average) and the method of valuing the inventory (cost, or lower of cost or market) should be shown. The details may be disclosed by a parenthetical note on the balance sheet or by a footnote.

IX. Estimating Inventory Cost.

A. In practice, an inventory amount may be needed to prepare an income statement when it is impractical to take a physical inventory or to maintain perpetual inventory records. In such cases, inventory estimation methods may be used.

B. The retail method of estimating inventory costs is based on the relationship of the cost of merchandise available for sale to the retail price of the same merchandise.

1. The retail prices of all merchandise acquired are accumulated.

2. The inventory at retail is determined by deducting sales for the period from the retail price of the goods that were available for sale during the period.

3. The inventory at retail is then converted to cost on the basis of the ratio of cost to selling (retail) price for the merchandise available for sale.

4. The retail method assumes that the "mix" of items in the ending inventory, in terms of percent of cost to selling price, is the same as the entire stock of merchandise available for sale.

5. One of the major advantages of the retail method is that it provides inventory figures for monthly or quarterly statements.

6. The retail method can be used with the periodic system when a physical inventory is taken at the end of the year.

C. The gross profit method of estimating inventory costs uses an estimate of the gross profit realized during the period to estimate the ending inventory.

1. The cost of merchandise available for sale is recorded in the accounting records.
2. An estimate of gross profit percentage is multiplied by the sales for the period to determine the estimated cost of merchandise sold.
3. Estimated ending inventory is then determined by subtracting from the merchandise available for sale the estimated cost of merchandise sold for the period.
4. The estimate of the gross profit rate is usually based on the actual rate for the preceding year, adjusted for any changes in the cost and sales prices during the current period.
5. The gross profit method may be used in estimating the cost of merchandise destroyed by fire or other disaster, or in preparing monthly or quarterly statements.

MATCHING

Instructions: A list of terms and related statements appear below. From the list of terms, select the one that relates to each statement. Print its identifying letter in the space provided.

A. Average cost method
B. Consignment inventory
C. First-in, first-out (FIFO) method

D. Gross profit method
E. Last-in, first-out (LIFO) method
F. Lower of cost or market

G. Merchandise inventory
H. Net realizable value
I. Physical inventory
J. Retail inventory method

____ 1. The inventory of merchandise purchased for resale is commonly called (?).

____ 2. The detailed listing of merchandise on hand.

____ 3. Merchandise that is shipped by a manufacturer to a retailer, who acts as the manufacturer's agent when selling the merchandise.

____ 4. An inventory method that treats the first merchandise acquired as the first merchandise sold.

____ 5. An inventory method in which the ending inventory is assumed to be composed of the earliest costs.

____ 6. An inventory method in which the weighted average unit costs are used in determining both ending inventory and cost of goods sold.

____ 7. A method of inventory pricing in which goods are valued at original cost or replacement cost, whichever is lower.

____ 8. The estimated selling price of inventory less any direct cost of disposition.

____ 9. An inventory method based on the relationship of the cost of merchandise available for sale to the retail price of the same merchandise.

____ 10. An inventory method which uses an estimate of the gross profit realized during the period to estimate the inventory at the end of the period.

TRUE / FALSE

Instructions: Indicate whether each of the following statements is true or false by placing a check mark in the appropriate column.

		True	False
1.	If merchandise inventory at the end of the period is understated, gross profit will be overstated..	____	____
2.	The two principal systems of inventory accounting are periodic and physical.......	____	____
3.	When terms of a sale are FOB destination, title usually does not pass to the buyer until the commodities are delivered.	____	____
4.	Ordinarily, specific identification inventory procedures are too costly and too time consuming to justify their use..	____	____
5.	During a period of rising prices, the inventory costing method which will result in the highest amount of net income is lifo.......................................	____	____
6.	If the cost of units purchased and the prices at which they were sold remained stable, all three inventory methods would yield the same results..................	____	____
7.	When the rate of inflation is high, the larger gross profits that result are frequently called inventory profits..	____	____
8.	As used in the phrase lower of cost or market, "market" means selling price........	____	____
9.	When the retail inventory method is used, inventory at retail is converted to cost on the basis of the ratio of cost to replacement cost of the merchandise available for sale.	____	____
10.	Merchandise inventory is usually presented on the balance sheet immediately following receivables..	____	____

MULTIPLE CHOICE

Instructions: Circle the best answer for each of the following questions.

1. If merchandise inventory at the end of the period is understated:
    a. gross profit will be overstated
    b. owner's equity will be overstated
    c. net income will be understated
    d. cost of merchandise sold will be understated

2. If merchandise inventory at the end of period 1 is overstated, and at the end of period 2 is correct:
    a. gross profit in period 2 will be understated
    b. assets at the end of period 2 will be overstated
    c. owner's equity at the end of period 2 will be understated
    d. cost of merchandise sold in period 2 will be understated

3. During a period of rising prices, the inventory costing method which will result in the lowest amount of the net income is:
    a. fifo
    b. lifo
    c. average cost
    d. perpetual

4. If the replacement price of an item of inventory is lower than its cost, the use of the lower of cost or market method:
    a. is not permitted unless a perpetual inventory system is maintained
    b. is recommended in order to maximize the reported net income
    c. tends to overstate the gross profit
    d. reduces gross profit for the period in which the decline occurred

5. When lifo is strictly applied to a perpetual inventory system, the unit cost prices assigned to the ending inventory will not necessarily be those associated with the earliest unit costs of the period if:
    a. a physical inventory is taken at the end of the period
    b. physical inventory records are maintained throughout the period in terms of quantities only
    c. at any time during a period the number of units of a commodity sold exceeds the number previously purchased during the same period
    d. moving average inventory cost is maintained

Name _____

EXERCISE 10-1

The net income, assets, and owner's equity of Ruby Co. for the past two fiscal years, ended December 31, are as follows:

	19XB	19XA
Net income..	$55,000	$40,000
Assets	$60,000	$55,000
Owner's equity	$50,000	$40,000

During 19XC, it was discovered that merchandise inventory had been understated by $5,000 at the end of year 19XA. The merchandise inventory was correct at the end of year 19XB.

Instructions: In the spaces provided below, indicate the effect of the error in the December 31, 19XA inventory on the net income, assets, and owner's equity in 19XA and 19XB. For each item, indicate (1) whether it is *understated*, *overstated*, or *correct*; and (2) the dollar amount of the error, if any.

	Net Income	Assets	Owner's Equity
19XA	(1) _____	(1) _____	(1) _____
	(2) _____	(2) _____	(2) _____
19XB	(1) _____	(1) _____	(1) _____
	(2) _____	(2) _____	(2) _____

EXERCISE 10-2

Instructions: Complete the following summary, which illustrates the application of the lower of cost or market rule to individual inventory items of Unks Co.

	Quantity	Unit Cost Price	Unit Market Price	Total Cost	Total Lower of C or M
Commodity A..................	750	$5.00	$4.80	$	$
Commodity B	460	6.00	7.00		
Commodity C..................	200	7.25	6.00		
Commodity D.................	300	4.80	4.30		
Total				$	$

PROBLEM 10-1

Hawkins Co. is a small wholesaler of hiking shoes. The accounting records show the following purchases and sales of the Mountain model during the first year of business.

Purchases				Sales	
Date	Units	Price	Total Cost	Date	Units
Jan. 10	10	$ 48	$ 480	Feb. 10	8
Feb. 15	100	54	5,400	Apr. 1	95
July 3	65	55	3,575	Aug. 10	65
Nov. 1	35	58	2,030	Nov. 15	30
Total	210		$11,485		198

A physical count of the Mountain model at the end of the year reveals that 12 are still on hand.

Instructions:
(1) Determine the cost of the Mountain model inventory as of December 31 by means of the average cost method with a periodic system.

INVENTORY (Average Cost)

Average unit cost = $_____ = $_____

_____ units in the inventory @ $_____ = $_____

(2) Determine the cost of the Mountain model inventory as of December 31 by means of the first-in, first-out (fifo) method with a periodic inventory system.

INVENTORY (Fifo Periodic)

Date Purchased	Units	Price	Total Cost

(3) Determine the cost of the Mountain model inventory as of December 31 by means of the first-in, first-out (fifo) method with a perpetual inventory system.

INVENTORY (Fifo Perpetual)

Date Purchased	Units	Price	Total Cost

(4) Determine the cost of the Mountain model inventory as of December 31 by means of the last-in, first-out (lifo) method with a periodic inventory system.

INVENTORY (Lifo Periodic)

Date Purchased	Units	Price	Total Cost

(5) Determine the cost of the Mountain Model inventory as of December 31 by means of the last-in, first-out (lifo) method with a perpetual inventory system.

INVENTORY (Lifo Perpetual)

Date Purchased	Units	Price	Total Cost

Name _____

PROBLEM 10-2

Bartle Co. began operating on January 1 of the current year. During the year, Bartle sold 28,000 units at an average price of $80 each, and made the following purchases:

Date of Purchase	Units	Unit Price	Total Cost
January 1	5,400	$50	$ 270,000
March 1..	4,100	54	221,400
June 1	4,800	56	268,800
September 1...	8,400	61	512,400
November 1...	5,400	69	372,600
December 1	1,900	73	138,700
	30,000		$1,783,900

Instructions: Determine the ending inventory, the cost of merchandise sold, and the gross profit for Bartle, using each of the following methods of inventory costing: **(1)** fifo, **(2)** lifo, and **(3)** average cost. (Round unit cost to two decimal places.)

	(1) Fifo	(2) Lifo	(3) Average Cost
Sales	$	$	$
Purchases..........................	$1,783,900	$1,783,900	$1,783,900
Less ending inventory			
Cost of merchandise sold	$	$	$
Gross profit........................	$	$	$

PROBLEM 10-3

Knish Co. operates a department store and takes a physical inventory at the end of each calendar year. However, Knish likes to have a balance sheet and an income statement available at the end of each month in order to study financial position and operating trends. Knish estimates inventory at the end of each month for accounting statement preparation purposes. The following information is available as of August 31 of the current year:

	Cost	Retail
Merchandise inventory, August 1	$118,500	$170,000
Purchases in August	307,125	481,400
Purchases returns and allowances—August...............................	8,000	8,900
Sales in August..		493,200
Sales returns and allowances—August....................................		14,200

Instructions:

(1) Determine the estimated cost of the inventory on August 31, using the retail method.

	Cost	Retail
Merchandise inventory, August 1	$_____	$_____
Purchases in August (net)	_____	_____
Merchandise available for sale	$_____	$_____

Ratio of cost to retail:

$$\frac{\$\rule{2cm}{0.4pt}}{\$\rule{2cm}{0.4pt}} = \quad \%$$

Sales in August (net)	_____
Merchandise inventory, August 31, at retail	$_____

Merchandise inventory, August 31, at estimated cost

($_____ × _____ %) .... | $_____ |

(2) Determine the estimated cost of inventory on August 31, using the gross profit method. On the basis of past experience, Knish estimates a rate of gross profit of 30% of net sales.

Merchandise inventory, August 1		$_____
Purchases in August (net)		_____
Merchandise available for sale		$_____
Sales in August (net)	$_____	
Less estimated gross profit		
($_____ × _____ %)	_____	
Estimated cost of merchandise sold..........................		_____
Estimated merchandise inventory, August 31		$_____

Chapter 11
Plant Assets and Intangible Assets

QUIZ AND TEST HINTS

The following hints may be helpful to you in preparing for a quiz or a test over the material covered in Chapter 11.

1. The chapter emphasizes the computation of depreciation. You should be able to compute depreciation using each of the four methods: straight-line, units-of-production, declining-balance, and sum-of-the-years-digits.

2. A common question on quizzes and tests involves the recording of plant asset disposals. You should be able to prepare general journal entries for disposals, including the exchange of similar assets. Exhibit 6 on pages 394-395 may be useful for reviewing the journal entries of exchanges of similar assets.

3. The chapter introduces a significant amount of new terminology. These terms lend themselves to numerous multiple-choice and matching questions. Review the Glossary of Key Terms.

4. You should expect some questions related to intangible assets. The computation of amortization is relatively simple, and it is similar to the units-of-production depreciation method. This section of the chapter lends itself to multiple-choice questions.

CHAPTER OUTLINE

I. Nature of Plant Assets and Intangible Assets.
   A. Plant assets are long-term or relatively permanent tangible assets that are used in the normal operations of the business. They are owned by the enterprise and are not held for sale in the ordinary course of the business.
      1. Another descriptive title often used is property, plant, and equipment.
      2. Plant assets may also be described in specific terms such as equipment, furniture, tools, machinery, buildings, and land.
   B. Long-term assets that are without physical attributes and not held for sale but are useful in the operations of an enterprise are classified as intangible assets. Intangible assets include such items as patents, copyrights, and goodwill.
   C. There is no standard rule as to the minimum length of life necessary for an asset

to be classified as a plant asset or intangible asset. In addition, an asset, such as standby equipment, need not actually be used on an ongoing basis or even often.
   D. Assets acquired for resale in the normal course of business are not classified as plant assets, regardless of their permanent nature or the length of time they are held.

II. Costs of Acquiring Plant Assets.
   A. The initial cost of acquiring a plant asset includes all expenditures necessary to get it in place and ready for use. Such expenditures include sales taxes, transportation charges, insurance, etc.
   B. The cost of constructing a building includes the fees paid to architects and engineers for plans and supervision, insurance, etc. Interest incurred during the construction should also be included in the cost of the building.

C. The cost of land includes not only the negotiated price but also broker's commissions, title fees, surveying fees, etc. If delinquent real estate taxes are assumed by the buyer, they are also chargeable to the land.

D. Expenditures for improvements that are neither as permanent as land nor directly associated with the building may be set apart in a land improvements account and depreciated accordingly. Such items include trees and shrubs, fences, and paved parking areas.

III. Nature of Depreciation.

A. Over time, all plant assets, with the exception of land, lose their ability to provide services. As a result, the cost of such assets should be transferred to expense accounts in a systematic manner during their expected useful life. This periodic cost expiration is called depreciation.

B. Factors that cause a decline in the ability of a plant asset to provide services include physical depreciation (e.g., wear and tear) and functional depreciation (e.g., obsolescence).

C. The meaning of the term *depreciation* as used in accounting may be misunderstood, because depreciation is not necessarily associated with declines in the market value of an asset. In addition, depreciation does not provide cash for the replacement of assets.

IV. Accounting for Depreciation.

A. Three factors are considered in determining the amount of depreciation expense to be recognized each period. These include (1) the plant asset's initial cost, (2) its expected useful life, and (3) its estimated value at the end of its useful life (residual value).

B. The straight-line method of determining depreciation provides for equal amounts of periodic expense over the estimated life of the asset.

1. The depreciable cost of the asset is determined by subtracting the estimated residual value from the initial cost of the asset.

2. The useful life of the asset is then divided into the depreciable cost.

3. The resulting amount is an annual depreciation charge which remains constant over the life of the asset.

4. Straight-line depreciation is often expressed by a percentage rate. The straight-line depreciation rate is equal to 100 divided by the useful life of the asset.

5. The straight-line method is widely used because of its simplicity.

C. The units-of-production method yields a depreciation expense that varies with the amount of the asset's usage.

1. The depreciable cost of the asset is determined by subtracting the estimated residual value from the initial cost of the asset.

2. The estimated life of the asset, expressed in terms of productive capacity, is then divided into the depreciable cost to arrive at the unit or hourly depreciation charge.

3. The actual amount of production usage is then multiplied by this rate to determine the depreciation charge.

D. The declining-balance method yields a declining periodic depreciation expense over the estimated life of the asset.

1. The double-declining balance method uses a rate of depreciation which is double the straight-line depreciation rate.

2. The declining-balance depreciation rate is then applied to the original cost of the asset for the first year, and thereafter to the book value (cost minus accumulated depreciation).

3. The residual value of the asset is not considered in determining the depreciation rate or the depreciation charge each period, except that the asset should not be depreciated below the estimated residual value.

E. The sum-of-the-years-digits method yields depreciation results which are similar to those of the declining-balance method.

1. The depreciable cost of the asset is determined by subtracting the estimated residual value from the initial cost of the asset.

2. The depreciation rate per year is determined by a fraction, whose numerator is the number of years of remaining life at the beginning of the year and the denominator is the sum of the years of useful life.

3. The depreciation charge for the period is determined by multiplying the sum-of-the-years-digits rate by the depreciable cost of the asset.

F. If the asset's first use does not coincide with the beginning of the fiscal year, each full year's depreciation should be allocated between the two years benefited.

G. The depreciation method chosen affects the amounts reported on the financial statements.

1. The straight-line method provides uniform periodic charges to depreciation expense over the life of the asset.

2. The units-of-production method provides for periodic charges to depreciation expense that may vary depending upon the amount of use of the asset.

3. Both the declining-balance and sum-of-the-years-digits methods provide for a higher depreciation charge in the first year of use of the asset and a gradually declining periodic charge thereafter. For this reason, these methods are referred to as accelerated depreciation methods.

H. Each of the four depreciation methods described above can be used to determine the amount of depreciation for federal income tax purposes for plant assets acquired prior to 1981.

I. For plant assets acquired after 1980 and before 1987, either the straight-line method or the Accelerated Cost Recovery System (ACRS) may be used to determine depreciation deductions for federal income tax purposes.

J. For plant assets acquired after 1986, either the straight-line method or Modified ACRS (MACRS) may be used.

K. Changes in the estimated useful lives and residual values of assets are accounted for by using the revised estimates to determine the amount of remaining undepreciated asset cost to be charged as an expense in future periods.

L. Revisions of the estimates used in the determination of depreciation does not affect the amounts of depreciation expense recorded in earlier years.

M. Depreciation may be recorded by an entry at the end of each month, or the adjust-ment may be delayed until the end of the year.

1. Depreciation is recorded by using a contra asset account, Accumulated Depreciation, or Allowance for Depreciation, so that the original cost of the asset can be reported along with the accumulated depreciation to date.

2. An exception to the general procedure of recording depreciation monthly or annually is made when a plant asset is sold, traded in, or scrapped, in which case depreciation must be brought up to date as of the date the asset is disposed of.

N. When depreciation is to be computed on a large number of individual assets, a subsidiary ledger is usually maintained.

1. Subsidiary ledgers for plant assets are useful to accountants in:
   a. Determining the periodic depreciation expense.
   b. Recording the disposal of individual items.
   c. Preparing tax returns.
   d. Preparing insurance claims in the event of insured losses.

2. Subsidiary ledger accounts may be expanded for accumulating data on the operating efficiency of the assets.

O. Subsidiary ledgers usually are not maintained for classes of plant assets that are made up of individual items of low unit cost. In such cases, the usual depreciation methods are not practical.

P. One common method of accounting for such assets is to treat them as expenses when they are acquired. Another method is to treat them as assets when acquired. An inventory of the items on hand at the end of the year is then taken and the assets' current value estimated. The difference between this value and the original cost or last year's value is debited to an expense account and credited to the plant asset account.

V. Composite-Rate Depreciation Method.

A. The composite-rate depreciation method determines depreciation for entire groups of assets by use of a single rate. The basis for grouping may be useful life estimates or other common traits.

B. When depreciation is computed on the basis of a composite group of assets of differing life spans, a rate based on averages must be developed using the following procedures:
  1. The annual depreciation for each asset is computed.
  2. The total annual depreciation is determined for the group of assets.
  3. The total annual depreciation divided by the total cost of the assets determines the composite rate.
C. Although new assets of differing life spans and residual values will be added to the group of assets and old assets will be retired, the "mix" of assets is assumed to remain relatively unchanged.
D. When a composite rate is used, it may be applied against total asset cost on a monthly basis, or some reasonable assumption may be made regarding the timing of increases and decreases in the group. A common practice is to assume that all additions and retirements have occurred uniformly throughout the year.
E. When assets within the composite group are retired, no gain or loss should be recognized. Instead, the asset account is credited for the cost of the asset and the accumulated depreciation account is debited for the excess of cost over the amount realized from the disposal.

VI. Capital and Revenue Expenditures.
  A. Expenditures for additions to plant assets or expenditures that add to the utility of plant assets for more than one accounting period are called capital expenditures.
    1. Expenditures for an addition to a plant asset should be debited to the plant asset account.
    2. Expenditures that increase operating efficiency or capacity for the remaining useful life of a plant asset are called betterments and should be debited to the plant asset account.
    3. Expenditures that increase the useful life of the asset beyond the original estimate are called extraordinary repairs and should be debited to the appropriate accumulated depreciation account.
  B. Expenditures that benefit only the current period and that are made in order to maintain normal operating efficiency of plant assets are called revenue expenditures.
    1. Expenditures for ordinary maintenance and repairs of a recurring nature are revenue expenditures and should be debited to expense accounts.
    2. Small expenditures are usually treated as repair expense, even though they may have characteristics of capital expenditures.

VII. Disposal of Plant Assets.
  A. A plant asset should not be removed from the accounts only because it has been depreciated for the full period of its estimated life. If the asset is still useful to the enterprise, the cost and accumulated depreciation should remain in the ledger. In this way, accountability for the asset is maintained.
  B. When plant assets are no longer useful to the business and have no residual market value, they are discarded.
    1. If the asset has been fully depreciated, then no loss is realized.
    2. The entry to record the disposal of a fully depreciated asset with no market value is to debit Accumulated Depreciation and credit the asset account.
    3. If the asset is not fully depreciated, depreciation should be brought up to date before the accumulated depreciation account is debited. The difference between the cost of the plant asset and its accumulated depreciation (book value) is recognized as a loss.
    4. Losses on discarding of plant assets are nonoperating items and are normally reported in the Other Expense section of the income statement.
  C. The entry to record the sale of a plant asset is similar to the entry to record the disposal of a plant asset.
    1. The first entry should be to record the depreciation expense for the period.
    2. Cash should be debited for the cash received from the sale of the plant asset.
    3. Accumulated Depreciation should be debited for its balance, the plant asset account should be credited for its cost, and any difference in the debits and credits to balance the entry should be

reported as a gain (credit) or a loss (debit) on the sale of the plant asset.

D. Plant assets may be traded in (exchanged) for new equipment having a similar use.
   1. The trade-in allowance is deducted from the price of the new equipment, and the balance owed is called boot.
   2. If the trade-in value of the plant asset is greater than its book value, the gain is not recognized for either financial reporting or tax purposes. The new asset's cost is the amount of boot given plus the book value of the old asset. In effect, the gain is indirectly recognized over the useful life of the asset as a reduction in the periodic depreciation charges which would otherwise be recognized.
   3. If the trade-in value of the plant asset is less than its book value, the loss is recognized for financial reporting purposes. For tax purposes, the loss is not recognized. Any loss on the exchange is added to the cost of the new asset.

VIII. Leasing Plant Assets.
   A. Instead of owning a plant asset, a business may acquire the use of a plant asset through a lease.
      1. A lease is a contract for the use of an asset for a stated period of time.
      2. The two parties to a lease are the lessor (the party who owns the asset) and the lessee (the party that obtains the rights to use the asset).
   B. Capital leases are defined as leases that include one or more of the following provisions:
      1. The lease transfers ownership of the leased asset to the lessee at the end of the lease term.
      2. The lease contains an option for a bargain purchase of the leased asset by the lessee.
      3. The lease term extends over most of the economic life of the leased asset.
      4. The lease requires rental payments which approximate the fair market value of the leased asset.
   C. Leases which do not meet the preceding criteria for capital leases are classified as operating leases.
   D. A capital lease is accounted for as if the lessee has, in fact, purchased the asset.

The lessee will debit an asset account for the fair market value of a leased asset and credit a long-term lease liability account.

E. In accounting for operating leases, rent expense is recognized as the leased asset is used.

F. Financial reporting disclosures require the presentation of future lease commitments in footnotes to the financial statements.

IX. Internal Control of Plant Assets.
   A. Effective internal controls over plant assets begin with authorization and approval for the purchase of plant assets.
   B. Once authorization and approval has been granted, procedures should exist to assure that the plant asset is acquired at the lowest possible cost.
   C. When the asset is received, it should be inspected and tagged for entry into the plant asset subsidiary ledger.
   D. A periodic physical inventory of plant assets should be performed to verify the accuracy of the accounting records. Such an inventory could detect missing, obsolete, or idle plant assets.
   E. Precautions should be taken to safeguard plant assets from possible theft, misuse, or other damage.
   F. All disposals of plant assets should be properly authorized and approved.

X. Depletion.
   A. The periodic allocation of the cost of metal ores and other minerals removed from the earth is called depletion.
   B. The periodic cost allocation is based upon a depletion rate which is computed as the cost of the mineral deposit divided by its estimated size. The amount of periodic depletion is determined by multiplying the depletion rate by the quantity extracted during the period.
   C. The adjusting entry for depletion is a debit to Depletion Expense and a credit to Accumulated Depletion. The accumulated depletion account is a contra account to the asset to which the cost of the mineral deposit was initially recorded.

XI. Intangible Assets.
   A. The basic principles of accounting for intangible assets are like those described earlier for plant assets. The major ac-

counting issues involve the determination of the initial costs and the recognition of periodic cost expiration, called amortization, due to the passage of time or a decline in usefulness of the intangible asset.

B. Patents provide exclusive rights to produce and sell goods with one or more unique features.
1. An enterprise may purchase patent rights from others or it may obtain patents on new products developed in its own research laboratories.
2. The initial cost of a purchased patent should be debited to an asset account and then written off, or amortized, over the years of its expected usefulness.
3. The straight-line method of amortization should be used unless it can be shown that another method is more appropriate.
4. A separate contra asset account is normally not credited for the write-off of patent amortization; the credit is recorded directly to the patent account.
5. Current accounting principles require that research and development costs incurred in the development of patents should be expensed as incurred.
6. Legal fees related to patent purchase or development should be recognized and amortized over the useful life of the patent.

C. The exclusive right to publish and sell a literary, artistic, or musical composition is obtained by a copyright.
1. The costs assigned to a copyright include all costs of creating the work plus the cost of obtaining the copyright.
2. A copyright that is purchased from another should be recorded at the price paid for it.
3. Because of the uncertainty regarding the useful life of a copyright, it is usually amortized over a relatively short period of time.

D. Goodwill is an intangible asset that attaches to a business as a result of such favorable factors as location, product superiority, reputation, and managerial skill.
1. Goodwill should be recognized in the accounts only if it can be objectively determined by an event or transaction, such as the purchase or sale of a business.
2. Goodwill should be amortized over the years of its useful life, which should not exceed 40 years.

XII. Financial Reporting for Plant Assets and Intangible Assets.
A. The amount of depreciation expense or amortization should be set forth separately in the income statement or disclosed in some other manner.
B. A general description of the method or methods used in computing depreciation or amortization should also be reported in the financial statements.
C. The balance of each major class of depreciable assets should be disclosed in the balance sheet or in notes thereto, together with the related accumulated depreciation, either by major class or in total.
D. Intangible assets are usually presented in the balance sheet in a separate section immediately following plant assets.

Name _____

MATCHING

Instructions: A list of terms and related statements appear below. From the list of terms, select the one that relates to each statement. Print its identifying letter in the space provided.

A. Accelerated depreciation method
B. Amortization
C. Betterments
D. Boot
E. Capital expenditures

F. Composite-rate method
G. Depletion
H. Depreciation
I. Extraordinary repairs
J. Goodwill
K. Lease

L. Residual value
M. Revenue expenditures
N. Straight-line method
O. Units-of-production method

H **1.** The allocation of the cost of an asset to expense over its expected useful life.

L **2.** The estimated value of a plant asset at the time that it is to be retired from service.

N **3.** A method of depreciation which provides for equal periodic charges to expense over the estimated life of the asset.

J **4.** An intangible asset that attaches to a business as a result of such favorable factors as location, product superiority, reputation, and managerial skill.

E **5.** Expenditures that add to the utility of the asset for more than one accounting period.

M **6.** Expenditures that benefit only the current period and that are made in order to maintain normal operating efficiency.

D **7.** The balance owed after the trade-in allowance is deducted from the price of new equipment acquired in a trade for equipment having similar uses.

A **8.** A depreciation method that provides for a high depreciation charge in the first year of use of an asset and gradually declining periodic charges thereafter.

G **9.** The periodic allocation of the cost of natural resources to expense as the units are removed.

B **10.** The allocation to expense of the cost of an intangible asset over the periods of its economic usefulness.

O **11.** A method of depreciation which yields a depreciation charge that varies with the amount of asset usage.

F **12.** A method of depreciation that applies a single depreciation rate to entire groups of assets.

C **13.** Expenditures that increase operating efficiency or capacity for the remaining useful life of a plant asset.

I **14.** Expenditures that increase the useful life of an asset beyond the original estimate.

K **15.** A contractual agreement that conveys the right to use an asset for a stated period of time.

TRUE / FALSE

Instructions: Indicate whether each of the following statements is true or false by placing a check mark in the appropriate column.

		True	False
1.	Both the declining-balance and the sum-of-the-years-digits methods provide for a higher depreciation charge in the first year of use of the asset, followed by a gradually declining periodic charge.	✓	
2.	The method of depreciation which yields a depreciation charge that varies with the amount of asset usage is known as the units-of-production method.	✓	
3.	The method of depreciation that, each year of an asset's estimated life, applies a successively smaller fraction to the original cost less the estimated residual value is called the declining-balance method.		✓
4.	In using the declining-balance method, the asset should not be depreciated below the net book value.		✓
5.	Accelerated depreciation methods are most appropriate for situations in which the decline in productivity or earning power of the asset is proportionately greater in the early years of its use than in later years.	✓	
6.	ACRS depreciation methods permit the use of asset lives that are often much shorter than the actual useful life.	✓	
7.	When an old plant asset is traded in for a new plant asset having a similar use, proper accounting treatment prohibits recognition of a gain.	✓	
8.	A procedure to determine depreciation for entire groups of assets by use of a single rate is called the composite-rate depreciation method.	✓	
9.	A lease which transfers ownership of the leased asset to the lessee at the end of the lease term should be classified as an operating lease.		✓
10.	Long-lived assets that are without physical characteristics but useful in the operations of an enterprise are classified as plant assets.		✓
11.	Fully depreciated assets should be retained in the accounting records until disposal has been authorized and they are removed from service.	✓	
12.	Intangible assets are usually reported in the balance sheet in the current asset section.		✓

MULTIPLE CHOICE

Instructions: Circle the best answer for each of the following questions.

1. If unwanted buildings are located on land acquired for a plant site, the cost of their removal, less any salvage recovered, should be charged to the:
   a. expense accounts
   b. building account
   c. land account
   d. accumulated depreciation account

2. The depreciation method used most often in the financial statements is the:
   a. straight-line method
   b. declining-balance method
   c. units-of-production method
   d. sum-of-the-years-digits method

3. The depreciation method that would provide the highest reported net income in the early years of an asset's life would be:
   a. straight-line
   b. declining-balance
   c. sum-of-the-years-digits
   d. accelerated

4. Equipment with an estimated useful life of 5 years and an estimated residual value of $600 is acquired at a cost of $13,800. Using the sum-of-the-years-digits method, what is the amount of depreciation for the first year of use of the equipment?
   a. $880
   b. $2,760
   c. $4,400
   d. $4,600

5. Equipment that cost $20,000 was originally estimated to have a useful life of 5 years and a residual value of $2,000. The equipment has been depreciated for 2 years using straight-line depreciation. During the third year it is estimated that the remaining useful life is 2 years (instead of 3) and that the residual value is $1,000 (instead of $2,000). The depreciation expense on the equipment in year 3 using the straight-line method would be: 3600/4p.   7,200
   a. $5,500
   b. $5,900
   c. $6,000
   d. $7,500

6. Assume that a drill press is rebuilt during its sixth year of use so that its useful life is extended 5 years beyond the original estimate of 10 years. In this case, the cost of rebuilding the drill press should be charged to the appropriate:
   a. expense account
   b. accumulated depreciation account
   c. asset account
   d. liability account

7. Old equipment which cost $11,000 and has accumulated depreciation of $6,300 is given, along with $9,000 in cash, for the same type of new equipment with a price of $15,600. At what amount should the new equipment be recorded?
   a. $15,600
   b. $15,300
   c. $13,700
   d. $9,000

8. Assume the same facts as in No. 7, except that the old equipment and $11,500 in cash is given for the new equipment. At what amount should the new equipment be recorded for financial accounting purposes?
   a. $16,200
   b. $15,600
   c. $11,500
   d. $10,900

9. In a lease contract, the party who legally owns the asset is the:
   a. contractor
   b. operator
   c. lessee
   d. lessor

10. Which of the following items would not be considered an intangible asset?
   a. lease
   b. patent
   c. copyright
   d. goodwill

EXERCISE 11-1

Dante Co. uses a composite rate of 25% for the depreciation of several pieces of equipment, based on the total of the annual depreciation charges on these assets divided by their total cost. Assuming that the balance of the equipment account at the end of the current year is $18,000 and that all of the equipment has been in use throughout the entire year, record the depreciation of Dante's equipment. (Omit explanation.)

JOURNAL   PAGE

	DATE	DESCRIPTION	POST. REF.	DEBIT	CREDIT	
1	Dec. 31	Depreciation Expense		4,500		1
2		Accum. Depreciation			4,500	2
3						3

EXERCISE 11-2

Bidwell Co. uses the units-of-production method for computing the depreciation on its machines. One machine, which cost $88,000, is estimated to have a useful life of 22,000 hours and no residual value. During the first year of operation, this machine was used a total of 5,200 hours. Record the depreciation of this machine at the end of the first year. (Omit explanation.)

JOURNAL   PAGE

	DATE	DESCRIPTION	POST. REF.	DEBIT	CREDIT	
1		Depr. Exp		20,800		1
2		Acc Exp			20,800	2
3						3

EXERCISE 11-3

On March 8, Tilly's Wholesale decides to sell for $2,000 cash some fixtures for which it paid $4,000 and on which it has taken total depreciation of $2,500 to date of sale. Record this sale. (Omit explanation.)

JOURNAL   PAGE

	DATE	DESCRIPTION	POST. REF.	DEBIT	CREDIT	
1		Cash		2,000		1
2		Accum. Depr.		2,500		2
3		Fixtures			4,000	3
4		Gain			500	4

Mine-It Co. paid $2,400,000 for some mineral rights in Idaho. The deposit is estimated to contain 800,000 tons of ore of uniform grade. Record the depletion of this deposit at the end of the first year, assuming that 80,000 tons are mined during the year. (Omit explanation.)

JOURNAL

PAGE

	DATE	DESCRIPTION	POST. REF.	DEBIT	CREDIT	
1		Depl. Exp		240 000		1
2		Acc. Depl.			240 000	2
3						3
4						4
5						5
6						6
7						7
8						8
9						9

Stables Co. acquires a patent at the beginning of its calendar (fiscal) year for $100,000. Although the patent will not expire for another ten years, it is expected to be of value for only five years. Record the amortization of this patent at the end of the fiscal year. (Omit explanation.)

JOURNAL

PAGE

	DATE	DESCRIPTION	POST. REF.	DEBIT	CREDIT	
1		Amort Expense		20 000		1
2		Patents			20 000	2
3						3
4						4
5						5
6						6
7						7
8						8
9						9
10						10
11						11
12						12
13						13
14						14
15						15
16						16
17						17
18						18
19						19

Name _____

PROBLEM 11-1

Bishop Company purchased equipment on January 1, 19XA, for $80,000. The equipment is expected to have a useful life of 4 years, and a residual value of $5,000.

Instructions: Determine the amount of depreciation expense for the years ended 19XA, 19XB, 19XC, and 19XD, for each method of depreciation in the table below.

Year	Straight-Line	Declining-Balance	Sum-of-the-Years-Digits
19XA	18,750	40,000	30,000
19XB	18,750	20,000	22,500
19XC	18,750	10,000	15,000
19XD	18,750	5,000	7,500
Total	75,000	75,000	75,000

PROBLEM 11-2

Getco Co. has a sales representative who must travel a substantial amount. A car for this purpose was acquired January 2, four years ago, at a cost of $20,000. It is estimated to have a total useful life of 4 years.

Instructions:
   (1) Record the annual depreciation on Getco's car at the end of the first and third years of ownership, using the straight-line method and assuming no salvage value. (Omit explanation.)
   (2) Record the annual depreciation on Getco's car at the end of the first and third years of ownership, using the declining-balance method at twice the straight-line rate. (Omit explanation.)
   (3) Record the annual depreciation on Getco's car at the end of the first and third years of ownership, using the sum-of-the-years-digits method and assuming no salvage value. (Omit explanation.)

JOURNAL   PAGE

	DATE	DESCRIPTION	POST. REF.	DEBIT	CREDIT	
1		Depr. Exp		5000		1
2		Accum Dep			5000	2
3		Depr Exp		5000		3
4		Accum Dep			5000	4
5		Depr. Exp		10 000		5
6					10 000	6
7		u		2500		7
8		u			2500	8
9				8000		9
10					8000	10
11				4000		11
12					4000	12
13						13
14						14
15						15
16						16
17						17
18						18
19						19
20						20
21						21
22						22
23						23
24						24
25						25
26						26
27						27
28						28
29						29

PROBLEM 11-3

(a)　Braso Co. is planning to trade in its present truck for a new model on April 30 of the current year. The existing truck was purchased May 1 three years ago at a cost of $15,000, and accumulated depreciation is $12,000 through April 30 of the current year. The new truck has a list price of $20,700. Ralston Motors agrees to allow Braso $3,500 for the present truck, and Braso agrees to pay the balance of $17,200 in cash.

Instructions: Record the exchange in general journal form according to acceptable methods of accounting for exchanges. (Omit explanation.)

JOURNAL　　　　　　　　　　　　　　　　PAGE

	DATE	DESCRIPTION	POST. REF.	DEBIT	CREDIT	
1		Truck		20500		1
2		accum Deps.		12000		2
3					15000	3
4					17200	4

(b)　Assume the same facts as in (a), except that the allowance on the present truck is $1,000 and that Braso agrees to pay the balance of $19,700 in cash.

Instructions:
(1)　Record the exchange according to acceptable methods of accounting for exchanges.
(2)　Record the exchange as in (1), except that the entry should be in conformity with the requirements of the Internal Revenue Code.

JOURNAL　　　　　　　　　　　　　　　　PAGE

	DATE	DESCRIPTION	POST. REF.	DEBIT	CREDIT	
1		accum Deps.		12000		1
2		Equip - Truck		20700		2
3		Loss on Sale of Truck		2000		3
4		Cash			19700	4
5		Equip - Truck			15000	5
6						6
7						7
8		accum Deps		12000		8
9		E - T		22700		9
10		cash			19700	10
11		Truck			15000	11
12						12
13						13
14						14
15						15
16						16
17						17

This page is blank.

Chapter 12
Payroll, Notes Payable, and Other Current Liabilities

QUIZ AND TEST HINTS

The following hints may be helpful to you in preparing for a quiz or a test over the material covered in Chapter 12.

1. If your instructor covered bonuses in class, expect a short problem or series of multiple-choice questions on the computation of bonuses. The chapter illustration is a good review.

2. A major focus of this chapter is on the computation of payroll. You should be able to compute total earnings, FICA tax, state and federal unemployment tax, and net pay and prepare the necessary journal entries. Review the chapter illustrations related to these computations.

3. The journal entries for vacation pay, pensions, and warranty expense are fairly easy to do. Spend a few minutes reviewing these entries.

4. Most instructors will ask some questions related to notes payable. You should be able to compute interest and prepare the necessary journal entries, including an adjusting entry for accrued interest. Also, carefully review the discounting of non-interest-bearing notes.

5. The Illustrative Problem in the Chapter Review is a good overall review of the types of journal entries you might have to prepare on a test or a quiz. Try to work the problem without looking at the solution. Check your answer. If you made any errors, review those sections of the chapter. If you still don't understand the answer, ask your instructor for help.

6. Review the Glossary of Key Terms.

CHAPTER OUTLINE

I. Payroll and Payroll Taxes.
  A. The term payroll refers to a total amount paid to employees for services provided during a period.
  B. Payroll expenditures are usually significant for a business enterprise for several reasons:
    1. Employees are sensitive to payroll errors or irregularities, and maintaining good employee morale requires that the payroll be paid on a timely, accurate basis.
    2. Payroll expenditures are subject to various federal and state regulations.
    3. Payroll expenditures and related payroll taxes have a significant effect on the net income of most business enterprises.
  C. Salary and wage rates are determined, in general, by agreement between the employer and employees. Enterprises engaged in interstate commerce must follow the requirements of the Fair Labor Standards Act. This act requires a minimum rate of 1½ times the regular rate for all hours worked in excess of 40 hours per week.
  D. The employee earnings for a period are determined by multiplying the hours worked up to 40 hours by the regular rate, and any overtime hours by 1½ times the regular rate.
  E. Many enterprises pay their employees an annual bonus in addition to their regular salary or wage. The method used in determining the amount of a profit-sharing

bonus may be expressed as a certain percentage of the following:

    1. Income before deducting the bonus and income taxes.

    2. Income after deducting the bonus but before deducting income taxes.

    3. Income before deducting the bonus but after deducting income taxes.

    4. Net income after deducting both the bonus and income taxes.

F. The total earnings of an employee for a payroll period, including bonuses and overtime pay, are often called the gross pay. From this amount is subtracted one or more deductions to arrive at net pay.

    1. Most employers are required by the Federal Insurance Contributions Act (FICA) to withhold a portion of the earnings of each of their employees as a deduction.

    2. Except for certain types of employment, all employers must withhold a portion of the earnings of their employees for payment of the employee's liability for federal income tax.

    3. Other deductions, such as union dues, employee insurance, etc., may be authorized by employees.

G. Gross earnings for a payroll period less the payroll deductions yields the amount to be paid to the employee.

H. Because there is a ceiling on annual earnings subject to FICA tax, when the amount of FICA tax to withhold from an employee is determined for a period, it is necessary to refer to one of the following cumulative amounts:

    1. Employee gross earnings for the year up to, but not including, the current payroll period.

    2. Employee tax withheld for the year up to, but not including, the current payroll period.

I. There is no ceiling on the amount of earnings subject to withholding for income taxes and hence no need to consider the cumulative earnings.

J. Most employers are subject to federal and state taxes based on the amount paid their employees. Such taxes are an operating expense of the business.

    1. Employers are required to contribute to the Federal Insurance Contributions

Act (FICA) program for each employee. The tax rates are the same as those for employees.

    2. Employers also are subject to federal and state unemployment compensation taxes on the pay of employees.

K. A few states also collect a state unemployment compensation tax from employees.

II. Accounting Systems for Payroll and Payroll Taxes.

A. The major parts common to most payroll systems are the payroll register, employee's earnings record, and payroll checks.

B. The multicolumn form used in assembling and summarizing the data needed at the end of each payroll period is called the payroll register. A payroll register will normally have columns for the following items:

    1. Total hours worked.

    2. Regular, overtime, and total earnings.

    3. Deductions for FICA, federal income tax, and other deductions.

    4. Total amount of deductions.

    5. The net amount of take-home pay.

    6. The check number of the payroll check issued to the employee.

    7. Distribution columns for the accounts to be debited for the payroll expense.

C. The payroll register serves as the basis for preparing the journal entries to record the payroll and related payroll tax expenses.

D. Payment of the liability for payroll and payroll taxes is recorded in the same manner as payment of other liabilities.

E. It is important to note that the payroll taxes levied against employers become liabilities at the time the payroll is paid to employees, rather than at the time the liability to the employees is incurred.

F. Detailed payroll data must be maintained for each employee in a record called the employee's earnings record. Such a record maintains data on total hours worked, total earnings, deductions, and net pay.

G. One of the principal outputs of most payroll systems is a series of payroll checks at the end of each pay period for distribution to employees.

    1. Most employers with a large number of employees use a special bank account

and payroll checks designed specifically for payroll.

2. Currency may be used to pay payroll when cashing checks is difficult for employees.

H. Through the use of diagrams, interrelationships of the principal parts of a payroll system may be shown.

   1. The outputs of the payroll system are the payroll register, the payroll check, earnings records, and reports for tax and other purposes.

   2. The basic data entering the payroll system are called the input of the system. Input data that remain relatively unchanged are characterized as constants. Those data that differ from period to period are termed variables.

I. The cash disbursement controls discussed in earlier chapters are applicable to payrolls. Thus, the use of the voucher system and the requirement that all payments be supported by vouchers are desirable.

J. Other controls include proper authorization for additions and deletions of employees, pay rate changes, and the maintenance of attendance records.

III. Employees' Fringe Benefits.

A. Many companies provide their employees a variety of benefits in addition to salary and wages earned. These benefits are called fringe benefits and include vacation pay and pensions.

B. To properly match revenue and expense, the employer should accrue the vacation pay liability as the vacation rights are earned.

C. The entry to accrue vacation pay is to debit Vacation Pay Expense and credit a liability, Vacation Pay Payable.

D. Retirement pension plans for employees may be classified as follows:

   1. A contributory plan requires the employer to withhold a portion of each employee's earnings as a contribution to the plan.

   2. A noncontributory plan requires the employer to bear the entire cost.

   3. A funded plan requires the employer to set aside funds to meet future pension benefits by making payments to an independent funding agency.

   4. An unfunded plan is managed entirely by the employer instead of by an independent agency.

   5. A qualified plan is designed to comply with federal income tax requirements which allow the employer to deduct pension contributions for tax purposes and which exempt fund income from tax. Most pension plans are qualified.

E. The recording of pension costs involves a debit to Pension Expense. If the pension cost is fully funded, the credit is to Cash. If the pension cost is partially funded, any unfunded amount is credited to Unfunded Pension Liability.

F. When an employer first adopts or changes a pension plan, the employer must consider whether to grant employees credit for prior years' service. If credit is granted for past service, a prior service cost obligation is recognized.

IV. Short-Term Notes Payable.

A. Notes may be issued to creditors to satisfy an account payable created earlier, or they may be issued at the time merchandise or other assets are purchased. The entries to record a note payable are:

   1. Debit Accounts Payable and credit Notes Payable for the issuance of a note to satisfy an account payable.

   2. Debit Cash or other asset and credit Notes Payable for notes initially issued.

B. Interest must be recognized on notes payable.

   1. An adjusting entry debiting Interest Expense and crediting Interest Payable must normally be made at the end of the year to record the accrual of any interest.

   2. When notes are paid at maturity, the entry is normally to debit Notes Payable, debit Interest Expense, and credit Cash for the maturity amount.

C. Notes may be issued when money is borrowed from banks. Such notes may be interest-bearing or non-interest-bearing.

   1. An interest-bearing note is recorded by debiting Cash and crediting Notes Payable for the face value of the note. At the due date, Notes Payable is debited for the face value of the note, Interest Expense is debited for the interest, and

Cash is credited for the total amount due.

2. When a non-interest-bearing note is issued to a bank, the bank discounts the note and remits the proceeds to the borrower.
3. The entry to record the discounted note is to debit Cash for the proceeds, debit Interest Expense for the difference between the face value of the note and the proceeds received, and credit Notes Payable for the amount of the face of the note. If the note is paid at maturity, Notes Payable is debited for the face value and Cash is credited.

V. Product Warranty Liability.
   A. At the time of sale, a company may grant a warranty on a product. If revenues and expenses are to be matched properly, a liability to cover the warranty must be recorded in the period of the sale.
   B. The entry to accrue warranty liability is to debit Product Warranty Expense and credit Product Warranty Payable.
   C. When a defective product is repaired, the repair cost should be recorded by debiting Product Warranty Payable and crediting Cash, Supplies, or another appropriate account.

MATCHING

Instructions: A list of terms and related statements appear below. From the list of terms, select the one that relates to each statement. Print its identifying letter in the space provided.

A. Discount
B. Employee's earnings record
C. FICA tax
D. Funded plan

E. Net pay
F. Noncontributory plan
G. Payroll register

H. Proceeds
I. Wages
J. W-4

_J_   1.   The Employee's Withholding Allowance Certificate.

_I_   2.   Remuneration for manual labor, computed on an hourly, weekly, or piecework basis.

_E_   3.   Gross pay less payroll deductions; the amount the employer is obligated to pay the employee.

_C_   4.   A tax used to finance federal programs for old-age and disability benefits and health insurance for the aged.

_G_   5.   Multicolumn form used in assembling and summarizing the data needed at the end of each payroll period.

_B_   6.   A detailed record of an employee's earnings for each payroll period and for the year.

_F_   7.   A pension plan requiring the employer to bear the entire cost.

_D_   8.   A pension plan requiring the employer to set aside funds to meet future pension benefits by making payments to an independent funding agency.

_A_   9.   The amount of interest deducted from a future value.

_H_ 10.   The net amount available to a borrower of funds.

Instructions: Indicate whether each of the following statements is true or false by placing a check mark in the appropriate column.

	True	False
1. The total earnings of an employee for a payroll period are called gross pay.........	✓	
2. Only employers are required to contribute to the Federal Insurance Contributions Act program.		✓
3. All states require that unemployment compensation taxes be withheld from employees' pay.............	✓	
4. The payroll register may be used as a posting medium in a manner similar to that in which the voucher register and the check register are used...........	✓	
5. The amounts withheld from employees' earnings have an effect on the firm's debits to the salary or wage expense accounts.		✓
6. All payroll taxes levied against employers become liabilities at the time the related remuneration is paid to employees.............	✓	
7. The recording procedures when special payroll checks are used are different from the procedures when the checks are drawn on the regular bank account...........		✓
8. Depending on when it is to be paid, vacation liability may be classified in the balance sheet as either a current liability or a long-term liability.		✓
9. If pension cost is partially funded, the employer's contribution to a pension plan for normal pension cost for a given year is recorded by a debit to Pension Expense and credits to Cash and Unfunded Pension Liability.............	✓	
10. In order for revenues and expenses to be matched properly, a liability to cover the cost of a product warranty must be recorded in the period when the product is repaired.		✓
11. When employees are paid and the voucher system is used, it is necessary to prepare a voucher for the net amount to be paid to the employees.............	✓	
12. All changes in the constants of the payroll system, such as changes in pay rates, should be properly authorized in writing.............	✓	

MULTIPLE CHOICE

Instructions: Circle the best answer for each of the following questions.

1. An employee's rate of pay is $8 per hour, with time and a half for hours worked in excess of 40 during a week. If the employee works 50 hours during a week, and has FICA tax withheld at a rate of 7.5% and federal income tax withheld at a rate of 15%, the employee's net pay for the week is:
   a. $440
   b. $374
   c. $341
   d. $310

2. For good internal control over payroll, which of the following is *not* desirable?
   a. all payments are made in cash
   b. all additions of employees are authorized in writing
   c. attendance records are controlled
   d. employee identification cards are used for clocking in

3. Which of the following items would not be considered a fringe benefit?
   a. vacations
   b. employee pension plans
   c. health insurance
   d. FICA benefits

4. For proper matching of revenues and expenses, the estimated cost of fringe benefits must be recognized as an expense of the period during which the:
   a. employee earns the benefit
   b. employee is paid the benefit
   c. fringe benefit contract is signed
   d. fringe benefit contract becomes effective

5. A pension plan which complies with federal income tax requirements which allow the employer to deduct contributions for tax purposes and which exempt pension fund income from tax is called a:
   a. contributory plan
   b. funded plan
   c. model plan
   d. qualified plan

6. The inputs into a payroll system may be classified as either constants or variables. All of the following are variables except for:
   a. number of hours worked
   b. vacation credits
   c. number of income tax withholding allowances
   d. number of days sick leave with pay

EXERCISE 12-1

Instructions: In each of the following situations, determine the correct amount.

(1) An employee of a firm operating under the Federal Wage and Hour Law worked 50 hours last week. If the hourly rate of pay is $14, what is the employee's gross earnings for the week?

_____ $ 770 _____

(2) During the current pay period, an employee earned $2,000. Prior to the current period, the employee earned (in the current year) $59,500. If the FICA tax is a combined rate of 7.5% on the first $60,000 of annual earnings and a rate of 1.5% on annual earnings from $60,000 to $140,000, what is the amount to be withheld from the employee's pay this period?

_____ $ 60 _____

(3) During the current pay period, an employee earned $3,000. Prior to the current period, the employee earned (in the current year) $137,800. Using the FICA rates and maximum bases in (2), compute the amount to be withheld from the employee's pay this period.

_____ $ 33 _____

(4) Using the rates and maximum bases in (2), compute the amount of FICA tax withheld from the pay of an employee who has earned $10,000 but has actually received only $9,700, with the remaining $300 to be paid in the next year.

_____ $ 727.50 _____

EXERCISE 12-2

Instructions: Prepare the general journal entries to record each of the following items for Wiler Co. (Omit explanations.)

(1) Accrued employee vacation pay at the end of the year is $3,225.

	DATE	DESCRIPTION	POST. REF.	DEBIT	CREDIT	
1		Vacation Exp				1
2		Vac Payable				2
3						3

(2) The estimated product warranty liability at the end of the year is 3% of sales of $150,000.

	DATE	DESCRIPTION	POST. REF.	DEBIT	CREDIT	
1		Warranty Exp		4500		1
2		Warr Payable			4500	2
3						3

(3) A partially funded pension plan is maintained for employees at an annual cost of $40,000. At the end of the year, $27,500 is paid to the fund trustee and the remaining accrued pension liability is recognized.

	DATE	DESCRIPTION	POST. REF.	DEBIT	CREDIT	
1		Pension Exp.				1
2		Pen - Payable				2
3		unfunded				3

204

PROBLEM 12-1

The weekly gross payroll of O'Brien Co. on December 7 amounts to $50,000, distributed as follows: sales salaries, $34,000; office salaries, $16,000. The following amounts are to be withheld: FICA tax $3,750; employees' income tax, $7,500; union dues, $900; and United Way, $450.

Instructions: Omitting explanations, prepare general journal entries to:
   (1) Record the payroll.

	DATE	DESCRIPTION	POST. REF.	DEBIT	CREDIT	
1		Sales Salaries		34000		1
2		Office Salaries		16000		2
3		FICA Tax			3750	3
4					7500	4
5					900	5
6					450	6
7		Sal Payable				7
8					37400	8

   (2) Record the payment of the payroll.

	DATE	DESCRIPTION	POST. REF.	DEBIT	CREDIT	
1		Salaries Payable		37400		1
2		Cash			37400	2
3						3

   (3) Record the employer's payroll taxes. Assume that the entire payroll is subject to FICA tax at 7.5%, federal unemployment tax of .8%, and state unemployment tax at 5.4%.

	DATE	DESCRIPTION	POST. REF.	DEBIT	CREDIT	
1		Payroll Taxes Expense		6850		1
2					3760	2
3					400	3
4					2700	4
5						5

   (4) Record the employer's payroll taxes. Assume that $40,000 of payroll is subject to FICA at 7.5% and $10,000 at 1.5% and that none of the payroll is subject to federal or state unemployment tax.

	DATE	DESCRIPTION	POST. REF.	DEBIT	CREDIT	
1						1
2						2
3						3
4						4
5						5

PROBLEM 12-2

The president of Soundlet Manufacturing Co. is to be granted a 6% profit-sharing bonus. The corporate income tax rate is 34%. The company's income before the deduction of the income tax and the bonus amounted to $500,000.

Instructions: Calculate the president's bonus under each of the following methods. (Show your work.)

(1) Bonus based on income before deducting either bonus or income tax.

$$30,000$$

(2) Bonus based on income after deducting bonus but before deducting income tax.

$$B = .06(500,000 - B) \quad 1.06\,B = 30,000$$
$$B = .30,000 - .06B \qquad B = {}^{+}28301.89$$

(3) Bonus based on income before deducting bonus but after deducting income tax.
$$B = .06(500,000 - T) \quad B = .06[500,000 - .34(500,000 - B)]$$
$$T = .34(500,000 - B) \quad B = .06(500,000 - 170,000 + .34B)$$
$$B = 30,000 - 10,200 + .0204B$$

(4) Bonus based on net income after deducting both bonus and income tax. $\quad 99.98\,B = 19,800$
$$B = .06(500,000 - B - T)$$
$$T = .34(500,000 - B)$$

PROBLEM 12-3

Instructions: For each of the employees listed below, compute the taxes indicated as well as the total of each tax. Assume the FICA tax is a combined rate of 7.5% on the first $60,000 of annual earnings and a rate of 1.5% on annual earnings from $60,000 to $140,000; a state unemployment tax rate of 5.4% on a maximum of $7,000; and a federal unemployment tax rate of .8% on a maximum of $7,000.

Employee	Annual Earnings	Employee's FICA Tax	FICA	State Unemployment	Federal Unemployment	Total
				Employer's Taxes		
Avery	$ 12,000					
Johnson	5,000					
Jones	59,000					
Smith	63,000					
Wilson	141,000					
Total	$280,000					

206

Name _____

PROBLEM 12-4

Instructions: Prepare the general journal entries to record the following transactions. (Omit explanations.)

    (1) Audrey Newman issued a 90-day, 12% note for $2,000 to Mayday Co. for a $2,000 overdue account.

	DATE	DESCRIPTION	POST. REF.	DEBIT	CREDIT	
1		Accounts Payable		2000		1
2		Notes Payable			2000	2
3						3
4						4
5						5

    (2) Newman paid the note in (1) at maturity.

	DATE	DESCRIPTION	POST. REF.	DEBIT	CREDIT	
1		Notes Payable		2000		1
2		Interest Expense		60		2
3		Cash			2060	3
4						4

    (3) Paula Wheat borrowed $8,000 from the bank and gave the bank a 90-day, 11% note.

	DATE	DESCRIPTION	POST. REF.	DEBIT	CREDIT	
1		Cash		8000		1
2		Notes Pay			8002	2
3						3
4						4

    (4) Wheat paid the note in (3) at maturity.

	DATE	DESCRIPTION	POST. REF.	DEBIT	CREDIT	
1		Notes Pay		8000		1
2		Int Exp		220		2
3		Cash			8220	3
4						4
5						5

(5) Randy Lucky borrowed $6,000 from the bank, giving a 60-day, non-interest-bearing note which was discounted at 9%.

	DATE		DESCRIPTION	POST. REF.	DEBIT	CREDIT	
1			Cash		5910		1
2			Int Exp		90		2
3			Notes Payable			6000	3
4							4
5							5

(6) Lucky paid the note recorded in (5) at maturity.

	DATE		DESCRIPTION	POST. REF.	DEBIT	CREDIT	
1			N P		6000		1
2			Cash			6000	2
3							3
4							4
5							5

Chapter 13
Concepts and Principles

The following hints may be helpful to you in preparing for a quiz or a test over the material covered in Chapter 13.

1. The chapter focuses on the ten concepts and principles of accounting. Carefully review the significance of each concept and principle. There is a significant amount of new terminology. Be sure to review the Glossary of Key Terms.

2. This information in this chapter lends itself to both true-false and multiple-choice questions.

Computational problems will involve either the installment method or percentage-of-completion method of recognizing revenue. Review the chapter illustrations for each of these methods. The Illustrative Problem in the Chapter Review provides a good review of the installment method.

CHAPTER OUTLINE

I. Development of Concepts and Principles.
  A. Accounting "principles" do not have the same universal authority as principles relating to the natural sciences. They represent guides based on reason and observation.
  B. The primary criterion of use of an accounting concept or principle is its general acceptance among users of financial statements and members of the accounting profession.
  C. The Financial Accounting Standards Board (FASB) is currently the primary body in the development of generally accepted accounting principles. The FASB replaced the Accounting Principles Board (APB) in 1973.
    1. After issuing discussion memoranda and preliminary proposals and evaluating comments from interested parties, the FASB issues *Statements of Financial Accounting Standards,* which become part of generally accepted accounting principles.
    2. The FASB also issues *Interpretations* which have the same authority as the standards.

  3. Presently, the FASB is in the process of developing a broad conceptual framework for financial accounting through the issuance of *Statements of Financial Accounting Concepts.* To date, six statements have been issued.
  D. The Governmental Accounting Standards Board (GASB) was formed in 1984 to establish accounting standards to be followed by state and municipal governments.
  E. Accounting organizations that are influential in the establishment of accounting principles include the American Institute of Certified Public Accountants (AICPA) and the American Accounting Association (AAA). Each of these organizations publishes a monthly or quarterly periodical and issues other publications in the form of research studies, technical opinions, and monographs.
  F. Governmental agencies with an interest in the development of accounting principles include the Securities and Exchange Commission (SEC) and the Internal Revenue Service (IRS).

G. Other influential organizations in the development of accounting principles include the Financial Executives Institute (FEI), the Institute of Management Accountants (IMA), the Financial Analysts Federation, and the Securities Industry Associates.

II. Business Entity Concept.
  A. The business entity concept assumes that a business enterprise is separate and distinct from the persons who supply its assets, regardless of the legal form of the entity.
  B. The business entity concept is implied by the accounting equation. The business owns the assets and must account for the use of the assets to the various equity holders (owners and creditors).

III. Going Concern Concept.
  A. The going concern concept assumes that a business entity expects to continue in business at a profit for an indefinite period of time.
  B. The going concern concept justifies recording plant assets at cost and depreciating them without reference to their current realizable (market) values.
  C. Doubt as to the continued existence of a firm may be disclosed in a note to the financial statements.
  D. When there is pervasive evidence that a business entity has a limited life, the accounting procedures should reflect the expected terminal date of the entity. For example, the financial statements should be prepared from a "quitting concern" or liquidation point of view rather than a "going concern" point of view.

IV. Objectivity Principle.
  A. To maintain the confidence of the many users of the financial statements, entries in the accounting records and the data reported on financial statements must be based on objective evidence.
  B. Judgments, estimates, and other subjective factors must be used in preparing financial statements. In such cases, the most objective evidence should be used.

V. Unit of Measurement Concept.
  A. All business transactions are recorded in terms of dollars. It is only through the record of dollar amounts that the diverse transactions and activities of a business may be measured, reported, and periodically compared.
  B. The scope of accounting reports is generally limited to those factors that can be expressed in monetary terms.
  C. As a unit of measurement, the value of the dollar, called its purchasing power, continually changes. However, assuming that the dollar is stable allows for greater objectivity in preparing financial statements.
    1. One method of supplementing the historical-dollar statements is to report current cost data.
      a. Current cost is the amount of cash that would have to be paid currently to acquire assets of the same age and same condition as existing assets.
      b. The use of current costs permits the identification of gains and losses that result from holding assets during periods of changes in price levels.
      c. The major disadvantage in the use of current costs is the lack of standards for determining such costs.
    2. Constant dollar data may also be used for supplementing historical-dollar financial statements.
      a. Constant dollar data are historical costs that have been restated to constant dollars through use of a price-level index.
      b. A price-level index is the ratio of the total cost of a group of goods at a specific time to the total cost of the same group of goods at an earlier base time.
  D. Current cost or constant dollar data are optional disclosures.

VI. Accounting Period Concept.
  A. A complete and accurate reporting of an enterprise's success or failure cannot be obtained until it discontinues operations, converts its assets into cash, and pays off its debts.
  B. Because many decisions must be made by management and interested outsiders throughout the life of a business entity, periodic reports are prepared on operations, financial position, and cash flows.

VII. Matching Concept.
  A. Determining periodic net income is a two-fold process of matching (1) revenue for the period with (2) expenses incurred in generating the revenues. The difference between the revenues and expenses is the net income or net loss for the period.
  B. Various criteria are acceptable for determining when revenue is realized. Generally, the criteria used should agree with any contractual terms with the customer and should be based on objective evidence.
    1. Revenue from the sale of merchandise is usually determined by the point-of-sale method, under which revenue is realized at the time title passes to the buyer.
    2. The recognition of revenue may be delayed until payment is received. When this criterion is used, revenue is considered to be realized at the time the cash is collected, regardless of when the sale was made. This method, referred to as the cash basis, has the practical advantage of simplicity, and may be used by professional services enterprises.
    3. Under the installment method of determining revenue (used primarily in the retail field), each receipt of cash is considered to be revenue and composed of part cost of merchandise sold and part gross profit on the sale.
    4. Under the percentage-of-completion method, the revenue to be recognized and the income for the period are determined by the estimated percentage of the contract that has been completed during the period. This estimated percentage can be developed by comparing the incurred costs with the most recent estimates by engineers, architects, or other qualified personnel of the progress of the work performed.
  C. Expenses are the using up of assets to generate revenues. The amount of an asset's cost that is used up is a measure of the expense.
    1. Each expense must be matched against its related revenue in order to properly determine the amount of net income or net loss for the period.
    2. Adjusting entries at the end of the period are often required to properly match revenues and expenses.

VIII. Adequate Disclosure Concept.
  A. Under the adequate disclosure concept, financial statements and their related footnotes or other disclosures should contain all the relevant data essential to the user's understanding of the entity's financial status.
  B. When there are several acceptable alternative accounting methods that could have a significant effect on amounts reported on the statements, the particular method used should be disclosed.
  C. In situations where an accounting estimate has been changed, any material effect of the change on net income should be disclosed in the financial statements for the year of the change.
  D. Contingent liabilities are potential obligations that will become liabilities only if certain events occur in the future.
    1. If the amount of the contingent liability is probable and can be reasonably estimated, it should be recorded in the accounts.
    2. If the amount of the contingent liability cannot be reasonably estimated, the details of the contingency should be disclosed.
    3. The most common contingent liabilities disclosed in notes to financial statements concern litigation, guarantees, and discounting receivables.
  E. To help financial statement users assess operating results of companies involved in more than one type of business activity or market, the financial statements should disclose information by segments. The information reported for each major segment includes: revenue, income from operations, and identifiable assets related to the segment.
  F. Significant events occurring after the close of the period should be disclosed.

IX. Consistency Concept.
  A. The concept of consistency does not completely prohibit changes in accounting principles used. However, changes in accounting principles must be justified and should be fully disclosed in the financial statements.

B. Different accounting methods may be used throughout an enterprise, such as the use of different depreciation methods for different classes of assets or different inventory methods for different classes of inventory.

X. Materiality Concept.

A. The concept of materiality refers to the relative importance of an event, accounting method, or change in methods that affects items on the financial statements.

B. In assessing materiality of an item, the size of the item, its nature, and relationship to other items in the financial statements should be considered.

C. The concept of materiality may also be applied to the recording of transactions. For example, small expenditures for plant assets may be treated as an expense of the period rather than as an asset.

XI. Conservatism Concept.

A. The concept of conservatism means that in selecting among alternatives, the method or estimates that yield the lesser amount of net income or asset value should be selected.

B. The conservatism concept is no longer considered to be the dominant factor in selecting among alternatives.

MATCHING

Instructions: A list of terms and related statements appear below. From the list of terms, select the one that relates to each statement. Print its identifying letter in the space provided.

A. Adequate disclosure
B. Business entity concept
C. Completed-contract method
D. Conservatism
E. Consistency concept

F. Current cost data
G. FASB
H. General price-level data
I. Going concern concept
J. Installment method
K. Matching

L. Materiality concept
M. Percentage-of-completion method
N. Point-of-sale method
O. SEC

B 1. The concept that assumes that a business enterprise is separate and distinct from the persons who supply its assets.

I 2. The concept that assumes that a business entity has a reasonable expectation of continuing in business at a profit for an indefinite period of time.

F 3. Data indicating the amount of cash that would have to be paid currently to acquire assets of the same age and in the same condition as existing assets.

H 4. Data indicating historical cost amounts that have been converted to constant dollars.

N 5. A method under which revenue is realized at the time title passes to the buyer.

J 6. A method under which each receipt of cash is considered to be revenue and to be composed of partial amounts of (1) the cost of merchandise sold and (2) gross profit on the sale.

M 7. A method under which revenue is realized over the entire life of a long-term contract.

E 8. The concept that enables financial statement users to assume that successive financial statements of an enterprise are based on the same generally accepted accounting principles.

L 9. The concept that permits accountants to treat small expenditures for plant assets as an expense rather than an asset.

D 10. The attitude that leads accountants to prefer the method or procedure that yields the lesser amount of net income or of asset value.

A 11. The concept that financial statements and their accompanying footnotes should contain all of the pertinent data believed essential to the reader's understanding of an enterprise's financial status.

C 12. The method that recognizes revenue from long-term construction contracts when the project is completed.

G 13. The current authoritative body for the development of accounting principles for all entities except state and municipal governments.

K 14. The principle of accounting that all revenues should be matched with the expenses incurred in earning those revenues during a period of time.

O 15. The federal agency that exercises a dominant influence over the development of accounting principles for most companies whose securities are traded in interstate commerce.

TRUE / FALSE

Instructions: Indicate whether each of the following statements is true or false by placing a check mark in the appropriate column.

		True	False
1.	There is likely to be less differentiation between "management" and "owners" in a business enterprise as it increases in size and complexity.		✓
2.	The "principles" used in accounting are similar to the natural laws relating to the physical sciences.		✓
3.	General acceptance among the members of the accounting profession is the criterion for determining an accounting principle.	✓	
4.	Responsibility for the development of accounting principles has rested primarily with the federal government.		✓
5.	The FASB replaced the Accounting Principles Board.	✓	
6.	The FASB's *Statements of Financial Accounting Concepts* are intended to provide a broad conceptual framework for accounting.	✓	
7.	The AICPA has responsibility for establishing the accounting standards to be followed by state and municipal governments.		✓
8.	The SEC is a branch of the FASB.		✓
9.	The business entity concept used in accounting for a sole proprietorship is the same as the legal concept of a sole proprietorship.		✓
10.	The going concern assumption supports the treatment of virtually unsalable prepaid expenses as assets.	✓	✓
11.	In a going concern, plant assets usually are recorded on the balance sheet at their estimated realizable values.		✓
12.	According to the objective evidence principle, entries in the accounting records and data reported on financial statements must be based on objectively determined evidence.	✓	
13.	The major disadvantage in the use of current costs is the absence of established standards and procedures for determining such costs.	✓	
14.	Large, publicly held companies are required to disclose both current cost and constant dollar information annually as supplemental data.		✓
15.	A complete and accurate picture of an enterprise's success or failure cannot be obtained until it discontinues operations, converts its assets into cash, and pays off its debts.	✓	
16.	In recent years, financial statement emphasis has shifted from the income statement to the balance sheet.		✓
17.	Revenue from the sale of goods generally is considered to be realized at the time title passes to the buyer.	✓	
18.	Revenue from the sale of services is normally realized when the services have been performed.	✓	

214

	True	False
19. On the cash basis, revenue is considered to be earned at the time the cash is collected, regardless of when the sale was made..................................	✓	
20. The percentage-of-completion method usually is more objective than the point-of-sale method...		✓
21. The amount of cash or equivalent given to acquire property or service is referred to as its cost.	✓	
22. The IRS's laws and regulations for preparing federal tax returns coincide with the generally accepted accounting principles used for preparing financial statements...		✓
23. Criteria for standards of disclosure must be based on objective facts rather than on value judgments..		✓
24. When there are several acceptable alternative accounting methods that could have a significant effect on amounts reported on the statements, the particular method used should be disclosed...	✓	
25. It is acceptable to revise accounting estimates based on additional information or subsequent developments..	✓	
26. If the amount of a contingent liability can be reasonably estimated, it should be recorded in the accounts.	✓	
27. The concept of consistency prohibits changes in accounting principles employed. ..		✓
28. The consistency concept requires that a specific accounting method be applied uniformly throughout an enterprise..		✓
29. If a lawsuit is filed against a company, the amount of the lawsuit must be recorded in the account as a liability and reported on the financial statements.		✓
30. If company A guarantees a loan for company B, company A is obligated to pay the loan if company B fails to make payment.	✓	

MULTIPLE CHOICE

Instructions: Circle the best answer for each of the following questions.

1. At the present time, the dominant body in the development of generally accepted accounting principles is the:
   a. AICPA
   b. FASB
   c. APB
   d. GASB

2. The statements of generally accepted accounting principles issued by the FASB are called:
   a. Statements of Accounting Principles
   b. Statements of FAF
   c. Statements of Financial Accounting Standards
   d. FASB Opinions

3. Of the various governmental agencies with an interest in the development of accounting principles, the one that has been the most influential has been the:
   a. SEC
   b. IRS
   c. GASB
   d. FEI

4. The organization of accountants that is primarily concerned with management's use of accounting information in directing business operations is the:
   a. FEI
   b. AAA
   c. AICPA
   d. IMA

5. For a number of reasons, including custom and various legal requirements, the maximum interval between accounting reports is:
   a. one month
   b. three months
   c. one year
   d. three years

6. When circumstances are such that the collection of receivables is not reasonably assured, a method of determining revenue that may be used is called the:
   a. installment method
   b. post-sale method
   c. gross profit method
   d. point-of-sale method

7. If property other than cash is given to acquire property, the cost of the acquired property is considered to be the:
   a. net realizable value of the acquired property
   b. current cost of the property given
   c. list price of the acquired property
   d. cash equivalent of the property given

8. If an enterprise suffers a major loss from a fire between the end of the year and the issuance of the financial statements, the enterprise should:
   a. not mention the loss in the statements because it occurred in a different accounting period
   b. disclose the loss in a note to the statements
   c. not mention the loss in the statements, but put out a separate announcement of the loss
   d. record the loss in the accounting records and in the statements

216

9. For each significant reporting segment of a business, an enterprise is required to disclose each of the following except:
   a. revenue
   b. income from operations
   c. identifiable assets associated with the segment
   d. identifiable liabilities associated with the segment

10. Of the following accounting concepts, the least important one in choosing among alternative accounting methods is:
    a. conservatism
    b. objectivity
    c. consistency
    d. materiality

11. All of the following are examples of contingent liabilities disclosed in notes to the financial statements except for:
    a. litigation
    b. guarantees
    c. receiving donated real estate
    d. discounting receivables

12. Entries in the accounting records and data reported on financial statements should be based on objective evidence. Of the following items of evidence, the least objective one is:
    a. bank statements
    b. vouchers for purchases
    c. physical counts of inventory
    d. estimates by the credit manager about the collectibility of accounts receivable

EXERCISE 13-1

During the current year, Wilton Construction Company contracted to build a new baseball stadium for the local university. The total contract price was $20,000,000 and the estimated construction costs were $16,500,000. At the end of the current year, the project was estimated to be 25% completed and the costs incurred totaled $4,100,000.

Instructions: Using the percentage-of-completion method of recognizing revenue, determine the following amounts:

(1) Revenue from the contract.. $ *5,000,000*

(2) Cost associated with the contract.. $ *4,100,000*

(3) Income from the contract recognized for the current year .... $ *900,000*

EXERCISE 13-2

Pasquale Co.'s net income for its first year of operations is $76,350, based on FIFO inventory and straight-line depreciation. Pasquale is considering making two accounting changes in the current year, as follows:

(1) From straight-line to declining-balance depreciation at twice the straight-line rate. Straight-line depreciation is $10,000, whereas declining-balance depreciation would be $12,000.
(2) From FIFO to LIFO inventory. FIFO inventory cost is $19,000, whereas LIFO inventory cost would be $13,800.

Instructions: In the space provided below, compute the net income if the two accounting changes are made.

Net income using straight-line and FIFO................................. $76,350

(1) Effect of depreciation change .... *−2,000*

(2) Effect of inventory change.. *5,200*

(3) Revised net income .... *$ 79,550*

218

Name _____

EXERCISE 13-3

Rista Co. reported net income for the current year of $37,600. In reviewing Rista's records, you discover the following items for which no adjustments were made at the end of the period.

(1) Supplies of $13 were on hand.
(2) Interest expense of $15 had accrued for 3 days on a note payable.
(3) Delivery charges of $6 on packages received in the current period were not entered until paid in the following period.
(4) Petty cash expenditures of $20 were not entered, because reimbursement of petty cash was not made at the end of the period.

Instructions:
(1) In the spaces provided below, compute the net income of Rista Co. for the year if adjustments were made for these items:

a.	Reported net income...	$37,600
b.	Supplies..	13
c.	Interest expense..	- 15
d.	Delivery charges..	- 6
e.	Petty cash expenditures...................................	-20
f.	Revised net income..	

(2) What accounting concept would support Rista's not making these adjustments?

PROBLEM 13-1

Instructions: In each of the following situations, determine the correct amounts.

(1) Ten years ago, Delaney Co. bought a building for $400,000. The company has taken depreciation of $15,000 a year on this building. Recently, the building was appraised at $300,000. Another firm offered to buy the building for $325,000. Delaney Co. should record this building on its balance sheet at the amount of . . . . $ _250,000_

(2) On January 1, Hillman Company paid $13,350 for a 3-year insurance policy. The company should report insurance expense for the second year in the amount of . . . . $ _4,450_

(3) Charo Company was organized on January 1. All sales are made on the installment plan and gross profits are calculated by the installment method. During the first year, sales amounted to $2,100,000; cost of sales, $1,365,000; and collections, $1,344,000. The gross profit for the first year was . . . . $ _470,400_

(4) Dutch Sales Company, organized January 1, makes all sales on the installment plan but calculates gross profits by using the point-of-sale method. During the first year, the company's sales amounted to $2,100,000; cost of sales, $1,365,000; and collections on installments, $1,344,000. The gross profit for the year was . . . . $ _735,000_

(5) V. Milano established a sole proprietorship business. During the first month, she wrote checks for $12,000 on the business bank account. Of this amount, she spent $6,750 for personal needs and $5,250 for merchandise for the business. The net worth of the business was decreased by . . . . $ _6,750_

2,100,000
– 1,365,000
—————
735,000

735,000
————— = .35 × 1,344.00
2100,000

Gross Profit
——————— = ratio of gross profit
Instal Sales

2,100,000
1,365,000
—————
735,000

Chapter 14
Partnership Formation, Income Division, and Liquidation

QUIZ AND TEST HINTS

The following hints may be helpful to you in preparing for a quiz or a test over the material covered in Chapter 14.

1. Review the Glossary of Key Terms that may be tested using true-false or multiple-choice questions.

2. You should be able to prepare journal entries for formation and dissolution of a partnership. Pay particular attention to the payment of a bonus on the admission of a new partner.

3. Expect at least one question involving distribution of partnership net income among the partners. This question may involve salary allowances and interest allowances on partners' capital balances. Remember, if the partnership agreement does not indicate how income is shared among the partners, it is shared equally. Also, be able to prepare the journal entries distributing a partnership net income or loss. The entry for distributing net income debits Income Summary and credits the partners' capital accounts.

4. If your instructor assigned a homework problem involving partnership liquidation or covered it in class, you may see a question related to liquidating a partnership. Review the chapter illustrations and the Illustrative Problem in the Chapter Review.

CHAPTER OUTLINE

I. Characteristics of Partnerships.
  A. The Uniform Partnership Act defines a partnership as "an association of two or more persons to carry on as co-owners a business for profit."
  B. Partnerships have several characteristics that have accounting implications.
    1. A partnership has a limited life. Dissolution of a partnership occurs whenever a partner ceases to be a member of the firm for any reason, or a new partner is admitted.
    2. Most partnerships are general partnerships, in which the partners have unlimited liability. Each partner is individually liable to creditors for debts incurred by the partnership.
    3. In some states, a limited partnership may be formed in which the liability of some partners may be limited to the amount of their capital investment. However, a limited partnership must have at least one general partner who has unlimited liability.
    4. Partners have co-ownership of partnership property. The property invested in a partnership by a partner becomes the property of all the partners jointly.
    5. The mutual agency characteristic of a partnership means that each partner is an agent of the partnership with the authority to enter into contracts for the partnership. Thus, the acts of each partner bind the partnership and become the responsibility of all partners.
    6. A significant right of partners is participation in income of the partnership. Net income and net loss are distributed among the partners according to their

agreement. In the absence of any agreement, all partners share equally.

7. Although partnerships are nontaxable entities and therefore do not pay federal income taxes, they must file an information return with the Internal Revenue Service.

C. A partnership is created by a contract containing all the elements essential to any other enforceable contract. This contract is known as the articles of partnership or partnership agreement.

II. Advantages and Disadvantages of Partnerships.

A. The advantages of a partnership form of organization include the following:

1. A partnership is relatively easy and inexpensive to organize, requiring only an agreement between two or more persons.

2. A partnership has the advantage of being able to bring together more capital, more managerial skill, and more experience than a sole proprietorship.

3. A partnership is a nontaxable entity; the combined income taxes paid by the individual partners may be lower than the income taxes that would be paid by a corporation.

B. The disadvantages of a partnership form of organization are as follows:

1. The partnership life is limited.

2. Each partner has unlimited liability.

3. One partner can bind the partnership to contracts.

4. Raising large amounts of capital is more difficult for a partnership than for a corporation.

III. Accounting for Partnerships.

A. Most of the day-to-day accounting for a partnership is the same as the accounting for any other form of business organization.

B. Differences in accounting arise primarily in the areas of formation, income distribution, dissolution, and liquidation of partnerships.

IV. Formation of a Partnership.

A. A separate entry is made for the investment of each partner in a partnership.

1. The various assets contributed by a partner are debited to the proper asset accounts.

2. If liabilities are assumed by the partnership, the liability accounts are credited.

3. The partner's capital account is credited for the net amount.

B. The monetary amounts at which noncash assets are recorded by a partnership are those agreed upon by the partners. The agreed upon values normally represent current market values.

C. Receivables contributed to the partnership are recorded at their face amount, with a credit to a contra account if provision is to be made for possible future uncollectibility.

V. Dividing Net Income or Net Loss.

A. Distribution and division of income or loss among partners should be in accordance with the partnership agreement. If the partnership agreement is silent on the matter, the law provides that all partners should share equally.

B. As a means of recognizing differences in ability and in amount of time devoted to the business, the partnership agreement may provide for the division of a portion of net income to the partners in the form of a salary allowance.

1. A clear distinction must be made between division of net income, which is credited to the capital accounts, and payments to the partners, which are debited to the drawing accounts.

2. In most cases, the amount of net income distributed to each partner's capital account at the end of the year will differ from the amount the partner withdraws during the year.

C. Partners may agree to allow salaries based on the services rendered and also to allow interest on their capital investments. The remainder is then divided as agreed.

D. If net income is less than the total of special allowances (salaries and interest), the "remaining balance" to be distributed will be a negative figure that must be divided among the partners as though it were a net loss.

VI. Financial Statements for Partnerships.

A. The division of net income should be disclosed in the financial statements prepared at the end of the fiscal period.

B. The changes in the owner's equity of a partnership during the period should also be presented in a statement of owner's equity.

VII. Partnership Dissolution.

A. One of the basic characteristics of the partnership form of organization is its limited life. Any change in the personnel of the ownership dissolves the partnership.

B. Dissolution of the partnership is not necessarily followed by the winding up of the affairs of the business. In many cases, the remaining partners may continue to operate the business. When this happens, a new partnership is formed and a new partnership agreement is prepared.

C. An additional person may be admitted to a partnership enterprise only with the consent of all the current partners.

D. An additional partner may be admitted to a partnership through either of two procedures:

1. A new partner may be admitted with the purchase of an interest from one or more of the current partners. In this case, neither the total assets nor the total owner's equity of the business is affected. The purchase price of the partnership share is paid directly to the selling partner or partners. The only accounting entry needed is to transfer the proper amounts of owner's equity from the capital accounts of the selling partner or partners to the capital account established for the incoming partner.

2. A new partner may be admitted to the partnership through the contribution of assets directly to the partnership. In this case, both the total assets and the total owner's equity of the business are increased. The assets contributed to the partnership are debited and the capital account of the incoming partner is credited.

E. Whenever a new partner is admitted to a partnership, the existing assets of the partnership should be adjusted to their fair market value. The net amount of the increases and decreases in asset values are then allocated to the capital accounts of the old partners according to their in-

come-sharing ratio. It is important that the assets be stated in terms of current prices at the time of admission of the new partner. Failure to recognize current prices may result in the new partner participating in gains or losses that arose in prior periods.

F. When a new partner is admitted to a partnership, the incoming partner may pay a bonus to the existing partners to join the partnership. The amount of any bonus paid to the partnership is distributed among the existing partners' capital accounts.

G. When a new partner is admitted to a partnership, the incoming partner may be paid a bonus to join the partnership. The amount of the bonus is debited to the capital accounts of the existing partners and credited to the capital account of the new partner.

H. When a partner retires or for some reason wishes to withdraw from the firm, one or more of the remaining partners may purchase the withdrawing partner's interest and the business may continue uninterrupted.

1. The settlement of the purchase and sale is made between the partners as individuals, in a manner similar to the admission of a new partner by purchase of interest, and thus is not recorded by the partnership.

2. The only entry required by the partnership is a debit to the capital account of the partner withdrawing and a credit to the capital account of the partner or partners acquiring the interest.

I. When a partner retires or for some other reason wishes to withdraw from the firm, the settlement with the withdrawing partner may be made by the partnership.

1. The effect of this withdrawal is to reduce the assets and the owner's equity of the firm.

2. To determine the ownership equity of the withdrawing partner, the asset accounts should be adjusted to current market prices. The net amount of the adjustment should be divided among the capital accounts of the partners according to the income-sharing ratio.

3. The entry to record the withdrawal is to debit the capital account of the withdrawing partner and credit the assets paid or liability incurred to the withdrawing partner.

J. The death of a partner dissolves the partnership. In the absence of any agreement, the accounts should be closed as of the date of death, and the net income for the part of the year should be transferred to the capital accounts.

1. The partnership agreement may indicate that the accounts remain open to the end of the fiscal year or until the affairs are wound up, if that should occur earlier.

2. The net income of the entire period is then divided, as provided by the agreement, between the periods occurring before and after the partner's death.

3. The balance in the capital account of the deceased partner is transferred to a liability account with the deceased's estate.

VIII. Liquidating Partnerships.

A. When a partnership goes out of business, it usually sells the assets, pays the creditors, and distributes the remaining cash or other assets to the partners. This winding-up process is called liquidation.

B. During the process of liquidation, the sale of assets is called realization. As cash is realized, it is applied first to the payment of the claims of creditors.

C. Any gains or losses realized from the sale of assets should be distributed to the capital accounts of the partners in their income-sharing ratios.

D. After all liabilities have been paid, the remaining cash should be distributed to the partners according to the balances in their capital accounts. Under no circumstances should the income-sharing ratio be used as a basis for distributing cash to the partners after payment of liabilities.

E. If the share of a loss from the realization of assets exceeds a partner's ownership equity (capital account balance), the resulting debit balance in the partner's capital account is called a deficiency.

1. Pending collection from the deficient partner, the partnership cash will not be sufficient to pay the other partners in full.

2. The affairs of the partnership are not completely wound up until the claims against the partners are settled. Payments to the firm by the deficient partner are credited to that partner's capital account. Any cash thus collected is distributed to the remaining partners.

3. Any uncollectible deficiency from a partner becomes a loss to the partnership and is written off against the capital accounts of the remaining partners according to their income-sharing ratios.

F. The type of error most likely to occur in the liquidation of a partnership is an improper distribution of cash to the partners. Errors of this type result from confusing the distribution of cash with the division of gains and losses on realization.

1. Gains and losses on realization result from the disposal of assets to outsiders. These gains and losses should be divided among the capital accounts in the same manner as net income or net loss from normal business operations, using the income-sharing ratio.

2. The distribution of cash (or other assets) to the partners upon liquidation is the exact reverse of the contribution of assets by the partners at the time the partnership was established. The distribution of assets to partners is equal to the credit balances of the partners' capital accounts after all gains and losses on realization have been divided and allowances have been made for any potential partner deficiencies.

MATCHING

Instructions: A list of terms and related statements appear below. From the list of terms, select the one that relates to each statement. Print its identifying letter in the space provided.

A. Articles of partnership   E. Limited life   H. Mutual agency
B. Deficiency   F. Limited partnership   I. Partnership
C. General partnership   G. Liquidation   J. Realization
D. Income statement

C   1.   A type of partnership in which the partners have unlimited liability.

F   2.   A type of partnership in which the liability of some partners may be restricted to the amount of their capital investment.

H   3.   A characteristic of a partnership that means that each partner has the authority to enter into contracts for the partnership.

A   4.   Another name for the partnership agreement or contract among the partners.

E   5.   A disadvantage of a partnership.

D   6.   A financial statement in which the details of the division of partnership net income would be disclosed.

I   7.   An unincorporated business of two or more persons to carry on as co-owners a business for profit.

G   8.   The winding-up process of a partnership may generally be called (?).

J   9.   When a partnership is going out of business, the sale of the assets is called (?).

B 10.   When a partnership is going out of business and the loss chargeable to a partner exceeds that partner's ownership equity, the resulting debit balance in the capital account is called a(n) (?)

TRUE / FALSE

Instructions: Indicate whether each of the following statements is true or false by placing a check mark in the appropriate column.

		True	False
1.	Partners are legally employees of the partnership and their capital contributions are considered a loan.		✓
2.	Each general partner is individually liable to creditors for debts incurred by the partnership.	✓	
3.	Salary allowances are treated as divisions of partnership net income and are credited to the partners' capital accounts.	✓	
4.	The property invested in a partnership by a partner remains identified as that partner's property.		✓
5.	A partner's claim against the assets of the partnership in the event of dissolution is measured by the amount of the partner's initial investment.	✓	✓
6.	A written contract is necessary to the legal formation of a partnership.		✓
7.	At the time a partnership is formed, the market values of the assets should be considered in determining each partner's investment.	✓	
8.	In the absence of an agreement for income or loss distributions among the partners, the partners should share income equally, even if there are differences in their capital contributions.	✓	
9.	Regardless of whether partners' salaries and interest are treated as expenses of the partnership or as a division of net income, the total amount allocated to each partner will not be affected.	✓	
10.	A partnership is required to pay federal income taxes.		✓
11.	Any change in the personnel of the ownership results in a dissolution of a partnership.	✓	
12.	A new partner may be admitted to a partnership with the consent of the majority of the old partners.		✓
13.	A partner's interest may be disposed of only with the consent of the remaining partners.		✓
14.	When a new partner is admitted by purchasing an interest from one or more of the old partners, the purchase price is recorded in the accounts of the partnership.		✓
15.	It is appropriate to adjust the old partnership assets to current market values at the time a new partner is admitted.	✓	
16.	At the time a new partner is admitted, a bonus may be paid to the incoming partner.	✓	
17.	A person may be admitted to a partnership by purchasing an interest from one or more of the existing partners. The only entry required by the partnership is to transfer owner's equity amounts from the capital accounts of the selling partners to the capital account of the new partner.	✓	

	True	False

18. As cash is realized from the sale of assets during the liquidation of a partnership, the cash is applied first to the payment of the claims of the limited partners. . . . .   _____   ✓

19. If the distribution of the loss on the sale of non-cash assets when a partnership goes out of business causes a partner's account to have a debit balance, this balance represents a claim of the partnership against the partner. . . . .   ✓   _____

20. If a deficiency of a partner is uncollectible, this represents a loss which is written off against the capital balances of the remaining partners. . . . .   ✓   _____

MULTIPLE CHOICE

Instructions: Circle the best answer for each of the following questions.

1. If a partnership agreement is silent on dividing net income or net losses, the partners:
   a. divide income/losses according to their original capital investments
   b. divide income/losses equally
   c. divide income/losses according to skills possessed by each partner
   d. divide income/losses on the basis of individual time devoted to the business

2. Which of the following is not an advantage of a partnership?
   a. It is possible to bring together more capital than in a sole proprietorship
   b. Partners' income taxes may be less than the income taxes would be on a corporation
   c. It is possible to bring together more managerial skills than in a sole proprietorship
   d. Each partner has limited liability

3. When a new partner is admitted to the partnership by a contribution of assets to the partnership:
   a. neither the total assets nor the total owner's equity of the business is affected
   b. only the total assets are affected
   c. only the owner's equity is affected
   d. both the total assets and the total owner's equity are increased

4. When a partner retires and the settlement with the partner is made by the partnership, the effect is to:
   a. reduce the assets and the owner's equity of the firm
   b. reduce the assets and increase the owner's equity of the firm
   c. increase the liabilities and the owner's equity of the firm
   d. leave the assets and the owner's equity unchanged

5. If there is a loss on the sale of noncash assets when a partnership goes out of business, the loss should be divided among the partners:
   a. according to their original capital investments
   b. according to their current capital balances
   c. according to their income-sharing ratio
   d. equally

EXERCISE 14-1

Ruth Cutco and Darrell Robbs formed a partnership. Cutco invested $100,000 cash and merchandise valued at $80,000. Robbs invested $10,000 cash, land valued at $115,000, equipment valued at $45,000, and merchandise valued at $5,000.

Instructions: Prepare the entries to record the investments of Cutco and Robbs on the partnership books. Use the current date.

JOURNAL

PAGE

	DATE	DESCRIPTION	POST. REF.	DEBIT	CREDIT	
1	Apr. 28	Cash		100 000		1
2		Merch. Ino.		80 000		2
3		D. R cap			180 000	3
4						4
5		Cash		10 000		5
6		Land		115 000		6
7		Equip		45 000		7
8		Merch		5 000		8
9		Cutco, cap			175 000	9
10						10
11						11
12						12
13						13
14						14
15						15
16						16
17						17
18						18
19						19
20						20
21						21
22						22
23						23
24						24
25						25
26						26
27						27
28						28
29						29
30						30
31						31
32						32
33						33
34						34
35						35

Name _____

EXERCISE 14-2

Ann Hartly, Barry Smetz, and Lynette Grasso are partners having capitals of $100,000, $55,000, and $35,000 respectively. They share net income equally.

Instructions: Prepare the entries to record each of the following situations. (Omit explanations.)

(1) On June 30, John Schafer is admitted to the partnership by purchasing one-fifth of the respective capital interests of the three partners. He pays $30,000 to Hartly, $15,000 to Smetz, and $10,000 to Grasso.

JOURNAL

PAGE _____

	DATE	DESCRIPTION	POST. REF.	DEBIT	CREDIT	
1				30 000		1
2				15 000		2
3				10 000		3
4					38 000	4

(2) On July 1, Laura Masko is admitted to the partnership for an investment of $50,000, and the parties agree to pay a bonus of $20,000 to Masko.

JOURNAL

PAGE _____

	DATE	DESCRIPTION	POST. REF.	DEBIT	CREDIT	
1						1
2						2
3						3
4						4
5						5
6						6
7						7
8						8
9						9
10						10
11						11
12						12
13						13
14						14
15						15
16						16
17						17
18						18
19						19
20						20
21						21
22						22
23						23
24						24

EXERCISE 14-3

Arway, Batts and Carlone are partners having capital balances of $65,000, $55,000, and $40,000 respectively. The partners share net income equally. Carlone has decided to leave the partnership.

Instructions: Prepare the entries to record each of the following situations. (Omit explanations.)
(1) The partners agree that the inventory of the partnership should be increased by $12,750 to recognize its fair market value. Arway buys Carlone's interest in the partnership for $53,000.

JOURNAL   PAGE

	DATE	DESCRIPTION	POST. REF.	DEBIT	CREDIT	
1						1
2						2
3						3
4						4
5						5
6						6
7						7

(2) The partners agree that the inventory of the partnership should be increased by $6,000 to recognize its fair market value. The partnership pays Carlone cash for her interest as reflected by the balance in her capital account.

JOURNAL   PAGE

	DATE	DESCRIPTION	POST. REF.	DEBIT	CREDIT	
1						1
2						2
3						3
4						4
5						5
6						6
7						7
8						8
9						9
10						10
11						11
12						12
13						13
14						14
15						15
16						16
17						17
18						18
19						19

PROBLEM 14-1

On January 2 of the current year, Bulley and Scram formed a partnership in which Bulley invested $300,000 and Scram invested $700,000. During the year, the partnership had a net income of $200,000.

Instructions: Show how this net income would be distributed under each of the following conditions:

(1) The partnership agreement says nothing about the distribution of net income.

Bulley's share	$ _100,000_
Scram's share	$ _100,000_
Total	$ _200,000_

(2) The partnership agreement provides that Bulley and Scram are to share net income in a 2:3 ratio respectively.

Bulley's share	$ _80,000_
Scram's share	$ _120,000_
Total	$ _200,000_

(3) The partnership agreement provides that Bulley and Scram are to share net income in accordance with the ratio of their original capital investments.

Bulley's share	$ _60,000_
Scram's share	$ _140,000_
Total	$ _200,000_

(4) The partnership agreement provides that Bulley is to be allowed a salary of $30,000 and Scram a salary of $50,000 with the balance of net income distributed equally.

Division of Net Income	Bulley	Scram	Total
Salary allowance	$ 30,000	$ 50,000	$ 80,000
Remaining income.................	60,000	60,000	120,000
Net income	$ 90,000	$ 110,000	$ 200,000

(5) The partnership agreement provides that interest at 5% is to be allowed on the beginning capital and that the balance is to be distributed equally.

Division of Net Income	Bulley	Scram	Total
Interest allowance	$ 15,000	$ 35,000	$ 50,000
Remaining income.................	75,000	75,000	150,000
Net income	$ 90,000	$ 110,000	$ 200,000

(6) The partnership agreement provides that Bulley is to be allowed a salary of $15,000 and Scram a salary of $25,000; that interest at 5% is to be allowed on beginning capital; and that the balance is to be distributed equally.

Division of Net Income	Bulley	Scram	Total
Salary allowance	$ 15,000	$ 25,000	$ 40,000
Interest allowance	15,000	35,000	50,000
Remaining income.................	55,000	55,000	110,000
Net income	$ 85,000	$ 115,000	$ 200,000

(7) The partnership agreement provides that Bulley is to be allowed a salary of $80,000 and Scram a salary of $78,000; that interest at 5% is to be allowed on beginning capital; and that the balance is to be distributed equally.

Division of Net Income	Bulley	Scram	Total
Salary allowance	$ 80,000	$ 78,000	$ 158,000
Interest allowance	15,000	35,000	50,000
Total	95,000	113,000	208,000
Excess of allowances over income....	– 4,000	– 4,000	8,000
Net income.......................	$ 91,000	$ 109,000	$ 200,000

PROBLEM 14-2

Prior to the liquidation of the partnership of Triste, Sandpipe, and Hinkle, the ledger contained the following accounts and balances: Cash, $100,000; Noncash Assets, $300,000; Liabilities, $120,000; Triste, Capital, $90,000; Sandpipe, Capital, $60,000; and Hinkle, Capital, $130,000. Assume that the noncash assets are sold for $400,000. Triste, Sandpipe, and Hinkle share profits in a 30:50:20 ratio.

Instructions:

(1) Complete the following schedule showing the sale of assets, payment of liabilities, and distribution of the remaining cash to the partners.

	Cash +	Noncash Assets	= Liabilities +	Triste 30%	Sandpipe 50%	Hinkle 20%
				Capital		
Balances before realization...........	$100,000	$300,000	$120,000	$90,000	$60,000	$130,000
Sale of noncash assets and division of gain						
Balances after realization						
Payment of liabilities................						
Balances after payment of liabilities ..						
Distribution of cash to partners						
Final balances						

(2) Assume that the noncash assets are sold for $130,000 and that the partner with a debit balance pays the entire deficiency. Complete the following schedule showing the sale of assets, payment of liabilities, and distribution of the remaining cash to the partners.

	Cash +	Noncash Assets	= Liabilities +	Triste 30%	Sandpipe 50%	Hinkle 20%
				Capital		
Balances before realization...........	$100,000	$300,000	$120,000	$90,000	$60,000	$130,000
Sale of noncash assets and division of loss.....................						
Balances after realization						
Payment of liabilities................						
Balances after payment of liabilities ..						
Receipt of deficiency						
Balances............................						
Distribution of cash to partners						
Final balances						

(3) Prepare the journal entries to record the liquidation of the partnership based on the facts in (2). Use the current date. (Omit explanations.)

JOURNAL

	DATE	DESCRIPTION	POST. REF.	DEBIT	CREDIT	
1						1
2						2
3						3
4						4
5						5
6						6
7						7
8						8
9						9
10						10
11						11
12						12
13						13
14						14
15						15
16						16
17						17
18						18
19						19
20						20
21						21
22						22
23						23
24						24
25						25
26						26
27						27
28						28
29						29
30						30
31						31
32						32
33						33
34						34
35						35
36						36
37						37

SOLUTIONS

CHAPTER 1

	MATCHING			*TRUE/FALSE*		*MULTIPLE CHOICE*	
1. F	6. C	11. H	1. T	6. T		1. d	4. d
2. D	7. A	12. E	2. F	7. F		2. c	5. a
3. G	8. L	13. I	3. F	8. T		3. b	
4. J	9. M	14. O	4. T	9. F			
5. N	10. B	15. K	5. F	10. F			

EXERCISE 1-1

	A	L	OE
1.	+	o	+
2.	+	+	o
3.	+	o	+
4.	+	o	+
5.	–	o	–
6.	+,–	o	o
7.	+,–	o	o
8.	–	–	o
9.	–	–	o
10.	–	o	–

PROBLEM 1-1

		Assets			=	Liabilities	+	Owner's Equity
	Cash	+	Supplies	+	Land	=	Accts. Pay.	+	Ed Casey, Capital
1.	$40,000								$40,000 I
2.			$2,000				$2,000		
Bal.	$40,000		$2,000				$2,000		$40,000
3.	-14,000				$14,000				
Bal.	$26,000		$2,000		$14,000		$2,000		$40,000
4.	- 1,800						–1,800		
Bal.	$24,200		$2,000		$14,000		$ 200		$40,000
5.	–2,000								– 2,000 D
Bal.	$22,200		$2,000		$14,000		$ 200		$38,000
6.	–2,800								– 2,800 E
Bal.	$19,400		$2,000		$14,000		$ 200		$35,200
7.							+ 900		– 900 E
Bal.	$19,400		$2,000		$14,000		$1,100		$34,300
8.	+10,000								+10,000 I
Bal.	$29,400		$2,000		$14,000		$1,100		$44,300
9.	+ 500								+ 500 R
Bal.	$29,900		$2,000		$14,000		$1,100		$44,800
10.			– 600						– 600 E
Bal.	$29,000		$1,400		$14,000		$1,100		$44,200

PROBLEM 1-2

(1)

Tom's Painting Service
Income Statement
For Year Ended December 31, 19—

Sales		$27,450
Operating Expenses:		
Supplies expense	$5,450	
Advertising expense	4,825	
Truck rental expense	1,525	
Utilities expense	700	
Misc. expense	1,400	13,900
Net income		$13,550

(2)

Tom's Painting Service
Statement of Owner's Equity
For Year Ended December 31, 19—

Investment, Jan. 1, 19—		$4,000
Additional investment by owner	$ 2,000	
Income for the year	13,550	
Less withdrawal	(1,000)	
Increase in owner's equity		14,550
Tom Wallace, capital, Dec. 31, 19—		$18,550

(3)

Tom's Painting Service
Balance Sheet
December 31, 19—

Assets

Cash	$10,050
Accounts receivable	8,950
Supplies	4,000
Total assets	$23,000

Liabilities

Accounts payable	$ 4,450

Owner's Equity

Tom Wallace, capital	18,550
Total liabilities & owner's equity	$23,000

CHAPTER 2

MATCHING			TRUE/FALSE		MULTIPLE CHOICE	
1. H	6. F	10. J	1. F	6. F	1. b	6. b
2. G	7. I	11. L	2. T	7. F	2. d	7. b
3. K	8. D	12. A	3. T	8. F	3. b	8. d
4. C	9. E		4. F	9. T	4. c	9. c
5. B			5. T	10. F	5. a	10. b

EXERCISE 2-1

Transactions	Account Debited Type	Effect	Account Credited Type	Effect
(1)	asset	+	capital	+
(2)	asset	+	liability	+
(3)	asset	+	liability	+
(4)	asset	+	revenue	+
(5)	liability	–	asset	–
(6)	expense	+	liability	+
(7)	asset	+	asset	–
(8)	drawing	+	asset	–

PROBLEM 2-1

(1) June 1 Cash 11   5,000

         Equipment.. 18   14,500

         Vehicles 19   21,000

            Joan Star, Capital... 31   40,500

    16 Equipment.. 18   5,500

            Accounts Payable 21   5,500

    28 Supplies.. 12   500

            Accounts Payable 21   500

    30 Accounts Payable 21   2,100

            Cash 11   2,100

(2) Account   Cash   Account No. 11

Date	Item	Post. Ref.	Debit	Credit	Balance Debit	Credit
19—						
June 1		1	5,000		5,000	
30		1		2,100	2,900	

Account   Supplies   Account No. 12

Date	Item	Post. Ref.	Debit	Credit	Balance Debit	Credit
19—						
June 28		1	500		500	

Account   Equipment   Account No. 18

Date	Item	Post. Ref.	Debit	Credit	Balance Debit	Credit
19—						
June 1		1	14,500		14,500	
16		1	5,500		20,000	

Account	Vehicles				Account No. 19
19—					
June 1		1	21,000		21,000

Account	Accounts Payable				Account No. 21
19—					
June 16		1		5,500	5,500
28		1		500	6,000
30		1	2,100		3,900

Account	Joan Star, Capital				Account No. 31
19—					
June 1		1		40,500	40,500

(3)

Star Service Company
Trial Balance
June 30, 19—

Cash	2,900	
Supplies	500	
Equipment	20,000	
Vehicles.	21,000	
Accounts Payable		3,900
Joan Star, Capital		40,500
	44,400	44,400

PROBLEM 2-2

(1)

	Cash		
(1)	20,000	(2)	2,500
(4)	19,600	(3)	1,000
		(5)	1,100
		(7)	2,600
		(8)	5,000
		(9)	800
		(11)	240
		(12)	1,700
		(13)	2,000
		(14)	5,000
		(15)	500

	Office Supplies	
(3)	1,000	
(6)	200	

	Prepaid Insurance	
(12)	1,700	

	Library	
(14)	5,000	

	Office Equipment	
(1)	13,200	

	Auto	
(7)	13,000	

	Accounts Payable		
(11)	240	(6)	200
(13)	2,000	(7)	10,400
		(10)	240

	Judy Turner, Capital	
		(1) 33,200

	Judy Turner, Drawing	
(8)	5,000	

Legal Fees				Telephone Expense		
		(4)	19,600	(10)	240	

Rent Expense			Auto Repairs & Maint. Expense		
(2)	2,500		(9)	800	

Salary Expense			Janitor Expense		
(5)	1,100		(15)	500	

(2)

Judy Turner
Trial Balance
January 31, 19—

Cash	17,160	
Office Supplies	1,200	
Prepaid Insurance	1,700	
Library	5,000	
Office Equipment	13,200	
Auto	13,000	
Accounts Payable		8,600
Judy Turner, Capital		33,200
Judy Turner, Drawing	5,000	
Legal Fees		19,600
Rent Expense	2,500	
Salary Expense	1,100	
Telephone Expense	240	
Auto Repairs & Maintenance Expense	800	
Janitor Expense	500	
	61,400	61,400

PROBLEM 2-3

(a)	Prepaid Insurance	1,000	
	Prepaid Rent		1,000
	To correct erroneous debit to Prepaid Rent.		
(b)	Accounts Receivable	200	
	Accounts Payable		200
	To correct erroneous credit to Accounts Receivable.		
(c)	Drawing	3,000	
	Cash		3,000
	To correct erroneous entry debiting Cash and crediting Drawing.		

CONTINUING PROBLEM

(2) The complete ledger for the Continuing Problem is at the end of the solution for Chapter 6.

(1)
1993

Dec.	1	Rent Expense	532	400	
		Cash	110		400
		Paid office rent for December.			
	1	Auto Expense	524	200	
		Cash	110		200
		Paid auto lease for December.			
	2	Prepaid Insurance	118	600	
		Cash	110		600
		Purchased 1-year prop. ins. policy.			
	2	Fees Receivable	112	9,800	
		Fees Earned	410		9,800
		Billed clients for performances in Oct. and Nov.			
	4	Cash	110	1,000	
		Fees Receivable	112		1,000
		Received payment for billings.			
	8	Cash	110	1,200	
		Fees Earned	410		1,200
		Received cash for performance.			
	11	Subcontractors Payable	214	750	
		Cash	110		750
		Paid George the Mysterious amount owed.			
	14	Theater Services Payable	213	2,005	
		Cash	110		2,005
		Paid Chi-Town Theater amount owed.			
	15	Supplies & Props	116	185	
		Accounts Payable	211		185
		Purchased supplies and props on account.			
	16	Equipment - Stage	123	1,200	
		Cash	110		200
		Accounts Payable	211		1,000
		Purchased equipment on account with down payment.			
	17	Accounts Payable	211	1,100	
		Cash	110		1,100
		Paid creditors.			

Dec. 18	Cash..	110	5,200	
	Fees Earned	410		5,200
	Received cash for December performances.			
21	Cosmetics Expense.......................	525	73	
	Cash.................................	110		73
	Paid cash for cosmetics.			
24	Furniture & Fixtures	121	7,000	
	Cash.................................	110		2,000
	Notes Payable	220		5,000
	Purchased furniture with cash and note.			
24	Cash...................................	110	5,200	
	Fees Receivable.......................	112		5,200
	Collected on December 2 billings.			
29	Telephone Expense	534	95	
	Cash.................................	110		95
	Paid telephone expense.			
30	Subcontractor Expense	522	450	
	Cash.................................	110		450
	Paid Jane the Fantastic for performance.			
31	Cosmetics Expense.......................	525	125	
	Cash.................................	110		125
	Paid cash for cosmetics.			
31	Auto Expense	524	150	
	Cash.................................	110		150
	Paid for gas for year.			

(3)

Egor the Magician
Trial Balance
December 31, 1993

Cash...	9,956	
Fees Receivable...	6,086	
Supplies & Props	1,268	
Office Supplies	789	
Prepaid Insurance	2,000	
Furniture & Fixtures	13,400	
Equipment - Stage	12,000	
Accounts Payable...		1,580
Notes Payable		6,500
E. J. Gribbet, Capital		21,852
E. J. Gribbet, Drawing..	400	
Fees Earned		31,300
Theater Services Expense	4,000	
Subcontractor Expense	2,460	
Auto Expense	3,250	
Cosmetics Expense..	428	
Rent Expense...	4,800	
Telephone Expense	395	
	61,232	61,232

CHAPTER 3

MATCHING		TRUE/FALSE		MULTIPLE CHOICE	
1. A	6. H	1. T	6. T	1. b	4. d
2. C	7. L	2. F	7. T	2. c	5. a
3. I	8. M	3. T	8. F	3. a	
4. G	9. K	4. F	9. T		
5. B	10. D	5. T	10. F		

EXERCISE 3-1

(1)

Cash				Insurance Expense		
	May 1	5,400		Dec. 31	1,200	

Prepaid Insurance				
May 1	5,400	Dec. 31	1,200	

(2) Unexpired insurance $4,200

(3) Insurance expense... $1,200

EXERCISE 3-2

(1)

Cash		
	Oct. 7	250
	14	250
	21	250
	28	250

Salary Expense		
Oct. 7	250	
14	250	
21	250	
28	250	
31	50	

Salaries Payable		
	Oct. 31	50

(2) Salary expense $1,050

(3) Salaries payable $50

EXERCISE 3-3

Unearned Rent		
Dec. 31 500	Dec. 1	6,000

Rent Income		
	Dec. 31	500

Dec. 31	Unearned Rent	500	
	Rent Income		500

EXERCISE 3-4

Interest Receivable		
Dec. 31	320	

Interest Income		
	Dec. 31	320

Dec. 31	Interest Receivable	320	
	Interest Income		320

PROBLEM 3-1

(1) and (2)

Bob's Service Company
Partial Work Sheet
For Month Ended July 31, 19—

	Trial Balance Dr.	Trial Balance Cr.	Adjustments Dr.	Adjustments Cr.	Adjusted Trial Balance Dr.	Adjusted Trial Balance Cr.
Cash.......................	9,218				9,218	
Accounts Receivable	7,277		(e) 2,100		9,377	
Supplies	2,750			(c) 1,750	1,000	
Prepaid Rent	8,712			(b) 726	7,986	
Tools/Equipment..............	21,829				21,829	
Accumulated Depreciation		1,535		(d) 400		1,935
Accounts Payable..............		7,117				7,117
Bob Jones, Capital..............		37,417				37,417
Bob Jones, Drawing	3,234				3,234	
Service Fees		28,699		(e) 2,100		30,799
Salary Expense	15,929		(a) 2,000		17,929	
Misc. Expense	5,819				5,819	
	74,768	74,768				
Salaries Payable				(a) 2,000		2,000
Rent Expense..................			(b) 726		726	
Supplies Expense			(c) 1,750		1,750	
Depr. Expense			(d) 400		400	
			6,976	6,976	79,268	79,268

CONTINUING PROBLEM

(4) and (5) See the Solution for the Continuing Problem in Chapter 4.

CHAPTER 4

MATCHING		TRUE/FALSE		MULTIPLE CHOICE	
1. K	6. F	1. F	6. T	1. a	4. b
2. A	7. J	2. F	7. F	2. a	5. c
3. H	8. N	3. T	8. F	3. c	
4. M	9. I	4. T	9. T		
5. G	10. L	5. F	10. T		

EXERCISE 4-1

Aug. 31	Salary Expense..		1,500	
	Salaries Payable..			1,500
31	Rent Expense		560	
	Prepaid Rent			560
31	Supplies Expense		700	
	Supplies..			700

Aug. 31	Depreciation Expense			1,000	
	Accumulated Depreciation				1,000
31	Accounts Receivable			3,200	
	Repair Fees...				3,200

EXERCISE 4-2

(1)

19—

Mar. 31	Service Fees		50	19,225	
	Income Summary		45		19,225
31	Income Summary		45	13,980	
	Salary Expense		58		8,550
	Supplies Expense		67		5,430

(2)

Account   Income Summary   Account No. 45

Date	Item	Post. Ref.	Debit	Credit	Balance Debit	Balance Credit
19—						
Mar. 31		8		19,225		19,225
31		8	13,980			5,245

Account   Service Fees   Account No. 50

Date	Item	Post. Ref.	Debit	Credit	Balance Debit	Balance Credit
19—						
Mar. 15		5		4,850		4,850
31		6		14,375		19,225
31		8	19,225			-0-

Account   Salary Expense   Account No. 58

Date	Item	Post. Ref.	Debit	Credit	Balance Debit	Balance Credit
19—						
Mar. 31		6	8,550		8,550	
31		8		8,550	-0-	

Account   Supplies Expense   Account No. 67

Date	Item	Post. Ref.	Debit	Credit	Balance Debit	Balance Credit
19—						
Mar. 15		5	2,430		2,430	
25		6	1,720		4,150	
31		6	1,280		5,430	
31		8		5,430	-0-	

PROBLEM 4-1

(1)

Castle Shop
Work Sheet
For Month Ended April 30, 19—

	Trial Balance Dr.	Trial Balance Cr.	Adjustments Dr.	Adjustments Cr.
Cash............................	10,056			
Accounts Receivable	7,938		(e) 3,000	
Supplies	3,000			(a) 1,200
Prepaid Rent	9,504			(b) 792
Tools/Equipment..................	23,814			
Accumulated Depreciation		1,674		(c) 1,000
Accounts Payable..................		7,764		
Unearned Fees		2,000	(f) 500	
Castle, Capital....................		38,818		
Castle, Drawing	3,528			
Service Fees		31,308		(e) 3,000
				(f) 500
Wages Expense....................	17,376		(d) 2,000	
Misc. Expense	6,348			
	81,564	81,564		
Wages Payable				(d) 2,000
Rent Expense.....................			(b) 792	
Supplies Expense..................			(a) 1,200	
Depr. Expense....................			(c) 1,000	
			8,492	8,492
Net Income				

Adjusted Trial Balance		Income Statement		Balance Sheet	
Dr.	Cr.	Dr.	Cr.	Dr.	Cr.
10,056				10,056	
10,938				10,938	
1,800				1,800	
8,712				8,712	
23,814				23,814	
	2,674				2,674
	7,764			7,764	
	1,500				1,500
	38,818				38,818
3,528				3,528	
	34,308		34,808		
19,376		19,376			
6,348		6,348			
	2,000				2,000
792		792			
1,200		1,200			
1,000		1,000			
87,564	87,564	28,716	34,808	58,848	52,756
		6,092			6,092
		34,808	34,808	58,848	58,848

(2)

Castle Shop
Income Statement
For Year Ended April 30, 19—

Service fees		$34,808
Operating expenses:		
Wages expenses	$19,376	
Misc. expenses	6,348	
Supplies expense	1,200	
Depreciation expense	1,000	
Rent expense	792	
Total operating expenses		28,716
Net income		$ 6,092

Castle Shop
Statement of Owner's Equity
For Year Ended April 30, 19—

Capital, May 1, 19—		$38,818
Income for the year	$ 6,092	
Less drawing for the year	3,528	
Increase in owner's equity		2,564
Capital, April 30, 19—		$41,382

Castle Shop
Balance Sheet
April 30, 19—

Assets

Current assets:

Cash	$10,056	
Accounts receivable	10,938	
Supplies	1,800	
Prepaid rent	8,712	
Total current assets		$31,506

Plant assets:

Office equipment	$23,814	
Less accumulated depreciation	2,674	21,140
Total assets		$52,646

Liabilities

Current liabilities:

Accounts payable	$ 7,764	
Wages payable	2,000	
Unearned fees	1,500	
Total liabilities		$11,264

Owner's Equity

Castle, capital	41,382
Total liabilities and owner's equity	$52,646

PROBLEM 4-2

19—	Adjusting Entries		
Apr. 30	Supplies Expense	1,200	
	Supplies		1,200
30	Rent Expense	792	
	Prepaid Rent		792
30	Depreciation Expense	1,000	
	Accumulated Depreciation		1,000
30	Wages Expense	2,000	
	Wages Payable		2,000
30	Accounts Receivable	3,000	
	Service Fees		3,000
30	Unearned Fees	500	
	Service Fees		500

19—   Closing Entries

Apr. 30 Service Fees 34,808
                Income Summary   34,808

      30 Income Summary 28,716
                Wages Expense   19,376
                Misc. Expense   6,348
                Supplies Expense   1,200
                Depreciation Expense   1,000
                Rent Expense   792

      30 Income Summary   6,092
                Castle, Capital   6,092

      30 Castle, Capital   3,528
                Castle, Drawing   3,528

CONTINUING PROBLEM

(4), (5), (6)

Egor the Magician
Work Sheet
For the Year Ended December 31, 1993

Account Titles	Trial Balance Dr.	Trial Balance Cr.	Adjustments Dr.	Adjustments Cr.
Cash	9,956			
Fees Receivable	6,086			
Supplies & Props	1,268			(b) 903
Office Supplies	789			(a) 579
Prepaid Insurance	2,000			(c) 1,450
Furn. & Fixtures	13,400			
Equipment—Stage	12,000			
Accounts Payable		1,580		
Theater Services Payable				(e) 850
Subcontractors Payable				(f) 600
Notes Payable		6,500		
E. J. Gribbet, Capital		21,852		
E. J. Gribbet, Drawing	400			
Fees Earned		31,300		
Theater Services Exp	4,000		(e) 850	
Subcontractor Exp	2,460		(f) 600	
Auto Expense	3,250			
Cosmetics Expense	428			
Rent Expense	4,800			
Telephone Expense	395			
	61,232	61,232		
Office Supplies Exp			(a) 579	
Supplies & Props Exp			(b) 903	
Insurance Expense			(c) 1,450	
Interest Expense			(d) 105	
Interest Payable				(d) 105
Depr. Exp.—Furn. & Fix			(g) 2,680	
Accum. Depr.—Furn. & Fix				(g) 2,680
Depr. Exp.—Equip			(h) 2,400	
Accum. Depr.—Equip				(h) 2,400
			9,567	9,567
Net Income				

Adjusted Trial Balance		Income Statement		Balance Sheet	
Dr.	Cr.	Dr.	Cr.	Dr.	Cr.
9,956				9,956	
6,086				6,086	
365				365	
210				210	
550				550	
13,400				13,400	
12,000				12,000	
	1,580				1,580
	850				850
	600				600
	6,500				6,500
	21,852				21,852
400				400	
	31,300		31,300		
4,850		4,850			
3,060		3,060			
3,250		3,250			
428		428			
4,800		4,800			
395		395			
579		579			
903		903			
1,450		1,450			
105		105			
	105				105
2,680		2,680			
	2,680				2,680
2,400		2,400			
	2,400				2,400
67,867	67,867	24,900	31,300	42,967	36,567
		6,400			6,400
		31,300	31,300	42,967	42,967

(7)

Egor the Magician
Income Statement
For the Year Ended December 31, 1993

Fees earned		$31,300
Operating expenses:		
Theater services expense	$4,850	
Rent expense	4,800	
Auto expense	3,250	
Subcontractor expense	3,060	
Depreciation expense—furn. & fix.	2,680	
Depreciation expense—equipment	2,400	
Insurance expense	1,450	
Supplies & props expense	903	
Office supplies expense	579	
Cosmetics expense	428	
Telephone expense	395	
Interest expense	105	
Total operating expenses		24,900
Net income		$ 6,400

Egor the Magician
Statement of Owner's Equity
For the Year Ended December 31, 1993

Egor J. Gribbet, capital, January 1, 1993		$21,852
Income for the year	$6,400	
Less drawing for the year	400	
Increase in owner's equity		6,000
Egor J. Gribbet, capital, December 31, 1993		$27,852

Egor the Magician
Balance Sheet
December 31, 1993

Assets

Current assets:

Cash...	$9,956	
Fees receivable	6,086	
Supplies & props	365	
Office supplies	210	
Prepaid insurance	550	
Total current assets		$17,167

Plant assets:

Furniture & fixtures	$13,400		
Less accumulated depreciation	2,680	$10,720	
Equipment—stage	$12,000		
Less accumulated depreciation	2,400	9,600	
Total plant assets.......................			20,320
Total assets			$37,487

Liabilities

Current liabilities:

Accounts payable.............................	$ 1,580	
Theater services payable	850	
Subcontractors payable	600	
Interest payable	105	
Total current liabilities.................		$3,135

Long-term liabilities:

Notes payable...............................		6,500
Total liabilities		$ 9,635

Owner's Equity

E. J. Gribbet, capital.........................		27,852
Total liabilities and owner's equity.............		$37,487

(8)

1993	Adjusting Entries			
Dec. 31	Office Supplies Expense....................	531	579	
	Office Supplies	117		579
31	Supplies & Props Expense.................	533	903	
	Supplies & Props	116		903
31	Insurance Expense........................	529	1,450	
	Prepaid Insurance	118		1,450
31	Interest Expense.........................	710	105	
	Interest Payable	215		105
31	Theater Services Expense.................	521	850	
	Theater Services Payable	213		850

Dec. 31	Subcontractor Expense	522	600	
	Subcontractors Payable	214		600
31	Depreciation Expense - Furniture & Fixtures	527	2,680	
	Accumulated Depreciation - Furniture & Fixtures	122		2,680
31	Depreciation Expense - Equipment	528	2,400	
	Accumulated Depreciation - Equipment	124		2,400

(9)

1993		Closing Entries			
Dec. 31	Fees Earned		410	31,300	
	Income Summary		312		31,300
31	Income Summary		312	24,900	
	Theater Services Expense		521		4,850
	Subcontractor Expense		522		3,060
	Auto Expense		524		3,250
	Cosmetics Expense		525		428
	Rent Expense		532		4,800
	Telephone Expense		534		395
	Office Supplies Expense		531		579
	Supplies & Props Expense		533		903
	Insurance Expense		529		1,450
	Interest Expense		710		105
	Depreciation Expense—Furn. & Fix.		527		2,680
	Depreciation Expense—Equip.		528		2,400
31	Income Summary		312	6,400	
	E. J. Gribbet, Capital		310		6,400
31	E. J. Gribbet, Capital		310	400	
	E. J. Gribbet, Drawing		311		400

CHAPTER 5

MATCHING		*TRUE/FALSE*		*MULTIPLE CHOICE*	
1. A	7. D	1. F	6. T	1. b	4. a
2. J	8. H	2. T	7. F	2. d	5. c
3. C	9. I	3. F	8. T	3. b	6. c
4. B	10. F	4. T	9. F		
5. K	11. G	5. F	10. T		
6. E	12. L				

EXERCISE 5-1

(1)	Purchases	5,000	
	Accounts Payable		5,000
(2)	Accounts Payable	5,000	
	Cash		4,900
	Purchases Discounts		100

(3)	Purchases	3,500	
	Transportation In	80	
	Accounts Payable		3,580
(4)	Accounts Payable	900	
	Purchases Returns and Allowances		900
(5)	Accounts Payable	2,680	
	Cash		2,628
	Purchases Discounts		52

EXERCISE 5-2

(1)	Accounts Receivable	3,150	
	Sales		3,150
(2)	Cash	2,850	
	Sales		2,850
(3)	Cash	3,050	
	Credit Card Collection Expense	100	
	Accounts Receivable		3,150
(4)	Accounts Receivable	4,500	
	Sales		4,500
	Accounts Receivable	150	
	Cash		150
(5)	Sales Returns and Allowances	400	
	Accounts Receivable		400
(6)	Cash	4,168	
	Sales Discounts	82	
	Accounts Receivable		4,250

PROBLEM 5-1

19—				
Sept.	3	Purchases	8,500	
		Accounts Payable		8,500
	4	Office Supplies	800	
		Cash		800
	6	Accounts Receivable	4,000	
		Sales		4,000
	7	Accounts Payable	2,000	
		Purchases Returns and Allowances		2,000
	10	Purchases	5,000	
		Cash		5,000
	12	Accounts Receivable	5,500	
		Sales		5,500
	13	Accounts Payable	6,500	
		Cash		6,435
		Purchases Discounts		65
	16	Cash	3,920	
		Sales Discounts	80	
		Accounts Receivable		4,000

Sept.	20	Cash	5,200	
		Nonbank Credit Card Expense	300	
		Accounts Receivable.........................		5,500
	24	Accounts Receivable...........................	3,000	
		Sales		3,000
	26	Cash	2,200	
		Sales		2,200
	30	Sales Returns and Allowances...................	1,000	
		Accounts Receivable.........................		1,000

PROBLEM 5-2

Cost of merchandise sold:

Merchandise inventory, July 1, 1993			$130,000
Purchases		$415,000	
Less: Purchases returns and allowances.........................	$3,780		
Purchases discounts.....................................	4,590	8,370	
Net purchases		$406,630	
Add transportation in...		2,970	
Cost of merchandise purchased			409,600
Merchandise available for sale			$539,600
Less merchandise inventory, June 30, 1994			155,000
Cost of merchandise sold.......................................			$384,600

CONTINUING PROBLEM

(11) The complete ledger for the Continuing Problem is at the end of the solutions for Chapter 6.

1994

Jan.	2	Rent Expense	532	2,400	
		Cash..	110		2,400
		Paid office rent for January-June.			
	2	Auto Expense.................................	524	2,400	
		Cash..	110		2,400
		Paid auto lease for year.			
	2	Notes Payable................................	220	1,500	
		Interest Payable	215	105	
		Cash..	110		1,605
		Paid note plus interest.			
	22	Cash	110	2,486	
		Fees Receivable..............................	112		2,486
		Received payment for billings.			
Feb.	11	Theater Services Payable.......................	213	850	
		Cash..	110		850
		Paid amount owed to theater.			
	24	Subcontractors Payable	214	600	
		Cash..	110		600
		Paid J.P. Magic amount owed.			
Mar.	15	Supplies and Props............................	116	840	
		Cash..	110		840
		Paid cash for props.			

Date		Account	Ref	Debit	Credit
Mar.	15	Salary Expense....................................	520	800	
		Cash..	110		800
		Paid part-time salary.			
	31	Cash	110	9,400	
		Fees Earned	410		9,400
		Received cash for performances.			
Apr.	11	Purchases	510	4,800	
		Accounts Payable............................	211		4,800
		Purchased merchandise from Magical Enterprises, 2/10, n/30.			
	20	Accounts Payable	211	4,800	
		Purchases Discounts	512		96
		Cash..	110		4,704
		Paid for purchase of April 11.			
May	15	Salary Expense..................................	520	800	
		Cash..	110		800
		Paid part-time salary.			
June	5	Accounts Receivable	111	2,200	
		Sales	411		2,200
		Sold merchandise to Jerome's Toys, 2/10, n/30.			
	5	Transportation Out.............................	535	45	
		Cash..	110		45
		Paid transportation costs.			
	30	Cash	110	2,200	
		Accounts Receivable	111		2,200
		Received payment from Jerome's Toys.			
July	1	Rent Expense..................................	532	2,400	
		Cash..	110		2,400
		Paid office rent July-Dec.			
	1	Interest Expense	710	150	
		Cash..	110		150
		Paid 6 months' interest on note.			
	2	Telephone Expense.............................	534	120	
		Cash..	110		120
		Paid telephone expense.			
	10	Accounts Payable	211	500	
		Cash..	110		500
		Paid creditors.			
July	15	Accounts Receivable	111	2,850	
		Sales	411		2,850
		Sold merchandise to Evan's Magic, 2/10, n/30.			
	15	Salary Expense..................................	520	800	
		Cash..	110		800
		Paid part-time salary.			
	18	Purchases	510	5,600	
		Transportation In	513	200	
		Accounts Payable............................	211		5,800
		Purchased merchandise from Magical Enterprises, 2/10, n/eom.			

257

July	20	Accounts Payable	211	400	
		Purchases Returns and Alllowances	511		400
		Returned merchandise purchased on 7/18.			
	24	Cash	110	2,793	
		Sales Discounts	413	57	
		Accounts Receivable	111		2,850
		Received payment on sale of 7/15.			
	28	Accounts Payable	211	5,400	
		Purchases Discounts	512		104
		Cash	110		5,296
		Paid for purchase of 7/18.			
	31	Accounts Receivable	111	4,600	
		Sales	411		4,600
		Sold merchandise to Toy Depot, n/30.			
Aug.	1	Transportation Out	535	75	
		Cash	110		75
		Paid transportation cost for 7/31 shipment.			
	3	Fees Receivable	112	9,200	
		Fees Earned	410		9,200
		Billed clients for performances in June and July.			
	16	Sales Returns and Allowances	412	500	
		Accounts Receivable	111		500
		Issued credit memo on sale of 7/31.			
	30	Cash	110	4,100	
		Accounts Receivable	111		4,100
		Received payment on sale of 7/31.			
Sept.	1	Cash	110	9,200	
		Fees Receivable	112		9,200
		Received payment for billings.			
	15	Cosmetics Expense	525	100	
		Cash	110		100
		Paid cash for cosmetics.			
	15	Salary Expense	520	800	
		Cash	110		800
		Paid part-time salary.			
Oct.	8	Subcontractors Expense	522	400	
		Cash	110		400
		Paid Jane the Fantastic for performance.			
Nov.	13	Theater Services Expense	521	600	
		Cash	110		600
		Paid Apollo Theater for its use.			
	15	Salary Expense	520	800	
		Cash	110		800
		Paid part-time salary.			
Dec.	2	Prepaid Insurance	118	600	
		Cash	110		600
		Prepaid 1-year property insurance policy.			

Dec.	2	Fees Receivable	112	8,100	
		Fees Earned	410		8,100
		Billed clients for performances in October and November.			
	11	Accounts Receivable	111	3,400	
		Sales	411		3,400
		Sold merchandise to Mystic Emporium, 2/10, n/30.			
	30	Telephone Expense..............................	534	135	
		Cash..	110		135
		Paid telephone expense.			

CHAPTER 6

MATCHING		TRUE/FALSE		MULTIPLE CHOICE	
1. E	6. D	1. F	6. F	1. c	4. d
2. J	7. F	2. F	7. F	2. a	5. b
3. C	8. A	3. T	8. T	3. d	
4. I	9. H	4. T	9. F		
5. B	10. G	5. T	10. T		

EXERCISE 6-1

19—

Dec.	31	Income Summary	150,000	
		Merchandise Inventory.........................		150,000
	31	Merchandise Inventory..........................	115,000	
		Income Summary		115,000

EXERCISE 6-2

(1)   Periodic Inventory System   **(2)**   Perpetual Invetory System

19—

Jan.	3	Purchases.................	25,000		Merchandise Inventory	25,000	
		Accounts Payable		25,000	Accounts Payable........		25,000
	5	Accounts Payable	5,000		Accounts Payable..........	5,000	
		Purchases Returns and Allowances		5,000	Merchandise Inventory ..		5,000
	12	Accounts Receivable.......	50,000		Accounts Receivable.......	50,000	
		Sales		50,000	Sales		50,000
	12	No entry.			Cost of Merchandise Sold ..	35,000	
					Merchandise Inventory ..		35,000
	13	Accounts Payable	20,000		Accounts Payable..........	20,000	
		Cash		19,600	Cash		19,600
		Purchases Discounts.....		400	Merchandise Inventory ..		400
	15	Sales Returns and Allow....	8,000		Sales Returns and Allow....	8,000	
		Accounts Receivable.....		8,000	Accounts Receivable.....		8,000

(1)   Periodic Inventory System
Jan. 15 No entry.

22 Cash.....................	41,580	
Sales Discounts...........	420	
Accounts Receivable.....		42,000

(2)   Perpetual Invetory System

Merchandise Inventory....	5,600	
Cost of Merchandise Sold		5,600
Cash.....................	41,580	
Sales Discounts...........	420	
Accounts Receivable		42,000

PROBLEM 6-1

Miller Company
Work Sheet
For Year Ended March 31, 19—

	Trial Balance Dr.	Trial Balance Cr.	Adjustments Dr.	Adjustments Cr.
Cash............................	43,100			
Notes Receivable	6,000			
Accounts Receivable	107,780			
Interest Receivable.................			(a) 520	
Merchandise Inventory	160,390		(c) 115,800	(b) 160,390
Office Supplies	10,350			(d) 9,100
Prepaid Insurance	24,740			(e) 16,000
Delivery Equipment	60,150			
Accum. Depr. - Delivery Equip.......		13,900		(f) 9,050
Accounts Payable..................		75,300		
Salaries Payable				(g) 2,000
Miller, Capital....................		193,650		
Miller, Drawing	30,000			
Income Summary...................			(b) 160,390	(c) 115,800
Sales.............................		1,016,700		
Sales Returns and Allowances	13,010			
Purchases.........................	642,900			
Purchases Discounts		6,430		
Sales Salaries Expense	77,120		(g) 1,130	
Advertising Expense................	13,090			
Delivery Expense..................	42,100			
Depreciation Exp.—Delivery Equip...			(f) 9,050	
Misc. Selling Expense	13,950			
Office Salaries Expense.............	54,930		(g) 870	
Office Supplies Expense............			(d) 9,100	
Insurance Expense.................			(e) 16,000	
Misc. Admin. Exp..................	6,870			
Interest Income...................		500		(a) 520
	1,306,480	1,306,480	312,860	312,860
Net Income				

Adjusted Trial Balance		Income Statement		Balance Sheet	
Dr.	Cr.	Dr.	Cr.	Dr.	Cr.
43,100				43,100	
6,000				6,000	
107,780				107,780	
520				520	
115,800				115,800	
1,250				1,250	
8,740				8,740	
60,150				60,150	
	22,950				22,950
	75,300				75,300
	2,000				2,000
	193,650				193,650
30,000				30,000	
160,390	115,800	160,390	115,800		
	1,016,700		1,016,700		
13,010		13,010			
642,900		642,900			
	6,430		6,430		
78,250		78,250			
13,090		13,090			
42,100		42,100			
9,050		9,050			
13,950		13,950			
55,800		55,800			
9,100		9,100			
16,000		16,000			
6,870		6,870			
	1,020		1,020		
1,433,850	1,433,850	1,060,510	1,139,950	373,340	293,900
		79,440			79,440
		1,139,950	1,139,950	373,340	373,340

PROBLEM 6-2A

Miller Company
Income Statement
For Year Ended March 31, 19—

Revenue from sales:		
Sales..	$1,016,700	
Less: Sales returns and allowances	13,010	
Net sales...		$1,003,690
Cost of merchandise sold:		
Merchandise inventory, April 1, 19—............................	$ 160,390	
Purchases $642,900		
Less: Purchases discounts 6,430		
Net purchases	636,470	
Merchandise available for sale	$796,860	
Less: Merchandise inventory, March 31, 19—......................	115,800	
Cost of merchandise sold......................................		681,060
Gross profit		$ 322,630
Operating expenses:		
Selling expenses:		
Sales salaries expense .... $ 78,250		
Advertising expense 13,090		
Delivery expense 42,100		
Depr. expense—delivery equip................................. 9,050		
Misc. selling expense.. 13,950		
Total selling expenses.......................................	$ 156,440	
Administrative expenses:		
Office salaries expense .... $ 55,800		
Office supplies expense 9,100		
Insurance expense 16,000		
Misc. administrative expenses 6,870		
Total administrative expenses	87,770	
Total operating expenses		244,210
Income from operations		$ 78,420
Other income:		
Interest income		1,020
Net income..		$ 79,440

PROBLEM 6-2B

Miller Company
Statement of Owner's Equity
For Year Ended March 31, 19—

Miller, capital, April 1, 19—......................................		$193,650
Net income for year..	$79,440	
Less withdrawals	30,000	
Increase in owner's equity		49,440
Miller, capital, March 31, 19—.....................................		$243,090

PROBLEM 6-2C

Miller Company
Balance Sheet
March 31, 19—

Assets

Current assets:

Cash..........	$ 43,100	
Notes receivable..............	6,000	
Accounts receivable	107,780	
Interest receivable	520	
Merchandise inventory	115,800	
Office supplies	1,250	
Prepaid insurance	8,740	
Total current assets		$283,190

Plant assets:

Delivery equipment	$ 60,150	
Less accumulated depreciation	22,950	
Total plant assets........		37,200
Total assets		$320,390

Liabilities

Current liabilities:

Accounts payable........	$ 75,300	
Salaries payable	2,000	
Total current liabilities........		$ 77,300

Owner's Equity

Miller, capital		243,090
Total liabilities and owner's equity........		$320,390

PROBLEM 6-3

(1)

Adjusting Entries

19—

(a)	Mar. 31	Interest Receivable.......................	520	
		Interest Income.......................		520
(b)	31	Income Summary.......................	160,390	
		Merchandise Inventory		160,390
(c)	31	Merchandise Inventory	115,800	
		Income Summary.......................		115,800
(d)	31	Office Supplies Expense..................	9,100	
		Office Supplies		9,100
(e)	31	Insurance Expense.......................	16,000	
		Prepaid Insurance		16,000

(f) Mar. 31 Depreciation Expense - Delivery Equipment   9,050
                    Accumulated Depreciation - Delivery Equipment..........   9,050

(g)   31 Sales Salaries Expense....................................   1,130
                 Office Salaries Expense...................................   870
                    Salaries Payable   2,000

(2)

Closing Entries

19—

Mar. 31 Sales 1,016,700
             Purchases Discounts.....................................   6,430
             Interest Income...   1,020
                 Income Summary.......................................   1,024,150

        31 Income Summary...   900,120
                 Sales Returns and Allowances   13,010
                 Purchases...   642,900
                 Sales Salaries Expense   78,250
                 Advertising Expense....................................   13,090
                 Delivery Expense......................................   42,100
                 Depreciation Expense - Delivery Equipment   9,050
                 Miscellaneous Selling Expense.........................   13,950
                 Office Salaries Expense   55,800
                 Office Supplies Expense................................   9,100
                 Insurance Expense.....................................   16,000
                 Miscellaneous Administrative Expense...................   6,870

        31 Income Summary..   79,440
                 Miller, Capital...   79,440

        31 Miller, Capital...   30,000
                 Miller, Drawing   30,000

PROBLEM 6-4

The work sheet for Problem 6-4 appears on pages 266-267.

PROBLEM 6-5

Zesta Company
Income Statement
For Year Ended December 31, 19—

Revenues:		
Net sales..		$757,500
Rent income..		1,600
Total revenues		$759,100
Expenses:		
Cost of merchandise sold...	$481,000	
Selling expenses...	91,900	
Administrative expenses	81,000	
Interest expense	11,500	
Total expenses		665,400
Net income...		$ 93,700

PROBLEM 6-6

Closing Entries

19—

Dec. 31	Sales..	777,000	
	Rent Income..	1,600	
	Income Summary.......................................		778,600
31	Income Summary...	684,900	
	Sales Returns and Allowances		12,000
	Sales Discounts...		7,500
	Cost of Merchandise Sold		481,000
	Sales Salaries Expense.....................................		67,500
	Advertising Expense.......................................		20,000
	Depreciation Expense - Store Equipment		8,100
	Store Supplies Expense....................................		1,400
	Miscellaneous Selling Expense.............................		4,400
	Office Salaries Expense....................................		32,200
	Rent Expense...		30,000
	Insurance Expense..		7,200
	Office Supplies Expense...................................		1,000
	Miscellaneous Administrative Expense......................		1,100
	Interest Expense..		11,500
31	Income Summary...	93,700	
	Zesta, Capital		93,700
31	Zesta, Capital	30,000	
	Zesta, Drawing...		30,000

PROBLEM 6-4

Zesta Company
Work Sheet
For Year Ended December 31, 19—

	Trial Balance Dr.	Trial Balance Cr.	Adjustments Dr.	Adjustments Cr.
Cash	35,800			
Accounts Receivable...............	88,300			
Merchandise Inventory	80,500			
Prepaid Insurance..................	11,500			(a) 7,200
Store Supplies.....................	2,300			(b) 1,400
Office Supplies....................	1,500			(c) 1,000
Store Equipment	166,600			
Accum. Depr.—Store Equipment		48,500		(d) 8,100
Accounts Payable		15,000		
Salaries Payable...................				(f) 4,700
Unearned Rent.....................		2,400	(e) 1,600	
Note Payable		100,000		
Zesta, Capital		136,100		
Zesta, Drawing....................	30,000			
Sales		777,000		
Sales Returns and Allowances........	12,000			
Sales Discounts	7,500			
Cost of Merchandise Sold	481,000			
Sales Salaries Expense	64,000		(f) 3,500	
Advertising Expense	20,000			
Depr. Exp.—Store Equipment			(d) 8,100	
Store Supplies Expense			(b) 1,400	
Misc. Selling Expense...............	4,400			
Office Salaries Expense	31,000		(f) 1,200	
Rent Expense	30,000			
Insurance Expense			(a) 7,200	
Office Supplies Expense			(c) 1,000	
Misc. Admin. Expense...............	1,100			
Rent Income				(e) 1,600
Interest Expense....................	11,500			
	1,079,000	1,079,000	24,000	24,000
Net Income				

Adj. Trial Balance		Income Statement		Balance Sheet	
Dr.	Cr.	Dr.	Cr.	Dr.	Cr.
35,800				35,800	
88,300				88,300	
80,500				80,500	
4,300				4,300	
900				900	
500				500	
166,600				166,600	
	56,600				56,600
	15,000				15,000
	4,700				4,700
	800				800
	100,000				100,000
	136,100				136,100
30,000				30,000	
	777,000		777,000		
12,000		12,000			
7,500		7,500			
481,000		481,000			
67,500		67,500			
20,000		20,000			
8,100		8,100			
1,400		1,400			
4,400		4,400			
32,200		32,200			
30,000		30,000			
7,200		7,200			
1,000		1,000			
1,100		1,100			
	1,600		1,600		
11,500		11,500			
1,091,800	1,091,800	684,900	778,600	406,900	313,200
		93,700			93,700
		778,600	778,600	406,900	406,900

267

CONTINUING PROBLEM

(2), (8), (9), (11)

Account   Cash   Account No. 110

DATE		ITEM	POST. REF.	DEBIT	CREDIT	BALANCE DEBIT	CREDIT
1993							
Nov.	30	Balance	✓			5,504	
Dec.	1		1		400	5,104	
	1		1		200	4,904	
	2		1		600	4,304	
	4		1	1,000		5,304	
	8		1	1,200		6,504	
	11		1		750	5,754	
	14		1		2,005	3,749	
	16		2		200	3,549	
	17		2		1,100	2,449	
	18		2	5,200		7,649	
	21		2		73	7,576	
	24		2		2,000	5,576	
	24		2	5,200		10,776	
	29		3		95	10,681	
	30		3		450	10,231	
	31		3		125	10,106	
	31		3		150	9,956	
1994							
Jan.	2		6		2,400	7,556	
	2		6		2,400	5,156	
	2		6		1,605	3,551	
	22		6	2,486		6,037	
Feb.	11		6		850	5,187	
	24		6		600	4,587	
Mar.	15		6		840	3,747	
	15		6		800	2,947	
	31		6	9,400		12,347	
Apr.	20		7		4,704	7,643	
May	15		7		800	6,843	
June	5		7		45	6,798	
	30		7	2,200		8,998	
July	1		7		2,400	6,598	
	1		7		150	6,448	
	2		8		120	6,328	
	10		8		500	5,828	
	15		8		800	5,028	
	24		8	2,793		7,821	
	28		8		5,296	2,525	
Aug.	1		9		75	2,450	
	30		9	4,100		6,550	
Sep.	1		9	9,200		15,750	
	15		9		100	15,650	
	15		9		800	14,850	
Oct.	8		10		400	14,450	
Nov.	13		10		600	13,850	
	15		10		800	13,050	
Dec.	2		10		600	12,450	
	30		10		135	12,315	

Account — Accounts Receivable — Account No. 111

DATE	ITEM	POST. REF.	DEBIT	CREDIT	BALANCE DEBIT	BALANCE CREDIT
1994						
June 5		7	2,200		2,200	
30		7		2,200	0	
July 15		8	2,850		2,850	
24		8		2,850	0	
31		9	4,600		4,600	
Aug. 16		9		500	4,100	
30		9		4,100	0	
Dec. 11		10	3,400		3,400	

Account — Fees Receivable — Account No. 112

DATE	ITEM	POST. REF.	DEBIT	CREDIT	BALANCE DEBIT	BALANCE CREDIT
1993						
Nov. 30	Balance	✓			2,486	
Dec. 2		1	9,800		12,286	
4		1		1,000	11,286	
24		2		5,200	6,086	
1994						
Jan. 22		6		2,486	3,600	
Aug. 3		9	9,200		12,800	
Sep. 1		9		9,200	3,600	
Dec. 2		10	8,100		11,700	

Account — Merchandise Inventory — Account No. 115

DATE	ITEM	POST. REF.	DEBIT	CREDIT	BALANCE DEBIT	BALANCE CREDIT
1994						
Dec. 31	Adjusting	11	2,370		2,370	

Account — Supplies & Props — Account No. 116

DATE	ITEM	POST. REF.	DEBIT	CREDIT	BALANCE DEBIT	BALANCE CREDIT
1993						
Nov. 30	Balance	✓			1,083	
Dec. 15		2	185		1,268	
31	Adjusting	4		903	365	
1994						
Mar. 15		6	840		1,205	
Dec. 31	Adjusting	11		945	260	

Account — Office Supplies — Account No. 117

DATE	ITEM	POST. REF.	DEBIT	CREDIT	BALANCE DEBIT	BALANCE CREDIT
1993						
Nov. 30	Balance	✓			789	
Dec. 31	Adjusting	4		579	210	
1994						
Dec. 31	Adjusting	11		110	100	

Account — Prepaid Insurance — Account No. 118

DATE	ITEM	POST. REF.	DEBIT	CREDIT	BALANCE DEBIT	BALANCE CREDIT
1993						
Nov. 30	Balance	✓			1,400	
Dec. 2		1	600		2,000	
31	Adjusting	4		1,450	550	
1994						
Dec. 2		10	600		1,150	
31	Adjusting	11		600	550	

Account — Furniture & Fixtures — Account No. 121

DATE	ITEM	POST. REF.	DEBIT	CREDIT	BALANCE DEBIT	BALANCE CREDIT
1993						
Nov. 30	Balance	✓			6,400	
Dec. 24		2	7,000		13,400	

Account — Accum. Depr.—Furniture & Fixtures — Account No. 122

DATE	ITEM	POST. REF.	DEBIT	CREDIT	BALANCE DEBIT	BALANCE CREDIT
1993						
Dec. 31	Adjusting	4		2,680		2,680
1994						
Dec. 31	Adjusting	11		2,680		5,360

Account — Equipment - Stage — Account No. 123

DATE	ITEM	POST. REF.	DEBIT	CREDIT	BALANCE DEBIT	BALANCE CREDIT
1993						
Nov. 30	Balance	✓			10,800	
Dec. 16		2	1,200		12,000	

Account — Accum. Depr.—Equipment-Stage — Account No. 124

DATE	ITEM	POST. REF.	DEBIT	CREDIT	BALANCE DEBIT	BALANCE CREDIT
1993						
Dec. 31	Adjusting	4		2,400		2,400
1994						
Dec. 31	Adjusting	11		2,400		4,800

Account — Accounts Payable — Account No. 211

DATE	ITEM	POST. REF.	DEBIT	CREDIT	BALANCE DEBIT	BALANCE CREDIT
1993						
Nov. 30	Balance	✓				1,495
Dec. 15		2		185		1,680
16		2		1,000		2,680
17		2	1,100			1,580
1994						
Apr. 11		7		4,800		6,380
20		7	4,800			1,580
July 10		8	500			1,080
18		8		5,800		6,880
20		8	400			6,480
28		8	5,400			1,080

Account — Salaries Payable — Account No. 212

DATE	ITEM	POST. REF.	DEBIT	CREDIT	BALANCE DEBIT	BALANCE CREDIT
1994						
Dec. 31	Adjusting	11		800		800

Account — Theater Services Payable — Account No. 213

DATE	ITEM	POST. REF.	DEBIT	CREDIT	BALANCE DEBIT	BALANCE CREDIT
1993						
Nov. 30	Balance	✓				2,005
Dec. 14		1	2,005			0
31	Adjusting	4		850		850
1994						
Feb. 11		6	850			0

Account   Subcontractors Payable   Account No. 214

DATE		ITEM	POST. REF.	DEBIT	CREDIT	BALANCE DEBIT	BALANCE CREDIT
1993							
Nov.	30	Balance	✓				750
Dec.	11		1	750			0
	31	Adjusting	4		600		600
1994							
Feb.	24		6	600			0

Account   Interest Payable   Account No. 215

1993							
Dec.	31	Adjusting	4		105		105
1994							
Jan.	2		6	105			0
Dec.	31	Adjusting	11		300		300

Account   Notes Payable   Account No. 220

1993							
Nov.	30	Balance	✓				1,500
Dec.	24		2		5,000		6,500
1994							
Jan.	2		6	1,500			5,000

Account   E.J. Gribbet, Capital   Account No. 310

1993							
Nov.	30	Balance	✓				21,852
Dec.	31	Closing	5		6,400		28,252
	31	Closing	5	400			27,852
1994							
Dec.	31	Closing	12		10,903		38,755

Account   E.J. Gribbet, Drawing   Account No. 311

1993							
Nov.	30	Balance	✓			400	
Dec.	31	Closing	5		400	0	

Account   Income Summary   Account No. 312

1993							
Dec.	31	Closing	4		31,300		31,300
	31	Closing	5	24,900			6,400
	31	Closing	5	6,400			0
1994							
Dec.	31	Adjusting	11		2,370		2,370
	31	Closing	11		40,350		42,720
	31	Closing	12	31,817			10,903
	31	Closing	12	10,903			0

Account   Fees Earned   Account No. 410

DATE	ITEM	POST. REF.	DEBIT	CREDIT	BALANCE DEBIT	CREDIT
1993						
Nov. 30	Balance	✓				15,100
Dec. 2		1		9,800		24,900
8		1		1,200		26,100
18		2		5,200		31,300
31	Closing	4	31,300			0
1994						
Mar. 31		6		9,400		9,400
Aug. 3		9		9,200		18,600
Dec. 2		10		8,100		26,700
31	Closing	11	26,700			0

Account   Sales   Account No. 411

DATE	ITEM	POST. REF.	DEBIT	CREDIT	BALANCE DEBIT	CREDIT
1994						
June 5		7		2,200		2,200
July 15		8		2,850		5,050
31		9		4,600		9,650
Dec. 11		10		3,400		13,050
31	Closing	11	13,050			0

Account   Sales Returns & Allowances   Account No. 412

DATE	ITEM	POST. REF.	DEBIT	CREDIT	BALANCE DEBIT	CREDIT
1994						
Aug. 16		9	500		500	
Dec. 31	Closing	12		500	0	

Account   Sales Discounts   Account No. 413

DATE	ITEM	POST. REF.	DEBIT	CREDIT	BALANCE DEBIT	CREDIT
1994						
July 24		8	57		57	
Dec. 31	Closing	12		57	0	

Account   Purchases   Account No. 510

DATE	ITEM	POST. REF.	DEBIT	CREDIT	BALANCE DEBIT	CREDIT
1994						
Apr. 11		7	4,800		4,800	
July 18		8	5,600		10,400	
Dec. 31	Closing	12		10,400	0	

Account   Purchases Returns & Allowances   Account No. 511

DATE	ITEM	POST. REF.	DEBIT	CREDIT	BALANCE DEBIT	CREDIT
1994						
July 20		8		400		400
Dec. 31	Closing	11	400			0

Account   Purchases Discounts   Account No. 512

DATE	ITEM	POST. REF.	DEBIT	CREDIT	BALANCE DEBIT	CREDIT
1994						
Apr. 20		7		96		96
July 28		8		104		200
Dec. 31	Closing	11	200			0

Account Transportation In   Account No. 513

DATE		ITEM	POST. REF.	DEBIT	CREDIT	BALANCE DEBIT	CREDIT
1994							
July	18		8	200		200	
Dec.	31	Closing	12		200	0	

Account Salary Expense   Account No. 520

DATE		ITEM	POST. REF.	DEBIT	CREDIT	BALANCE DEBIT	CREDIT
1994							
Mar.	15		6	800		800	
May	15		7	800		1,600	
July	15		8	800		2,400	
Sep.	15		9	800		3,200	
Nov.	15		10	800		4,000	
Dec.	31	Adjusting	11	800		4,800	
	31	Closing	12		4,800	0	

Account Theater Services Expense   Account No. 521

DATE		ITEM	POST. REF.	DEBIT	CREDIT	BALANCE DEBIT	CREDIT
1993							
Nov.	30	Balance	✓			4,000	
Dec.	31	Adjusting	4	850		4,850	
	31	Closing	5		4,850	0	
1994							
Nov.	13		10	600		600	
Dec.	31	Closing	12		600	0	

Account Subcontractor Expense   Account No. 522

DATE		ITEM	POST. REF.	DEBIT	CREDIT	BALANCE DEBIT	CREDIT
1993							
Nov.	30	Balance	✓			2,010	
Dec.	30		3	450		2,460	
	31	Adjusting	4	600		3,060	
	31	Closing	5		3,060	0	
1994							
Oct.	8		10	400		400	
Dec.	31	Closing	12		400	0	

Account Auto Expense   Account No. 524

DATE		ITEM	POST. REF.	DEBIT	CREDIT	BALANCE DEBIT	CREDIT
1993							
Nov.	30	Balance	✓			2,900	
Dec.	1		1	200		3,100	
	31		3	150		3,250	
	31	Closing	5		3,250	0	
1994							
Jan.	2		6	2,400		2,400	
Dec.	31	Closing	12		2,400	0	

Account Cosmetics Expense   Account No. 525

DATE		ITEM	POST. REF.	DEBIT	CREDIT	BALANCE DEBIT	CREDIT
1993							
Nov.	30	Balance	✓			230	
Dec.	21		2	73		303	
	31		3	125		428	
	31	Closing	5		428	0	
1994							
Sep.	15		9	100		100	
Dec.	31	Closing	12		100	0	

Account	Depreciation Expense—Furniture & Fixtures				Account No. 527	
DATE	ITEM	POST. REF.	DEBIT	CREDIT	BALANCE DEBIT	CREDIT
1993						
Dec. 31	Adjusting	4	2,680		2,680	
31	Closing	5		2,680	0	
1994						
Dec. 31	Adjusting	11	2,680		2,680	
31	Closing	12		2,680	0	

Account	Depreciation Expense—Equipment				Account No. 528	
1993						
Dec. 31	Adjusting	4	2,400		2,400	
31	Closing	5		2,400	0	
1994						
Dec. 31	Adjusting	11	2,400		2,400	
31	Closing	12		2,400	0	

Account	Insurance Expense				Account No. 529	
1993						
Dec. 31	Adjusting	4	1,450		1,450	
31	Closing	5		1,450	0	
1994						
Dec. 31	Adjusting	11	600		600	
31	Closing	12		600	0	

Account	Office Supplies Expense				Account No. 531	
1993						
Dec. 31	Adjusting	4	579		579	
31	Closing	5		579	0	
1994						
Dec. 31	Adjusting	11	110		110	
31	Closing	12		110	0	

Account	Rent Expense				Account No. 532	
1993						
Nov. 30	Balance	✓			4,400	
Dec. 1		1	400		4,800	
31	Closing	5		4,800	0	
1994						
Jan. 2		6	2,400		2,400	
July 1		7	2,400		4,800	
Dec. 31	Closing	12		4,800	0	

Account	Supplies & Props Expense				Account No. 533	
1993						
Dec. 31	Adjusting	4	903		903	
31	Closing	5		903	0	
1994						
Dec. 31	Adjusting	11	945		945	
31	Closing	12		945	0	

Account	Telephone Expense					Account No. 534

DATE		ITEM	POST. REF.	DEBIT	CREDIT	BALANCE DEBIT	CREDIT
1993							
Nov.	30	Balance	✓			300	
Dec.	29		3	95		395	
	31	Closing	5		395	0	
1994							
July	2		8	120		120	
Dec.	30		10	135		255	
	31	Closing	12		255	0	

Account	Transportation Out					Account No. 535

DATE		ITEM	POST. REF.	DEBIT	CREDIT	BALANCE DEBIT	CREDIT
1994							
June	5		7	45		45	
Aug.	1		9	75		120	
Dec.	31	Closing	12		120	0	

Account	Interest Expense					Account No. 710

DATE		ITEM	POST. REF.	DEBIT	CREDIT	BALANCE DEBIT	CREDIT
1993							
Dec.	31	Adjusting	4	105		105	
	31	Closing	5		105		
1994							
July	1		7	150		150	
Dec.	31	Adjusting	11	300		450	
	31	Closing	12		450	0	

(12), (13), (14)

Egor the Magician
Work Sheet
For the Year Ended December 31, 1994

	Trial Balance Dr.	Trial Balance Cr.	Adjustments Dr.	Adjustments Cr.
Cash..................................	12,315			
Accounts Receivable	3,400			
Fees Receivable.....................	11,700			
Supplies & Props	1,205			(b) 945
Office Supplies	210			(a) 110
Prepaid Insurance	1,150			(d) 600
Furniture & Fixtures	13,400			
Accum. Depr.—Furn. & Fixtures		2,680		(g) 2,680
Equipment - Stage	12,000			
Accum. Depr.—Equipment		2,400		(h) 2,400
Accounts Payable...................		1,080		
Notes Payable		5,000		
E.J. Gribbet, Capital.................		27,852		
Fees Earned		26,700		
Sales................................		13,050		
Sales Returns and Allowances	500			
Sales Discounts.....................	57			
Purchases	10,400			
Purchases Returns and Allowances...		400		
Purchases Discounts		200		
Transportation In	200			
Salary Expense	4,000		(f) 800	
Theater Services Expense............	600			
Subcontractor Expense	400			
Auto Expense	2,400			
Cosmetics Expense..................	100			
Rent Expense.......................	4,800			
Telephone Expense	255			
Transportation Out	120			
Interest Expense	150		(e) 300	
	79,362	79,362		
Office Supplies Expense.............			(a) 110	
Supplies & Props Expense			(b) 945	
Insurance Expense...................			(d) 600	
Interest Payable				(e) 300
Salaries Payable				(f) 800
Depr. Exp.—Furn. & Fixtures			(g) 2,680	
Depr. Exp.—Equipment			(h) 2,400	
Merchandise Inventory..............			(c) 2,370	
Income Summary				(c) 2,370
			10,205	10,205
Net Income.........................				

| Adj. Trial Balance | | Income Statement | | Balance Sheet | |
Dr.	Cr.	Dr.	Cr.	Dr.	Cr.
12,315				12,315	
3,400				3,400	
11,700				11,700	
260				260	
100				100	
550				550	
13,400				13,400	
	5,360				5,360
12,000				12,000	
	4,800				4,800
	1,080				1,080
	5,000				5,000
	27,852				27,852
	26,700		26,700		
	13,050		13,050		
500		500			
57		57			
10,400		10,400			
	400		400		
	200		200		
200		200			
4,800		4,800			
600		600			
400		400			
2,400		2,400			
100		100			
4,800		4,800			
255		255			
120		120			
450		450			
110		110			
945		945			
600		600			
	300				300
	800				800
2,680		2,680			
2,400		2,400			
2,370				2,370	
	2,370		2,370		
87,912	87,912	31,817	42,720	56,095	45,192
		10,903			10,903
		42,720	42,720	56,095	56,095

Egor the Magician
Income Statement
For the Year Ended Dec. 31, 1994

Fees earned			$26,700
Sales		$13,050	
Less: Sales returns and allowances	$500		
Sales discounts	57	557	
Net sales		$12,493	
Less cost of goods sold:			
Purchases	$10,400		
Less: Purchases returns and allowances	$400		
Purchases discounts	200	600	
Net purchases	$ 9,800		
Plus transportation	200		
Net cost of purchases	$10,000		
Less ending merchandise inventory	2,370		
Cost of goods sold		7,630	
Gross profit			4,863
Total net revenues			$31,563
Operating expenses:			
Selling expenses:			
Salary expense	$ 4,800		
Rent expense	4,800		
Depreciation expense - equipment	2,400		
Auto expense	2,400		
Supplies & props expense	945		
Theater services expense	600		
Subcontractor expense	400		
Telephone expense	255		
Transportation out	120		
Cosmetics expense	100		
Total selling expenses		$16,820	
Administrative expenses:			
Depreciation expense - furniture & fixtures	$ 2,680		
Insurance expense	600		
Office supplies expense	110		
Total administrative expenses		3,390	
Total operating expenses			20,210
Operating income			$11,353
Other expense:			
Interest expense			450
Net income			$10,903

Egor the Magician
Statement of Owner's Equity
For the Year Ended Dec. 31, 1994

Egor J. Gribbet, capital, January 1, 1994	$27,852
Income for the year	10,903
Egor J. Gribbet, capital, December 31, 1994	$38,755

Egor the Magician
Balance Sheet
Dec. 31, 1994

Assets

Current assets:

Cash	$12,315	
Accounts receivable	3,400	
Fees receivable.	11,700	
Merchandise inventory	2,370	
Supplies & props.	260	
Office supplies.	100	
Prepaid insurance.	550	
Total current assets		$30,695

Plant assets:

Furniture & fixtures	$13,400		
Less accumulated depreciation	5,360	$ 8,040	
Equipment - stage.	$12,000		
Less accumulated depreciation	4,800	7,200	
Total plant assets			5,240
Total assets			$45,935

Liabilities

Current liabilities:

Accounts payable	$ 1,080	
Interest payable.	300	
Salaries payable.	800	
Total current liabilities		$2,180

Long-term liabilities:

Notes payable		5,000
Total liabilities		$ 7,180

Owner's Equity

E.J. Gribbet, capital	38,755
Total liabilities and owner's equity.	$45,935

(16)   Adjusting Entries

Dec.	31	Office Supplies Expense	531	110	
		Office Supplies	117		110
	31	Supplies & Props Expense	533	945	
		Supplies & Props	116		945
	31	Merchandise Inventory.	115	2,370	
		Income Summary.	312		2,370
	31	Insurance Expense	529	600	
		Prepaid Insurance	118		600
	31	Interest Expense	710	300	
		Interest Payable	215		300
	31	Salary Expense.	520	800	
		Salaries Payable	212		800
	31	Depreciation Expense - Furn. & Fix.	527	2,680	
		Accum. Depr. - Furn. & Fix.	122		2,680
	31	Depreciation Expense - Equipment	528	2,400	
		Accum. Depr. - Equipment	124		2,400

(17)

Dec.	31	Fees Earned.....................................	410	26,700	
		Sales	411	13,050	
		Purchases Returns & Allowances	511	400	
		Purchases Discounts............................	512	200	
		Income Summary	312		40,350

Closing Entries

Dec.	31	Income Summary	312	31,817	
		Sales Returns & Allowances	412		500
		Sales Discounts..............................	413		57
		Purchases	510		10,400
		Transportation In	513		200
		Salary Expense	520		4,800
		Theater Services Expense......................	521		600
		Subcontractor Expense	522		400
		Auto Expense	524		2,400
		Cosmetics Expense............................	525		100
		Depreciation Expense—Furn. & Fix..............	527		2,680
		Depreciation Expense—Equipment..............	528		2,400
		Insurance Expense	529		600
		Office Supplies Expense	531		110
		Rent Expense.................................	532		4,800
		Supplies & Props Expense	533		945
		Telephone Expense	534		255
		Transportation Out	535		120
		Interest Expense	710		450
	31	Income Summary	312	10,903	
		E.J. Gribbet, Capital...........................	310		10,903

CHAPTER 7

MATCHING		*TRUE/FALSE*			*MULTIPLE CHOICE*	
1. H	7. A	1. F	6. F	11. T	1. d	4. a
2. J	8. B	2. T	7. T	12. F	2. b	5. a
3. D	9. K	3. F	8. F	13. T	3. c	6. d
4. L	10. E	4. F	9. T	14. T		
5. G	11. C	5. T	10. T	15. F		
6. F	12. I					

EXERCISE 7-1

Feb. 1	Purchases Journal
6	Cash Receipts Journal
8	General Journal
11	Cash Payments Journal
18	Sales Journal
28	Cash Receipts Journal

EXERCISE 7-2
Purchases Journal

Date	Accounts Credited	Post. Ref.	Accounts Payable Cr.	Purchases Dr.	Store Supplies Dr.	Office Supplies Dr.
19—						
Mar. 2	Eastside Co..........................		15,250	15,250		
8	Bench Co............................		3,500	3,500		
28	James & Co..........................		900		800	100

Cash Payments Journal

Date	Ck. No.	Account Debited	Post. Ref.	Other Accounts Dr.	Accounts Payable Dr.	Purchases Discounts Cr.	Cash Cr.
19—							
Mar. 16	230	Bench Co.....................			3,500	70	3,430
20	231	Purchases		1,500			1,500
27	232	Eastside Co.			14,630		14,630

Journal

19—				
Mar. 9	Accounts Payable—Eastside Co.		620	
	Purchases Returns and Allowances.....................			620

EXERCISE 7-3
Sales Journal

Date	Invoice No.	Account Debited	Post. Ref.	Accts. Rec. Dr. Sales Cr.
19—				
Oct. 3	2883	Blanders Co..		8,250
4	2884	Montana Co.		5,000

Cash Receipts Journal

Date	Account Credited	Post. Ref.	Other Accounts Cr.	Sales Cr.	Accounts Receivable Cr.	Sales Discounts Dr.	Cash Dr.
19—							
Oct. 13	Blanders Co.................				7,250	145	7,105
14	Montana Co.................				5,000	100	4,900
25	Office Supplies.............		300				300
31	Sales			39,600			39,600

Journal

19—			
Oct. 8	Sales Returns and Allowances.............................	1,000	
	Accounts Receivable—Blanders Co.		1,000

PROBLEM 7-1

(1)

Purchases Journal

Date	Account Credited	Post. Ref.	Accounts Payable Cr.	Purchases Dr.	Store Supplies Dr.	Office Supplies Dr.	Other Accounts Dr. Account	Post. Ref.	Amount
19—									
Apr. 2	Gudorf Co.		7,010	7,010					
14	Mills Co.		300		300				
16	Quick Co.		175			175			
22	Mills Co.		5,250				Store Equip.	121	5,250
26	Gudorf Co.		6,925	6,925					
30	Mills Co.		280		280				
			19,940	13,935	580	175			5,250
			(211)	(511)	(115)	(116)			

(2) and (3)

GENERAL LEDGER

Store Supplies 115

Apr. 30	580	

Office Supplies 116

Apr. 30	175	

Store Equipment 121

Apr. 22	5,250	

Accounts Payable 211

	Apr. 30	19,940

Purchases 511

Apr. 30	13,935	

ACCOUNTS PAYABLE LEDGER

Gudorf Co.

	Apr. 2	7,010
	26	6,925

Mills Co.

	Apr. 14	300
	22	5,250
	30	280

Quick Co.

	Apr. 16	175

(4)

Gudorf Co.	$13,935
Mills Co.	5,830
Quick Co.	175
Total accounts payable	$19,940

PROBLEM 7-2

(1)

Purchases	6,000	Accounts Payable	8,430
Store Supplies	640		
Office Supplies	800		
Other Accounts	990		
Debit Totals	8,430	Credit Totals	8,430

(2) Purchases Journal

Date	Post. Ref.	Accounts Payable Cr.	Purchases Dr.	Store Supplies Dr.	Office Supplies Dr.	Other Accounts Dr. Account	Post. Ref.	Amount
19—								
Oct. 31	✓	620				Store Equip.	121	620
31	✓	8,430	6,000	640	800			990
		(211)	(511)	(115)	(116)			

GENERAL LEDGER

Store Supplies 115	
Oct. 31 640	

Accounts Payable 211	
	Oct. 31 8,430

Office Supplies 116	
Oct. 31 800	

Purchases 511	
Oct. 31 6,000	

Store Equipment 121	
Oct. 31 620	

PROBLEM 7-3

(1) Sales Journal

Date	Invoice No.	Account Debited	Post. Ref.	Accts. Rec. Dr. Sales Cr.
19—				
Sept. 8	210	Robert Poon	✓	220
12	225	Jeff Lucas	✓	50
24	260	Pamela Stark	✓	70
30	290	Steve Kocan	✓	400
				740
				(113)(411)

(2) and (3)

GENERAL LEDGER	ACCOUNTS RECEIVABLE LEDGER

Accounts Receivable 113

Sept. 30   740 |

Sales 411

| Sept. 30   740

Steve Kocan

Sept. 30   400 |

Jeff Lucas

Sept. 12   50 |

Robert Poon

Sept. 8   220 |

Pamela Stark

Sept. 24   70 |

(4)

Steve Kocan	$400
Jeff Lucas	50
Robert Poon	220
Pamela Stark	70
Total accounts receivable	$740

CHAPTER 8

MATCHING		TRUE/FALSE			MULTIPLE CHOICE	
1. E	6. H	1. F	5. T	9. T	1. b	4. d
2. C	7. J	2. F	6. F	10. F	2. a	5. c
3. G	8. B	3. F	7. F	11. T	3. c	
4. A	9. F	4. T	8. T	12. F		
5. I	10. D					

EXERCISE 8-1

(2) Cash in Bank	1,920	
Notes Receivable		1,800
Interest Income		120
(3) Miscellaneous Administrative Expense	28	
Cash in Bank		28
(6) Accounts Payable—Charlie's Optical Supply	100	
Cash in Bank		100

EXERCISE 8-2

Jan. 8 Purchases	4,900	
Accounts Payable		4,900
10 Purchases	11,880	
Accounts Payable		11,880
20 Accounts Payable	11,880	
Cash in Bank		11,880

Feb. 9	Accounts Payable	4,900	
	Discounts Lost	100	
	Cash in Bank		5,000

EXERCISE 8-3

| (1) | Petty Cash | 400.00 | |
| | Accounts Payable | | 400.00 |

| (2) | Accounts Payable | 400.00 | |
| | Cash in Bank | | 400.00 |

(3)	Office Supplies	80.25	
	Miscellaneous Selling Expense	115.33	
	Miscellaneous Administrative Expense	78.05	
	Cash Short and Over		1.97
	Accounts Payable		271.66

| (4) | Accounts Payable | 271.66 | |
| | Cash in Bank | | 271.66 |

PROBLEM 8-1
Dumont Co.

(1)

Bank Reconciliation
September 30, 19—

Balance according to bank statement		$8,510
Add deposit not recorded		1,900
		$10,410
Deduct outstanding checks:		
No. 255	$325	
No. 280	100	
No. 295	700	1,125
Adjusted balance		$ 9,285
Balance according to depositor's records		$7,540
Add: Error in recording Check No. 289	$270	
Error in a deposit	720	
Note and interest collected by bank	780	1,770
		$ 9,310
Deduct bank service charge		25
Adjusted balance		$ 9,285

(2) Sept. 30	Cash in Bank	1,745	
	Miscellaneous Administrative Expense	25	
	Vouchers Payable		270
	Accounts Receivable		720
	Notes Receivable		700
	Interest Income		80

PROBLEM 8-2

(1) Voucher Register

Date	Vou. No.	Payee	Date Paid	Ck. No.	Accounts Payable Cr.	Purchases Dr.
4/1	325	Sillo Co.	4/5	810	700	700
4/1	326	Cross Inc.	4/15	812	525	525
4/1	327	Leo's Co.	4/8	811	1,000	1,000

(2) Check Register

Date	Ck. No.	Payee	Vou. No.	Accounts Payable Dr.	Purchases Discounts Cr.	Cash in Bank Cr.
4/5	810	Sillo Co.	325	700	14	686
4/8	811	Leo's Co.	327	1,000	10	990
4/15	812	Cross Inc.	326	525		525

CHAPTER 9

MATCHING			TRUE/FALSE		MULTIPLE CHOICE	
1. K	5. G	9. A	1. F	6. F	1. c	5. b
2. F	6. B	10. L	2. T	7. T	2. d	6. c
3. J	7. E	11. C	3. T	8. T	3. b	
4. D	8. H	12. I	4. F	9. T	4. a	
			5. F	10. F		

EXERCISE 9-1

1. $80	5. $35
2. $35	6. $270
3. $60	7. $210
4. $80	

EXERCISE 9-2

	(1)	(2)
Face value..	$12,000.00	$15,000.00
Interest on face value......................................	360.00	400.00
Maturity value...	12,360.00	15,400.00
Discount on maturity value.................................	288.40	299.44
Proceeds..	12,071.60	15,100.56

EXERCISE 9-3

(1) Aug. 31	Uncollectible Accounts Expense...........................	550	
	Accounts Receivable—D. Shore...........................		550
(2) Oct. 8	Accounts Receivable—D. Shore...........................	550	
	Uncollectible Accounts Expense...........................		550
8	Cash...	550	
	Accounts Receivable—D. Shore...........................		550

EXERCISE 9-4

$68,000

EXERCISE 9-5

Walton Company
Balance Sheet
December 31, 19—

Assets

Current assets:

Cash..		$ 37,500
Marketable equity securities.......................	$55,000	
Less allowance for decline to market.............	2,000	53,000
Notes receivable....................................		20,000
Accounts receivable	$35,000	
Less allowance for doubtful accounts	1,200	33,800
Interest receivable		9,900
Total current assets		$154,200

PROBLEM 9-1

(1)	Notes Receivable	8,000.00	
	Accounts Receivable—Dave Davidson		8,000.00
(2)	Cash..	8,092.00	
	Interest Income...		92.00
	Notes Receivable		8,000.00
(3)	Accounts Receivable - Dave Davidson.....................	8,160.00	
	Cash		8,160.00
(4)	Cash..	8,184.93	
	Interest Income...		24.93
	Accounts Receivable—Dave Davidson		8,160.00
(5)	Notes Receivable	3,000.00	
	Accounts Receivable—Sue Smith		3,000.00
(6)	Accounts Receivable—Sue Smith	3,075.00	
	Interest Income...		75.00
	Notes Receivable		3,000.00

PROBLEM 9-2

(1)	Uncollectible Accounts Expense	24,000	
	Allowance for Doubtful Accounts........................		24,000
(2)	Uncollectible Accounts Expense	5,955	
	Allowance for Doubtful Accounts........................		5,955
(3)	Allowance for Doubtful Accounts..........................	3,500	
	Accounts Receivable—Bentley Co........................		3,500

(4) Accounts Receivable—Apple Co..............................		1,235	
Allowance for Doubtful Accounts.........................			1,235
Cash..		1,235	
Accounts Receivable—Apple Co...........................			1,235

CHAPTER 10

MATCHING		TRUE/FALSE		MULTIPLE CHOICE	
1. G	6. A	1. F	6. T	1. c	4. d
2. I	7. F	2. F	7. T	2. a	5. c
3. B	8. H	3. T	8. F	3. b	
4. C	9. J	4. T	9. F		
5. E	10. D	5. F	10. T		

EXERCISE 10-1

		Net Income	Assets	Owner's Equity
19XA	(1)	under	(1) under	(1) under
	(2)	$5,000	(2) $5,000	(2) $5,000
19XB	(1)	over	(1) correct	(1) correct
	(2)	$5,000	(2)	(2)

EXERCISE 10-2

		Total
	Cost	Lower of Cost or Market
Commodity A......................	$3,750	$3,600
Commodity B	2,760	3,220
Commodity C......................	1,450	1,200
Commodity D......................	1,440	1,290
Total	$9,400	$9,310

PROBLEM 10-1

(1)

$$\text{Average unit cost: } \frac{\$11,485}{210} = \$54.69$$

12 units in the inventory @ $54.69 = $656.28

(2) Date Purchased	Units	Price	Total Cost
November 1	12	$58	$696
Total	12		$696

(3) Date Purchased	Units	Price	Total Cost
November 1	12	$58	$696
Total	12		$696

(4) Date Purchased	Units	Price	Total Cost
January 10	10	$48	$480
February 15	2	54	108
Total	12		$588

(5) Date Purchased	Units	Price	Total Cost
January 10	2	$48	$ 96
February 15	5	54	270
November 1	5	58	290
Total	12		$656

PROBLEM 10-2

	(1) Fifo	(2) Lifo	(3) Average Cost
Sales	$2,240,000	$2,240,000	$2,240,000
Ending inventory	145,600	100,000	118,920
Cost of merchandise sold	1,638,300	1,683,900	1,664,980
Gross profit	601,700	556,100	575,020

COMPUTATION OF ENDING INVENTORY

	Date Purchased	Units	Price	Total Cost
FIFO:	November 1	100	$69	$ 6,900
	December 1	1,900	73	138,700
	Total	2,000		$145,600
LIFO:	January 1	2,000	50	$100,000

AVERAGE COST:
   Average Unit Cost:

$$\frac{\$1,783,900}{30,000} = \$59.46$$

$$\$59.46 \times 2,000 = \$118,920$$

PROBLEM 10-3

(1)

	Cost	Retail
Merchandise inventory, August 1	$118,500	$170,000
Purchases in August (net)	299,125	472,500
Merchandise available for sale	$417,625	$642,500

Ratio of cost to retail:

$$\frac{\$417,625}{\$642,500} = 65\%$$

Sales in August (net)		479,000
Merchandise inventory, August 31, at retail		$163,500
Merchandise inventory, August 31, at estimated cost ($163,500 × 65%)		$106,275

(2)

Merchandise inventory, August 1		$118,500
Purchases in August (net)		299,125
Merchandise available for sale		$417,625
Sales in August (net)	$479,000	
Less estimated gross profit ($479,000 × 30%)	143,700	
Estimated cost of merchandise sold		335,300
Estimated merchandise inventory, August 31		$ 82,325

CHAPTER 11

MATCHING			TRUE/FALSE		MULTIPLE CHOICE	
1. H	6. M	11. O	1. T	7. T	1. c	6. b
2. L	7. D	12. F	2. T	8. T	2. a	7. c
3. N	8. A	13. C	3. F	9. F	3. a	8. b
4. J	9. G	14. I	4. F	10. F	4. c	9. d
5. E	10. B	15. K	5. T	11. T	5. b	10. a
			6. T	12. F		

EXERCISE 11-1

Dec. 31	Depreciation Expense—Equipment........................	4,500	
	Accumulated Depreciation—Equipment..................		4,500

EXERCISE 11-2

Dec. 31	Depreciation Expense—Equipment........................	20,800	
	Accumulated Depreciation—Equipment..................		20,800

EXERCISE 11-3

Mar. 8	Accumulated Depreciation—Fixtures......................	2,500	
	Cash..	2,000	
	Fixtures..		4,000
	Gain on Disposal of Assets		500

EXERCISE 11-4

Dec. 31	Depletion Expense	240,000	
	Accumulated Depletion—Mineral Rights		240,000

EXERCISE 11-5

Dec. 31	Amortization Expense—Patents...........................	20,000	
	Patents..		20,000

PROBLEM 11-1
Depreciation Expense

Year	Straight-Line	Declining-Balance	Sum-of-the-Years-Digits
19XA	$18,750	$40,000	$30,000
19XB	18,750	20,000	22,500
19XC	18,750	10,000	15,000
19XD	18,750	5,000	7,500
Total	$75,000	$75,000	$75,000

PROBLEM 11-2

(1) Dec. 31	Depr. Expense—Automobile	5,000	
	Accum. Depr.—Automobile		5,000
31	Depr. Expense—Automobile	5,000	
	Accum. Depr.—Automobile		5,000
(2) Dec. 31	Depr. Expense—Automobile	10,000	
	Accum. Depr.—Automobile		10,000
31	Depr. Expense—Automobile	2,500	
	Accum. Depr.—Automobile		2,500
(3) Dec. 31	Depr. Expense—Automobile	8,000	
	Accum. Depr.—Automobile		8,000
31	Depr. Expense—Automobile	4,000	
	Accum. Depr.—Automobile		4,000

PROBLEM 11-3

(a)		Apr. 30 Accumulated Depr.—Truck	12,000	
		Truck	20,200	
		Truck		15,000
		Cash		17,200
(b)	(1)	Apr. 30 Accumulated Depr.—Truck	12,000	
		Truck	20,700	
		Loss on Disposal of Plant Assets	2,000	
		Truck		15,000
		Cash		19,700
	(2)	Apr. 30 Accumulated Depr.—Truck	12,000	
		Truck	22,700	
		Truck		15,000
		Cash		19,700

CHAPTER 12

MATCHING		TRUE/FALSE			MULTIPLE CHOICE	
1. J	6. B	1. T	5. F	9. T	1. c	4. a
2. I	7. F	2. F	6. T	10. F	2. a	5. d
3. E	8. D	3. F	7. F	11. T	3. d	6. c
4. C	9. A	4. T	8. T	12. T		
5. G	10. H					

EXERCISE 12-1

(1) $770
(2) $60
(3) $33
(4) $727.50

EXERCISE 12-2

(1) Dec. 31	Vacation Pay Expense		3,225	
	Vacation Pay Payable			3,225

(2) Dec. 31	Product Warranty Expense		4,500	
	Product Warranty Payable			4,500

(3) Dec. 31	Pension Expense		40,000	
	Cash			27,500
	Unfunded Pension Liability			12,500

PROBLEM 12-1

(1) Dec. 7	Sales Salaries Expense		34,000	
	Office Salaries Expense		16,000	
	FICA Tax Payable			3,750
	Employees Income Tax Payable			7,500
	Union Dues Payable			900
	United Way Payable			450
	Salaries Payable			37,400

(2) Dec. 7	Salaries Payable		37,400	
	Cash			37,400

(3) Dec. 7	Payroll Taxes Expense		6,850	
	FICA Tax Payable			3,750
	State Unemployment Tax Payable			2,700
	Federal Unemployment Tax Payable			400

(4) Dec. 7	Payroll Taxes Expense		3,150	
	FICA Tax Payable			3,150

PROBLEM 12-2

(1) $\quad B = .06\ (\$500,000)$
$\quad\quad B = \$30,000$

(2) $\quad B = .06\ (\$500,000 - B)$
$\quad\quad B = \$30,000 - .06B$
$\quad 1.06B = \$30,000$
$\quad\quad B = \$28,301.89$

(3) $\quad B = .06\ (\$500,000 - T)$
$\quad\quad T = .34\ (\$500,000 - B)$
$\quad\quad B = .06\ [\$500,000 - .34\ (\$500,000 - B)]$
$\quad\quad B = .06\ (\$500,000 - \$170,000 + .34B)$
$\quad\quad B = \$30,000 - \$10,200 + .0204B$
$\quad .9796B = \$19,800$
$\quad\quad B = \$20,212.33$

(4)

$$B = .06 (\$500{,}000 - B - T)$$
$$T = .34 (\$500{,}000 - B)$$
$$B = .06 [\$500{,}000 - B - .34 (\$500{,}000 - B)]$$
$$B = .06 (\$500{,}000 - B - \$170{,}000 + .34B)$$
$$B = \$30{,}000 - .06B - \$10{,}200 + .0204B$$
$$1.0396B = \$19{,}800$$
$$B = \$19{,}045.79$$

PROBLEM 12-3

Employee	Annual Earnings	Employee's FICA Tax	FICA	State Unemployment	Federal Unemployment	Total
Avery	$ 12,000	$ 900	$ 900	$ 378	$ 56	$ 1,334
Johnson	5,000	375	375	270	40	685
Jones	59,000	4,425	4,425	378	56	4,859
Smith	63,000	4,545	4,545	378	56	4,979
Wilson	141,000	5,700	5,700	378	56	6,134
	$280,000	$15,945	$15,945	$1,782	$264	$17,991

PROBLEM 12-4

(1)	Accounts Payable—Mayday Co.	2,000	
	Notes Payable		2,000
(2)	Notes Payable	2,000	
	Interest Expense	60	
	Cash		2,060
(3)	Cash	8,000	
	Notes Payable		8,000
(4)	Notes Payable	8,000	
	Interest Expense	220	
	Cash		8,220
(5)	Cash	5,910	
	Interest Expense	90	
	Notes Payable		6,000
(6)	Notes Payable	6,000	
	Cash		6,000

CHAPTER 13

MATCHING		TRUE/FALSE			MULTIPLE CHOICE	
1. B	9. L	1. F	11. F	21. T	1. b	7. d
2. I	10. D	2. F	12. T	22. F	2. c	8. b
3. F	11. A	3. T	13. T	23. F	3. a	9. d
4. H	12. C	4. F	14. F	24. T	4. d	10. a
5. N	13. G	5. T	15. T	25. T	5. c	11. c
6. J	14. K	6. T	16. F	26. T	6. a	12. d
7. M	15. O	7. F	17. T	27. F		
8. E		8. F	18. T	28. F		
		9. F	19. T	29 F		
		10. T	20. F	30. T		

EXERCISE 13-1	EXERCISE 13-2	EXERCISE 13-3	PROBLEM 13-1
(1) $5,000,000	$76,350	(1) a. $37,600	(1) $250,000
(2) $4,100,000	(1) (2,000)	b. 13	(2) $4,450
(3) $900,000	(2) (5,200)	c. (15)	(3) $470,400
	(3) $69,150	d. (6)	(4) $735,000
		e. (20)	(5) $6,750
		f. $37,572	
		(2) Materiality	

CHAPTER 14

MATCHING		TRUE/FALSE			MULTIPLE CHOICE	
1. C	6. D	1. F	8. T	15. T	1. b	4. a
2. F	7. I	2. T	9. T	16. T	2. d	5. c
3. H	8. G	3. T	10. F	17. T	3. d	
4. A	9. J	4. F	11. T	18. F		
5. E	10. B	5. F	12. F	19. T		
		6. F	13. F	20. T		
		7. T	14. F			

EXERCISE 14-1

Cash	100,000	
Merchandise Inventory	80,000	
Cutco, Capital		180,000
Cash	10,000	
Land	115,000	
Equipment	45,000	
Merchandise Inventory	5,000	
Robbs, Capital		175,000

EXERCISE 14-2

(1) June 30 Hartly, Capital... 20,000

Smetz, Capital 11,000

Grasso, Capital 7,000

Schafer, Capital...................................... 38,000

(2) July 1 Cash.. 50,000

Hartly, Capital.. 7,000

Smetz, Capital 7,000

Grasso, Capital 7,000

Mesko, Capital.. 71,000

EXERCISE 14-3

(1) Inventory 12,750

Arway, Capital 4,250

Batts, Capital 4,250

Carlone, Capital 4,250

Carlone, Capital 44,250

Arway, Capital 44,250

(2) Inventory 6,000

Arway, Capital 2,000

Batts, Capital 2,000

Carlone, Capital 2,000

Carlone, Capital 42,000

Cash... 42,000

PROBLEM 14-1

(1) Bulley's share... $100,000

Scram's share... 100,000

Total.. $200,000

(2) Bulley's share... $ 80,000

Scram's share... 120,000

Total.. $200,000

(3) Bulley's share... $ 60,000

Scram's share... 140,000

Total.. $200,000

(4)

	Bulley	Scram	Total
Salary allowance..................................	$30,000	$ 50,000	$ 80,000
Remaining income	60,000	60,000	120,000
Net income......................................	$90,000	$110,000	$200,000

(5)

Interest allowance.................................	$15,000	$ 35,000	$ 50,000
Remaining income	75,000	75,000	150,000
Net income......................................	$90,000	$110,000	$200,000

(6)

Salary allowance.................................	$15,000	$ 25,000	$ 40,000
Interest allowance.................................	15,000	35,000	50,000
Remaining income	55,000	55,000	110,000
Net income......................................	$85,000	$115,000	$200,000

(7)

	Bulley	Scram	Total
Salary allowance	$80,000	$ 78,000	$158,000
Interest allowance	15,000	35,000	50,000
Total	$95,000	$113,000	$208,000
Excess of allowances over income	4,000	4,000	8,000
Net income	$91,000	$109,000	$200,000

PROBLEM 14-2

	Cash +	Noncash Assets	= Liabilities +	Capital		
				Triste +	Sandpipe +	Hinkle
(1) Balances before realization	$100,000	$300,000	$120,000	$ 90,000	$ 60,000	$130,000
Sale of noncash assets and division of gain	+400,000	−300,000		+ 30,000	+ 50,000	+20,000
Balances after realization	$500,000	-0-	$120,000	$120,000	$110,000	$150,000
Payment of liabilities	−120,000		−120,000			
Balances after payment of liabilities	$380,000	-0-	-0-	$120,000	$110,000	$150,000
Distribution of cash to partners	−380,000			−120,000	−110,000	− 150,000
Final balances	-0-	-0-	-0-	-0-	-0-	-0-
(2) Balances before realization	$100,000	$300,000	$120,000	$ 90,000	$60,000	$130,000
Sale of noncash assets and division of loss	+130,000	−300,000		− 51,000	− 85,000	− 34,000
Balances after realization	$230,000	-0-	$120,000	$ 39,000	$ 25,000 Dr.	$ 96,000
Payment of liabilities	−120,000		−120,000			
Balances after payment of liabilities	$110,000	-0-	-0-	$ 39,000	$ 25,000 Dr.	$ 96,000
Receipt of deficiency	+ 25,000				+ 25,000	
Balances after receipt of deficiency	$135,000	-0-	-0-	$ 39,000	-0-	$ 96,000
Distribution of cash to partners	−135,000			− 39,000		− 96,000
Final balances	-0-	-0-	-0-	-0-	-0-	0

(3)

Cash	130,000	
Loss and Gain on Realization	170,000	
Noncash Assets		300,000
Triste, Capital	51,000	
Sandpipe, Capital	85,000	
Hinkle, Capital	34,000	
Loss and Gain on Realization		170,000
Liabilities	120,000	
Cash		120,000
Cash	25,000	
Sandpipe, Capital		25,000
Triste, Capital	39,000	
Hinkle, Capital	96,000	
Cash		135,000